Urban Recycling Cooperatives
Building resilient communities

Solid waste is a major urban challenge worldwide and decisions over which technologies or methods to apply can have beneficial or detrimental immediate and long-term consequences, locally and globally. Inappropriate management of solid waste leads to damaging environmental impacts, particularly visible in the megacities of the Global South.

Urban Recycling Cooperatives explores the multiple narratives and interdisciplinary nature of waste studies, drawing attention to the pressing social, economic, cultural and environmental challenges related to waste and waste management. The book asks questions such as: how do we define waste and our relation to it; who is involved in dealing with waste; and what power interactions become manifest over issues of accessing and dealing with waste? In recent years, cooperatives, small entrepreneurial enterprises and community-based organizations have emerged, devoted to recovering and recycling household and business waste. These workers are able to reclaim significant amounts of natural resources and thus contribute to the saving of resources and reductions in waste management expenditures.

With particular reference to the Brazilian megalopolis of São Paulo, this book describes the paradigm shift in the general understanding of waste as unwanted discard and yet profitable resource and commodity, to the recognition that waste should not be produced. Reuse and recycling offer new potentials for addressing waste in innovative forms, acknowledging local practices. There are new ways of engaging with waste, ways that generate work and income, stimulate the local economy, develop appropriate technology and open up alternative solutions to urban challenges. The book is of interest to students and policy makers working in international development and waste management.

Jutta Gutberlet is Associate Professor in the Geography Department at the University of Victoria, Canada.

Routledge advances in regional economics, science and policy

Urban Recycling Cooperatives
Building resilient communities

Jutta Gutberlet

Routledge
Taylor & Francis Group
LONDON AND NEW YORK

First published 2016
by Routledge

2 Park Square, Milton Park, Abingdon, Oxfordshire OX14 4RN
52 Vanderbilt Avenue, New York, NY 10017

Routledge is an imprint of the Taylor & Francis Group, an informa business

First issued in paperback 2019

British Library Cataloguing in Publication Data
A catalogue record for this book is available from the British Library

Library of Congress Cataloging in Publication Data
Names: Gutberlet, Jutta, author.
Title: Urban recycling cooperatives: building resilient communities/
Jutta Gutberlet.
Description: Abingdon, Oxon; New York, NY: Routledge, 2016. | Includes
bibliographical references.
Subjects: LCSH: Recycling cooperatives. | Refuse and refuse disposal–
Environmental aspects. | Urban ecology (Sociology) | Sustainable urban
development.
Classification: LCC HD4482.G87 2016 | DDC 334/.6813637282–dc23
LC record available at
http://lccn.loc.gov/2015047856

ISBN: 978-1-138-92116-0 (hbk)
ISBN: 978-0-367-87367-7 (pbk)

DOI: 10.4324/9781315686523

Typeset in Times New Roman
by Sunrise Setting Ltd, Brixham, UK

This book is dedicated to the waste pickers who recover uncountable amounts of recyclable materials, every day, redirecting these materials into new production cycles. Uncollected, these materials would become an environmental hazard and burden future generations. Most of the recyclers work 'informally', receive very low pay, and are often not recognized by governments or the public.

Dona Selma and Vilma Moura were two waste pickers in the metropolitan region of São Paulo, leaders in the National Recyclers' Movement (MNCR), and were exemplary through their everyday commitment as recyclers, political leaders, and as friends. Unfortunately, both women recently died from diseases that could have been prevented with early care.

Contents

Photographs

Figures

Tables

Boxes

Acknowledgements

The present book would not have been written without the participation of many individuals, whose important contributions I want to acknowledge here. First come the many *catadores* in Brazil and *waste pickers* from other countries that I had the opportunity to interact with and who have taught me about their everyday experiences and livelihood situations. Here I want to mention specifically their leaders: Maria da Penha Aparecida Guimarães, Joana D'Arc P. Costa, José Gomes Aveiro, Maria Brito, Maria Mônica Silva, Wilma Moura de Souza, Francisca Maria Lima Araujo, Claudemir Sebastião, Aparecida Margarete de Souza, Guiomar dos Santos, Paulo Renato dos Prazeres, Luzia Maria Honorato, Rosilda Lopes dos Santos, Francisca Rabelo, Kelly Janaína Monteiro, José Lacerda Borges, Maria das Dores Silva, Armando Octaviano Júnior, Damaris Cristina Costa, Célia Aparecida dos Santos and Vanda Bacelar Reis, among many others. My colleagues in Brazil, with whom we created the *Participatory Sustainable Waste Management* project and follow ups, since 2005. These action-oriented scholars and practitioners have deeply inspired me with their thoughts and experiences, including Maria Ruth Takahashi, Fabio Luiz Cardozo, Ana Maria Marins, Professor Nidia Nacib Pontuschka, Professor Angela Martins Baeder, Sonia Felipone, Tereza dos Santos and Solanje Dias de Araujo. I would also like to acknowledge the critical administrative support received during the research from Fundação de Apoio à Faculdade de Educação da Universidade de São Paulo. I especially thank the students and volunteers that have comprised our research team throughout the years with their insights, motivation and energy including Crystal Tremblay, Bruno de Oliveira Jayme, Clécio Varjão, Emma Taylor, Neil Nunn, Julian Yates, Megan King, Eric Binion, Rhianna Nagel, Vanuza de Araujo Ramos and Dibya Shrestha. I want to thank my husband Greg for his always thought-provoking reflections and my son Kauê for his happiness, a source of inspiration throughout the writing process.

Generous funding to support the research described in this book was given primarily by: the Canadian International Development Agency (CIDA), the International Development Research Centre Canada (IDRC), Human Resources and Social Development Canada (HRSDC) and the Social Sciences and Humanities Research Council (SSHRC).

1 Waste governance

An introduction

DOI: 10.4324/9781315686523-1

Summary

Solid waste is a major urban challenge worldwide and reclaiming the materials embedded in waste streams is a necessary response to it. The form in which we manage our waste matters and decisions over which technology or method to apply can have beneficial or detrimental long-term consequences. This book discusses many different social, cultural, economic and environmental facets of waste management and recycling. In Chapter 1, I introduce the multiple narratives and the interdisciplinary nature of waste studies. I describe the broad scenarios related to waste, from production and consumption to discard and recycling. The debate draws the attention to the wide-reaching, and pressing social, economic and environmental challenges related to waste management, particularly in Southern city contexts. In cities in the global South approximately 0.5 to 1 per cent of the population works in informal household waste collection and separation of recyclables.

Collective and institutionalized forms of resource recovery, such as those involving recycling cooperatives, associations, or small social/environmental entrepreneurs, are introduced as alternatives in waste management co-production. Inclusive waste management requires a governance shift, allowing for deep levels of participation and deliberative conditions through which social and environmental justice issues are tackled. Key themes discussed in the following nine chapters are briefly outlined here and the notion of inclusive recycling and waste management contributing towards sustainable and more resilient communities and ultimately more inclusive cities becomes delineated.

1.1 Introduction: why research waste?

Waste has many contested facets encompassing social, cultural, political, economic and ecological aspects. Waste creates different narratives, by those who produce it and by those who work with it, or on waste issues. Waste embodies conflicting, rationalities, for example, between those perceiving waste as common property resource and those who see it as profitable commodity. Objects made of natural resources and transformed through industrial processes can become threats to the environment, human health and sustainability once discarded. At the same time these objects and materials become resources to those who collect, separate and transform them. Inappropriate solid waste management causes environmental impacts and generates health risks affecting the quality of life of urban populations worldwide, particularly in the global South, where thousands of waste pickers collect recyclable household and business waste, and classify and redirect these materials to the recycling industry. Local governments have challenging decisions to make on how to best deal with the city's growing waste. Residents live in crisis situations because of the lack of household waste collection so common in informal settlements throughout the global South. Other cities have encountered calamity due to a temporary waste management breakdown, as happened in Naples in 2008. In many countries large numbers of waste pickers work on landfills and surrounding dumps (Photograph 1.1). City administrations are mostly failing to address these issues with safer working arrangements for informal workers. Instead they often apply repressive measures to avoid their presence in public spaces. Consequently the livelihoods of waste pickers are most often threatened.

Waste prevention and resource conservation should always be the first priority, followed by reuse and recycling. Waste disposal and treatment needs to be precaution-oriented, which means that those materials that are problematic and not yet recycled should be avoided at first place. In hindsight avoidance is often cheaper and more effective, but it is more difficult to implement. Society at large still does not adequately reintegrate wastes into production processes and resource extraction continues at full steam. These problematic realities obviously require robust solutions. Today, geo-engineering is the dominant discourse on waste, while social and cultural aspects are often demeaned as irrelevant when dealing with solid waste. Privatization in waste services and treatment is a growing trend in the global South, with corporate investors becoming the brokers in waste collection and management.

Photograph 1.1 Waste pickers at the landfill *Gramacho* in Rio de Janeiro, Brazil.

From this perspective the more waste we generate, the larger the profits for these companies. Thus waste prevention and waste reduction do not become priorities. We see corporations substituting local entrepreneurs and particularly the informal waste collection sector as a consequence of modernizing waste management (Zapata Campos and Hall, 2013). In many places incineration and waste-to-energy technology have generated overcapacities, requiring waste to be imported – sometimes from large distances. There are many examples of overcapacity in waste incineration in Europe (Mallorca, Germany, the Netherlands, Sweden, etc.), perpetuating the growth in waste generation and further adding to the environmental footprint of waste (Amengual, 2014). Waste-to-energy technology also generates impacts on recycling markets and waste treatment prices besides producing intricate social and environmental consequences, which are discussed in this book.

Waste is hybrid and political. It has multiple facets, with obvious links between the ecological (*waste understood as a natural resource X waste seen as discard*), the social (*workers educated to recover resources X machines recovering or destroying resources*), the cultural (*consumers reduce, reuse and recycle X consumers reiterate mass consumption*) and the economic (*inclusive waste management under a social and solidarity perspective X profit-oriented waste management geared towards the commodification of waste*) dimensions. Putting on a historical lens further distinguishes the meanings and everyday praxes related to waste generation and waste management. Humans have always produced waste. Yet it is not until recently that extensive, long-lasting, negative impacts have become the consequence of human consumption. Since the middle of the nineteenth century industrialization, rapid urbanization and the influence of economic globalization have turned waste into the problem we are discussing today. Reuse and recycling concepts are not new and have been practiced at various degrees in different time periods and under different political systems.

1.1.1 Ecological paradigm

Given its pervasiveness, complexity and multi-dimensional aspects, waste has turned into a 'super wicked' global problem – a simultaneous failure of product, production and socioeconomic design – and yet we continuously produce more of it (Levin *et al.*, 2012; Zaman and Lehmann, 2013). The generation of solid waste is still on the rise, coupled with growing Gross Domestic Product (GDP). Data from the 15 European Union states, the OECD and North America, for example, demonstrate a per capita increase in municipal waste production of 54 per cent, 35 per cent and 29 per cent, respectively, between 1980 and 2005 (Sjöström and Östblom, 2010). In transitional economies (e.g. the BRIC countries: Brazil, Russia, India and China) the rise is underway; while in many other countries in the global South, GDP and consumption are either already on the rise or are expected to increase in the near future. We live with an unprecedented waste dilemma, in terms of quantity, complexity and toxicity of materials produced and discarded every day and everywhere, resulting in an unparalleled environmental crisis.

Waste is the epitomized result of growth-oriented production and consumption. An increasing number of scientists believe that human action, largely under industrial capitalism, has driven the world into a new geological epoch, the

Anthropocene (Crutzen and Stoermer, 2010, see also Hamilton, Gemenne and Bonneuil, 2015). The term calls attention to the negative effects humankind has had on the planet, causing mass extinctions of plant and animal species, pollution of the oceans and soils, and altered atmosphere among other lasting impacts in the planetary boundaries. The expansion of human populations and the unlimited extraction of the earth's resources are generating alarming environmental impacts. Not everybody of course is equally accountable for the current environmental destruction and impacts. The global economic and political elite and in particular white, male supremacy are the primary responsible forces in these negative developments. Production, consumption and waste disposal are interlinked to these transforming forces that change the planet in countless, problematic ways.

1.1.2 Social paradigm

The 2008 global economic recession has impacted on many countries and regions. While some economies have been able to recover more quickly, others still suffer the effects through high unemployment rates. According to the *World of Work Report 2014,* by the International Labour Organization, key challenges remain, "including rising youth unemployment, . . . stubbornly high employment informality and significant income inequalities" (ILO, 2014: v). Quality employment remains weak and core labour standards are not properly enforced, even in some emerging economies with significant institutional capacity. A shortage of jobs drives the most marginalized populations in urban regions to work in the 'informal' economy as a means of survival, often due to the lack of decent employment opportunities in the formal sector (Tokman, 2007). The term 'informal' denotes the often precarious and undervalued working and livelihood conditions of these individuals. I do not want to reiterate the conventional binary hierarchical representation of a formal/informal economy dualism, which understands informal employment as marginal with largely negative consequences for economic development and is thus often deterred. However, I suggest a different reading of the 'informal' as creative, diverse, often emancipatory and empowering to individuals that perform 'informal' work.

We need many more jobs in the global South. According to the ILO, approximately 200 million new jobs over the next five years are needed in order to accompany the growing working-age population in emerging and developing countries (ILO, 2014). Youth unemployment is already over 12 per cent in most countries in the global South. The many different forms of inclusive waste management based on *decent work* opportunities and supported with adequate public policies directly generate new jobs and can reverse this situation.

The 'informal' waste economy embodies many opportunities that immediately generate income. Among waste collectors in neglected settlements, waste pickers and recyclers perform different tasks, which can range from collection, separation and commercialization to adding value through transformation (e.g. plastic into pellets for recycling; PET bottles into washing line; Tetra Pack packaging into building material). These workers often also act as environmental stewards, educating the public about more responsible consumption and clean source separation. Through their praxis, organized waste pickers have accumulated everyday knowledge in managing waste and if organized and in a supportive political environment they have the potential to grow and develop. Recycling cooperatives generate social goods. The cooperatives also include individuals who are difficult to employ, because of long-term unemployment, lack of skills and literacy, and often also because of physical and mental handicaps. These social benefits of organized recycling are often overlooked.

1.1.3 Economic paradigm

The Social and Solidarity Economy is defined by values of trust, participatory democracy, reciprocity, respect and inclusive actions. Most experiences are small scale and restricted to initiatives described as fair trade, microcredit, microfinance, alternative or parallel currencies, bartering clubs or cooperatives (Laville 1992). These initiatives are bottom-up, and can encompass the voluntary sector as much as new institutionalized economic experiences. According to Moulaert and Ailenei, "solidarity economy thus creates synergies between actors (local authorities, private enterprises, state, citizens) and generates workplaces by offering new services" (2005: 2042). The Social and Solidarity Economy sees the intrinsic contributions of organized recycling to the human, the social and the economy.

Sufficiency and *zero waste* are discussed under Ecological Economy theory, but they are rarely applied to key urban development issues, including energy use and transportation or, material and food consumption. Nevertheless, sufficiency is a key concern in shifting towards greater sustainability, given that often well-meaning innovations can trigger additional energy and material flows. Mainstream economic thought understands growth as wealth creation under a free market system, attributed to efficiency (Adam Smith) and innovation (Joseph Schumpeter). In this case, consumerism is based on the unlimited and cheap supply of fossil fuel energy, as well as the externalization of all environmental costs. The sufficiency strategy, discussed by Paech (2009) as alternative economic approach for *de-growth* and de-materialization, includes strategies to regionalize the economy (regional markets, shortened supply chains, regional currencies, local employment, etc.), to 'reduce' and 'slow down' (consumption and lifestyles), to expand self-sufficiency and reduce the dependence on global production and markets, and to promote institutional innovations as well as 'material zero-sum'. After exhausting reduction and reuse, resource recovery and recycling are the elements of an adaptive co-evolutionary strategy striving for greater sufficiency.

1.2 Key terms and key perspectives discussed

Throughout the text I adopt the term municipal solid waste for the waste generated by households, commerce, offices and public institutions, including street sweeping and yard waste (EEA, 2013). While environmental and human health hazards linked to trash are obvious to most people, the socio-materiality of it – the different ways in which waste is socially defined and thus dealt with – only becomes visible to those familiar with waste. These are important considerations for sustainability.

Access to these resources as an urban common good, particularly to those who have historically accessed them, but who have lifelong been dispossessed and excluded from material well being, is yet another facet that defines waste.

The main protagonists in this book are waste pickers and organized recyclers, also called 'informal' recyclers or just recyclers. Recyclers work on their own or with family members, in the streets or on dumpsites. Recyclers have different names in each country or region. They are called *waste pickers* or *rag pickers* in India and other English speaking countries in the global South, *catadores* in Brazil, *recolectores* in Chile, *recuperadores* in Peru, *classificadores* in Uruguay, *zabaleen* in Egypt, *cartoneros* in Argentina, *recicladores* in Colombia, *mikhali* in Morocco, *minadores* in Ecuador and *pepenadores* in Mexico.

As already hinted earlier the term 'informal' is used as synonym for not recognized, nor protected by the public authorities in terms of health, and social benefits provision, encompassing different forms of survival activities of those working in the marginal or peripheral segments of the economy (ILO, 2002). I use the term organized recyclers to distinguish those waste pickers that have organized into a cooperative, association or trade union. Most of them still remain 'informal', because their work often continues unrecognized and unremunerated by the government.

This book in part reflects my own personal history and trajectory related to waste and my work related to waste pickers and *catadores*. Since I first started to study waste my initial focus on the environmental and social problems of waste widened to an interdisciplinary, integrated, global, participatory and action-oriented perspective applying complementary theoretical conceptions. The following box (Box 1.1) highlights some of the key concerns on waste that are tackled within the book.

BOX 1.1: Key perspectives on waste and waste governance

Why a book on waste?

- multifaceted perspectives and approaches to waste
- personal histories and trajectories related to waste studies
- ubiquitous topic touching everybody, everywhere
- experiences such as the *Participatory Sustainable Waste Management* project (PSWM)

Definition of waste

- historical perspective: waste in the past, present and future
- cultural understandings of waste: from nuisance to resource
- hybrid, multifaceted and political performance of waste

Environmental aspects of waste

- growth-oriented development driving consumption
- environmental crisis and the *Anthropocene*
- opportunities: resource recovery and recycling reducing greenhouse gas (GHG) emissions
- environmental education and *conscientization*

Social and economic aspects of waste

- social/economic crisis due to unemployment and underemployment
- livelihood opportunities in diverse economies
- building social assets, social cohesion, social resilience

Southern perspectives

- the colonial condition: racism, imperialism, white supremacy and consequent hegemonies
- unequal distribution of public services (e.g. lack of waste collection in informal settlements)
- poverty, lack of access to formal education
- community-based initiatives, collectivization, social movements

'Informal' and organized selective waste collection and recycling

- co-production, inclusive recycling
- social/environmental entrepreneurship
- cooperative recycling

Political ecology

- social and environmental justice
- inappropriate technologies: waste-to-energy, incineration, automatization
- decolonization

Theoretical framework

- situated Urban Political Ecology
- Ecological Economy (urban metabolism, industrial ecology, resilience, *zero waste*, environmental health)
- Social and Solidarity Economy (sustainable livelihoods, social and human capital, *decent work*)
- Participatory Action Research
- knowledge democratization
- localized, reflexive ecofeminist epistemology and ontology

1.3 Introduction to the content of the book

Chapter 2 provides an introduction to the overarching theoretical framework applied to the themes described, analysed and debated in the book. The research informing these discussions is situated in the context of postcolonial, critical social theory – particularly Southern theory– seeking to understand cities, actors and processes in the global South. This chapter introduces the situated Urban Political Ecology framework applied to the discussions on waste and those that work with it. This framework is particularly suitable because it draws attention to questions of social justice, inequality and the connection between political economy and everyday material lives. Urban metabolism analysis further helps understand waste flows and reveals who is involved in these flows as well as the social and power relations that underpin the predominant forms of generating and managing waste. Finally, Participatory Action Research (PAR) is outlined as inclusive research methodology and epistemology, where knowledge is co-created and jointly validated by the participants. Here, the research process itself is a major result and has potential for transformation.

The empirical research for most of the case study data presented in the book stems from participatory action methodology embedded in a long-term international research experience, the PSWM. In Chapter 3, I describe this research collaboration, formalized between the University of Victoria, Canada, and the University of São Paulo, and conducted with 32 recycling cooperatives in the metropolitan region of São Paulo, Brazil.[1] The interactive qualitative research has allowed for the co-creation and mobilization of specific knowledge for recycling cooperatives and agents working in solid waste management.[2] The long-term collaboration has created multiple results and products including many benefits to the participants, from diverse capacity building activities, input in policy design and diverse knowledge on collectively organizing and managing recycling cooperatives, to creating theory and specific knowledge within the geographies of waste.

Chapter 4 presents and analyses various forms of 'informal' recycling performed by individuals and groups in different geographic contexts in the global South. The chapter begins with a brief definition of the 'informal' economy. Recyclers and waste pickers ('informal' and organized) are situated within the context of informality, given that they operate outside of the formal economy, often under non-standard, atypical, alternative, irregular or precarious conditions. Gathering recyclables can be done under very different conditions, from separating at waste dumps, in the street or at home, to working in cooperatives and associations. The chapter introduces basic socioeconomic characteristics of the recyclers, social entrepreneurs and recycling cooperative members. The second part of this chapter describes the social movement that has been formed by waste pickers and organized recyclers in Brazil and other Latin American countries, contesting social injustices and inequalities, and demanding participatory deliberation on waste management issues. The chapter concludes with an examination of pro-active legislation from Brazil, exemplifying drivers for institutional change towards *decent work* for the 'informal' sector and organized cooperative recyclers.

Everyday experiences of waste pickers everywhere are pervaded by stigmatization and exclusion. Chapter 5 highlights the persisting social and cultural challenges recyclers are exposed to in their daily experience of working with waste. Social exclusion becomes manifested in dispossession, exploitation, oppression, aggression and stigmatization. The theoretical debate on agency and empowerment is readdressed through a participatory and gender-specific lens. There are processes that facilitate social inclusion and create agency for recyclers, thus empowering them. The chapter discusses the social benefits of organized recycling, particularly the generation of work, recovery of citizenship and potential for human development. Appropriate policies are key to safeguarding the social dimension of inclusive waste management. Cooperatives are life-transforming spaces, particularly for women. Cooperative recycling and solid waste co-management generate undeniable social benefits, as discussed through several case studies and particularly through the example of the recycling cooperative network COOPCENT-ABC, in the metropolitan region of São Paulo. Historically, there has been a strong gender dimension to waste collection and separation in the global North, transparent in contemporary recycling strategies of women organized in cooperatives and associations in many places in the global South.

Multifarious health risks are present in the daily work performed by the 'informal' recyclers, particularly the waste pickers that still work on waste dumps and landfills. Most waste pickers work under unhealthy and risky conditions. Health problems are related to chemical and biological hazards, musculoskeletal damage, mechanical trauma and poor emotional wellbeing. In Chapter 6, some research results are presented to better understand the work of the recyclers and the related health and safety threats. As a recycler it is common to experience body pain, injuries and accidents, and even within the cooperative there can be precarious and unsafe work conditions. The workers suffer from social stigma experienced in the streets and during social interactions with government, police or the general public. Difficulties in their interpersonal relationships within the cooperative as well as demonstrations of solidarity and friendship also affect their emotional wellbeing. Other more specific health implications of which most recyclers are not yet aware of derive from separating the waste of electrical and electronic equipment (WEEE). This is a major health challenge, given the recent exponential increase in the generation of this type of waste and the expanding recovery of it in the global South. Appropriate policies and other specific measures present urgent demands to make the work of the recyclers more humane, safe and efficient. Finally, this chapter reiterates the important contribution of the recyclers as environmental stewards improving environmental health.

In cities of the global South, more than 70 per cent of the waste generated is of organic matter, yet almost exclusively these organic resources are lost. There are few examples in the global South of formal initiatives to collect and redirect these materials into composting or other upstream activities. Chapter 7 explains some of the problems related to the formal recycling of organic municipal waste. The recovery of the organic, compostable fraction of household waste and the use of these materials for composting and community gardens, or for other forms of urban agriculture, are discussed here. The theoretical framework on urban sustainability and the application of the urban metabolism concept allows for a detailed visual understanding of organic waste flows and retrieval. What happens to the organic part of our waste and what are the environmental concerns with the recovery or the discard of organic waste are some of the questions answered in this chapter, aside from showcasing examples of organic waste recovery and composting for community gardens. The chapter concludes by highlighting persisting governance challenges in integrated organic waste recovery.

Selective, inorganic waste collection and recycling generates many environmental benefits, which are usually not accounted for. Chapter 8 discusses the research findings on greenhouse gas accounting and estimates for energy reduction due to recycling. This methodology explains some of the environmental benefits of collecting and recycling materials from the waste stream. Of course, recycling can also generate impacts. It uses water and energy during the transformation process and still requires mostly fossil fuels for the transportation of materials to and from the recycling centre. Sometimes solid waste and retrieved recyclable materials travel far, and even globally. These aspects are important to consider when conducting environmental balances. Ecological Economy attempts to assess the real costs of environmental damage. As such, the framework can also be applied to evaluate the environmental effect of recycling. A case study describes a simplified methodology to calculate the energy and GHG emission savings from recycling operations. This calculator can be applied by recycling cooperatives worldwide.

Basic infrastructure and public services are crucial to healthy life in the city. Decision-making, planning and the implementation of public infrastructure and services are dependent on local government and the quality of its governance. Over the past decades, neoliberal policies have heavily impacted water and solid waste management in many cities in the world. Particularly, since the 1980s, many local governments in the global South have privatized their water and waste management services, some of which have completely shifted towards private operators. These decisions have serious consequences for communities, raising the costs in accessing water and waste services and sometimes pushing out and dispossessing residents individual workers and micro entrepreneurs in waste and water management, particularly in poor neighbourhoods. Allowing large companies to carry out the collection of waste and recyclables impacts the livelihoods of those who were previously providing the service informally. Chapter 9 discusses the challenges that come with these transformations in Southern cities, specifically with regards to solid waste management. Key questions here are, on the one hand, the absence of the state in providing services and infrastructure in poor and informal settlements and, on the other hand, the trend towards privatization in solid waste management. The chapter examines the challenges involved in co-producing waste collection and recycling services. The assets and barriers of recycling cooperatives and networks working with local governments are analysed, applying a critical, Southern city perspective based on case study data.

Finally, Chapter 10 reminds us of the big social, economic and environmental challenges ahead that result from the waste regime of industrial capitalism that characterizes contemporary times. The concept of 'waste regime' is applied here to understand the politics and social relations related to waste production and waste management. In order to address the current complex challenges, a new waste regime needs to evolve which is characterized by radical transformations toward sustainable practices in production and consumption. This new waste regime embraces the idea of *zero waste* as the environmental ethic required to meet the political, societal and environmental challenges related to waste. Cooperative recycling and co-production in solid waste management, as practiced in many parts of the global South, embody important transitional approaches toward building sustainable and resilient communities. The chapter ends by reiterating the key benefits of inclusive recycling and waste collection to the resilience of

Southern cities and by alerting to remaining challenges during the transition towards a new waste regime.

Notes

1 All research conducted under the PSWM project umbrella was approved by the Human Research Ethics Board at the University of Victoria with the Protocol number 05-129 and with subsequent amendments for specific projects.
2 To protect the participants all names for the direct quotes have been changed into fictitious names.

2 Situated theoretical framework for waste governance

DOI: 10.4324/9781315686523-2

Summary

The research presented in this book is primarily situated within critical social theory adopting a postcolonial Southern perspective that seeks to understand cities, actors and processes involved in solid waste issues through an everyday life experience lens from the city actors in the global South. The current chapter tries to make sense of this overarching theoretical framework and introduces the situated urban political ecology concept applied in the many-sided discussions on waste presented here. This framework draws attention to questions of social and environmental justice, inequality and the connection between the political economies and everyday material lives in the city. To imagine the urban space as metabolism helps to identify the material flows and their impacts. Urban metabolism analysis maps waste flows and key actors and materialities involved, thus it identifies the social and power relations that underpin predominant forms of generating and managing waste. Participatory Action Research methodology has produced part of the data discussed in this book. This chapter briefly describes the research methodology and discusses how inclusive research processes can create new epistemologies, where knowledge is co-created and jointly validated. In this case, the research process in itself has become as important as the results.

2.1 Introduction to the theoretical background

This chapter outlines the overarching theoretical framework that has informed most of the research reflections discussed in this book. Solid waste and resource recovery (recycling) are hybrid and multifaceted topics, and as such, require a plural, interdisciplinary and yet situated approach. In this context Participatory Action Research (PAR), community-based inquiry and popular education are instrumental in this research methodology, for generating meaningful data through a transformative approach. The theoretical pillars in the discussion on waste are political ecology, social economy and Ecological Economy (Figure 2.1). These overlapping lenses provide insights into questions related to sustainability, justice, ethics, development and social innovation that derive from modern waste generation and waste management. The case studies and reflections presented in this

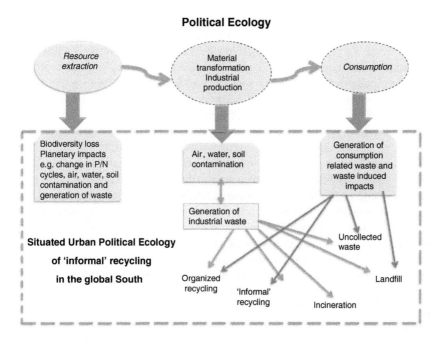

Figure 2.1 Simplified solid waste scenario in the global South through the lens of situated Urban Political Ecology.

book emphasize the necessity for a paradigm shift in our thinking and acting related to production, consumption and waste. The narratives, theories and practical examples provided in this book point towards the urgency to change perceptions on waste and waste workers. The overall tenor of the discussion suggests a radical shift in the politics of waste, cross-cutting individual behaviours and actions as well as changes at governmental, business and civil society levels. Best practices need to be scaled up, multiplied and transferred to other communities, cities and regions, while, of course, respecting specific local contexts.

Situated Urban Political Ecology (UPE), as a theoretical framework, brings in ideas from Ecological Economy (EE) and from Social and Solidarity Economy (SSE). Urban metabolism, industrial ecology, resilience, *de-growth, zero waste*, sustainability and environmental health are central concepts debated in Ecological Economy theory. Scholars have long been demanding the recognition of the *true* costs of production, consumption and transportation. Shifting into a post-mass-production paradigm has become a key topic within these debates (Niemann *et al.*, 2009).

Social and Solidarity Economy, complements this approach by bringing in theories on sustainable livelihoods, cooperatives, social enterprises, social and human assets, heterodox approaches to economy, *decent work* and other contentious social and economic questions closely related to the geographies of waste

(Arruda, 2008; Harnecker, 2005; Puntasen *et al.*, 2008). Integrating EE and SSE is essential in order to provide more overarching and long-term answers and strategies to address a system change shift to our current waste problem.

Solid waste is a central factor affecting global sustainability. Waste is a driver of environmental and social impacts, and, at the same time, dealing with waste allows for finding pathways out of larger socio-ecological dilemmas. With waste being a resource, waste management then becomes a form of resource management, involving different actors who pursue different interests, often resulting in conflicting outcomes and new negative impacts. In order to understand the economic and political processes that determine current waste management, the key actors involved need to be identified (Schmink and Wood, 1987). This also means studying the economic and political power structures and the policies and infrastructures supporting existing waste management systems. Aside from local governments and private businesses, there is a diverse spectrum of other 'informal' and organized actors that work in household waste collection and resource recovery (recycling) in most Southern cities and sometimes also in cities in the global North. This book focuses on the specific groups of waste-related actors.

A participatory and community-based epistemology, with a Southern perspective, is crucial to understanding what it means to work in the 'informal' and organized waste sector. Southern theory seeks to view cities in the global South in their own context and on their own terms, not necessarily through theories developed in the global North. This book proposes to learn from Southern examples, because many patterns here are indicative of future possibilities and challenges for other cities in the global South and beyond. In the resource rich, large and populous BRIC countries (Brazil, Russia, India and China) in particular, consumption is rapidly growing in line with rising incomes. Increasing inequality and socioeconomic polarization is another social characteristic of these countries. Extreme poverty and lack of economic opportunities drive this population into waste collection and resource recovery.

Local governments need to be informed about the assets of and barriers to 'informal' and organized recycling, and the policies, infrastructures, and technical as well as financial resources required for inclusive solid waste management (co-management). Some cities in the South already have progressive regulations in solid waste management and are experimenting with innovative forms of inclusive, selective household waste collection. These cases are still rare and are sometimes disputed by those actors that defend the use of labour saving, expensive technologies in waste management. The diverse case studies and experiences from different parts of the global South discussed in this book provide important insights to, and lessons on, the opportunities, possibilities, challenges and barriers related to inclusive and participatory solid waste management.

2.2 The overarching frame of situated Urban Political Ecology

2.2.1 Critical theory

The research is situated in the context of *critical theory*, seeking to understand broad human–environmental challenges related to production, consumption and waste; involving, particularly, city actors and urban processes in the global South. Critical theory has originated out of the *Frankfurt School of Sociology*, influencing contemporary research in many different fields, including social theory, philosophy, communications theory, human geography cultural studies and other disciplines (see Wiggershaus, 1986). Critical methodology distinguishes itself as a critique of positivism (e.g. Adorno's critique of science and technology), questioning accepted mainstream views, deconstructing ideologies and conventional interpretations, and making visible the hidden facets in society. Critical theorists were among the first to question mass consumption and consumer society. They developed "critiques of the mass society and provided early warnings concerning the decline of individuality and freedom and threats to democracy in the brave new world of consumer capitalism" (Kellner, n.d.: 2). The notion of critical theory is connected to decolonizing ways of thinking and acting, as, for example, *Feminist and Anarchist theories* demand. Radical thinking also gained popularity in geography in the early 1980s, with the establishment of an annual meeting for critical geography (Peet, 1977, 1998).

Critical theory perspectives recognize subjectivity, self-reflexivity and the awareness of social and political embeddedness, refocusing on the potentially mundane and everyday experiences (Blomley, 2006). As to Herbert Marcuse, a prominent member of the *Frankfurt School*:

> To investigate the roots of [social] developments and examine their historical alternatives is part of the aim of a critical theory, a theory which analyzes society in the light of its used and unused or abused capacities for improving the human condition.
>
> (Bauder and Engel-Di-Mauro, 2008: 1)

Recent critical theorists work in an interdisciplinary way and attempt to articulate the interrelations between economy, state, society, culture and individual everyday experiences. Scholars like Jürgen Habermas, Hannah Arendt and Michel Foucault, for example, have widely influenced current social and political debates. They are cited in the context of critical geography and have been prominent in critiquing consumer capitalism and suggesting a new perspective also from within political ecology.

2.2.2 Political ecology

Political ecology has its roots in social theory – specifically in cultural studies and political theory (particularly in political economy) – and attempts to better understand relationships and interactions between society and the natural world (Braun and Castree, 1998; Fischer and Hajer, 1999, Heynen *et al.*, 2006). The increasingly complex societal challenges related to environmental change most often lack an ethics of environmental justice and social change (Bryant, 1998). Political ecology tries to reveal and comprehend the intricate and multifaceted environmental and social impacts of human activities. The approach seeks to politicize understandings of the distribution or absence of resources. Political ecology theory helps us comprehend existing social and environmental injustices, and is often inspired by a practical, grass-roots method. Beyond questioning distributive issues posthumanism sees the elimination of the existing divide between humans and nature as the most important paradigm shift in order to transcend current global societal challenges.

The production of urban nature has mostly been the domain of architects, engineers or planners, with not much attention given to the profoundly political aspect of the arrangement of roads, trail tracks, paths, waterways or landfills. The transformation of nature becomes perceptible, both in its physical form and its socio-ecological outcomes. Cities most often are the result of a profoundly transformed nature, destroyed in its essence and reproduced as a sterile *green environment*, without biodiversity, giving rise to what Lefebvre has termed "second nature" (1976). These new urban environments often contain nothing that resembles nature. Endless landscapes of suburbia, with collated houses and an absence of trees or bushes, extend for many kilometres particularly in the megacities with extreme examples such as Mexico City, São Paulo, Kuala-Lumpur and many others.

2.2.3 Urban Political Ecology

Political ecology in the specific urban context

> recognizes that the material conditions that comprise urban environments are controlled, manipulated and serve the interests of the elite at the expense of marginalized populations. These conditions, in turn, are not independent from social, political and economic processes and from cultural constructions of what constitutes the "urban" or the "natural".
>
> (Heynen *et al*., 2006: 6)

While most early work in political ecology was focused on socio-political questions and power struggles in rural environments, some scholars (Bryant, 1998) noted early the need for a focus on the urban perspective in the global South, where rapid and unequal rates of urbanization became evident in recent decades.

In their edited book *In The Nature of Cities* (Heynen *et al*., 2006), the authors apply the evolving political ecology theory to the city environment, enquiring who produces what kind of socio-ecological outcomes and for whom. Urban political ecology has become a far-reaching theoretical approach to urban research, with a strong political notion that attempts to explain particularly those processes that lead to uneven urban environments. "Environmental transformations are not independent of class, gender, ethnicity, or other power struggles". [These processes] ... "produce socio-environmental conditions that are both enabling, for powerful individuals and groups, and disabling, for marginalized individuals and groups" (Heynen *et al*., 2006: 10). David Harvey introduces the phenomena of *accumulation by dispossession*, where the urban poor are removed from more central spaces, dedicated to economic accumulation (2012). Throughout Southern cities the economy of dispossession of vulnerable populations is evident almost everywhere and it is perpetuated by urban capital, which accumulates in the large centres in particular.

2.2.4 *Urban metabolism*

The concept of urban metabolism gives us a systems perspective of the city, where everything (social processes, spatial form and the material/energy metabolism) is connected and interwoven, as noted by Swyngedouw and Heynen (2003). Together with the *ecological footprint* analysis (Wackernagel and Rees, 1996) and the water footprint analysis (Hoekstra *et al.*, 2009) the concept of urban metabolism is useful for identifying and understanding material flows and their impacts on the city and its inhabitants. The analysis studies the entry, transformation and storage of materials and energy and the discharge of waste and unwanted products. Here, infrastructure and service provision play crucial roles in maintaining cities and providing for the residents (see Figure 2.1).

In this context the authors describe the city as a *socio-natural landscape*, transformed by human activity, with physical and socio-ecological consequences. Urban metabolism is a complex systems approach with a cyclical perspective, which when applied to planning and development, shows where cities are not livable, or are unhealthy and unsustainable (Newman and Jennings, 2008). A major goal is to strive for greater resilience to inevitable internal and external shocks that might impact the city. From an industrial ecology perspective, material and energy flows are quantified and studied to make cities more self-sufficient (Gandy, 2004). This approach helps identify inefficiencies, patterns, drivers and lifestyles that cause environmental problems. The knowledge is used to improve metabolic efficiency and to reduce the quantity of resources used per person or unit of economic output, by applying a cradle-to-cradle design. These are strategies and methods that help implement dematerialization, also discussed under decoupling in a post-capitalist society (Czech and Daly, 2004; Jackson, 2009b). Steady-state economy, involving stabilizing the economy without growth in consumption, will require, according to Jackson (2009a), the development of a new macroeconomic model.

2.2.5 *Cyborg*

Recently, some authors have been reinterpreting cities away from a dualistic and towards a socio-natural hybrid perspective, called *cyborg* (Kaika and Swyngedouw, 2000; Gandy, 2006). Material and energy flows, but also political, technical, economic, ecologic and social processes and relations are considered in such urban analyses. Cyborg emphasizes the overlap between the body and the city, particularly the connection between physical infrastructure and technological networks, and the human body. Introducing the concept of hybrids draws attention to the physical materiality and importance of infrastructure and technology. Cities depend on their hinterlands as important interfaces between nature and society, not only for resource extraction and energy supply, but also for waste disposal, to move waste out of sight of urban inhabitants. Urban metabolism analysis provides for a better understanding of waste flows and who is involved in these flows, as well as the social and power relations that underpin the predominant forms of generating and managing waste.

2.2.6 Power structures and relations

Urban Political Ecology literature is recently shifting from the purely class-oriented perspectives of distributional inequities to views that also recognize racism as a factor in environmental injustices (Keil, 2013). Citizenship, political rights and social movements become central lenses in UPE studies. Through participatory democratic deliberation citizens acknowledge the potential impacts that the civil society has in transforming the urban environment.

Theoretical developments give rise to a change in perspective from government to governance and more specifically, to urban and environmental governance and the underlying governmentality (a term coined by Michel Foucault expressing the ways in which the state governs and exercises control over its population) (Gibbs and Jonas, 2000). Nevertheless, it often takes a long time for theoretical understandings to translate into wider praxis. Everyday practices by which urban flows are governed and the role power relations play in this are of recent focus and help fill that gap. Too often, social movements, individual resistance and civil disobedience are curtailed by the dominant power structures that maintain current situations and yet they are the necessary seeds for future change.

Power provides an actor with the means to control resources or the environment of others and to maintain the status quo. As Schmink and Wood pointed out almost 20 years ago, "ideas are never innocent but either reinforce or challenge existing social and economic arrangements" (1987: 51). Economic and political elites invariably seek to maintain and justify existing, often highly unequal patterns of resource use. As a consequence disadvantaged groups have been more adversely affected than others, which sometimes even manifests in patterns of human health, disease and mortality (Mayer, 1996).

Deprivation is not a uniform process (Bryant, 1998). A colonial legacy, still alive in many countries, is the widespread accumulation of wealth and power of political and economic elites, while large parts of society are deprived. The exploitation of resources and human populations and the subjugation and maintenance of hegemonic economic and political power structures during the colonial empire (until the early nineteenth century in Latin America and until the beginning to mid-twentieth century in Africa and Asia), often followed later by military dictatorships, have cemented highly unequal and unjust social relations and a political system characterized by neo-patrimony (burdened with over-bureaucracy and corruption) (Erdmann and Engel, 2006). As a counter-reaction, subordinate groups typically try to challenge these elites, partly by developing a culture of resistance to the existing dominant group. Grass-roots activism and social movements propose a rupture of persisting unequal power relations. Furthermore, feminist political ecology perspectives uncover specific gender-related inequities and female oppression, but also multiple incidents of women's resistance and emancipation. Miraftab (2004a) argues that trash has historically been linked to women, given the patriarchal gender ideology which defines the home and neighbourhood as spaces to be overseen by women. McGurty (1998) provides an account based on Chicago, where during the last century, when cities were facing serious public health issues with the lack of sanitation and hygiene, women's clubs and associations took on a leading role in the development of proper waste collection strategies and in demanding the state's duty and participation in waste management. In the contemporary Southern city context we see a strong involvement of women in waste-related work, from exploitive working conditions to empowering collective forms of organization (Kerstenetzky, 2007). In the case of Cape Town, South Africa, Samson (2003) details how women were contracted as cheap labour, on a short-term basis, for waste collection and as volunteers for street sweeping. Samson (2009) later describes several cases were women recyclers have consciously chosen to form women-only cooperatives (*Coopcarmo*, Brazil and *Indepenencia de la Mujer*, Uruguay), in order to build their confidence and challenge gender stereotypes, demonstrating that they are able to do the same work as men. Women have found opportunities to build their agency through work in recycling cooperatives, permitting them to take up leadership roles and assume more responsibility in the work within the cooperative and in the organization of their category.

2.2.7 Situating urban political ecology

Applying a situated context in urban political ecology means recognizing the differences and valuing everyday praxis for generating solutions to pressing urban problems. Situated urban political ecology is, then, a useful framework for understanding the complexity of daily material lives confronted with social justice, poverty and inequality realities, as well as their environmental and ecological dimensions, mostly constituted through unequal power relations.

The interesting part of actor-network theory is that it recognizes non-human actors as part of the political universe and it does not see people as particularly special compared to other forms of life, but rather understands society as a heterogeneous network bound together. Humans are not put on a higher value scale than plants and animals. Such a perspective acknowledges new forms of encounters between human and non-humans, giving rise to new relations and political practices (in the literature discussed under posthumanism). Actor-network theory studies "ways in which patterning generates institutional and organizational effects, including hierarchy and power" (Law, 1992: 2). Further, actor-network theory writers suggest "that the social is nothing other than patterned networks of heterogeneous materials [and that] . . . these networks are composed not only of people, but also of machines, animals, texts, money, architectures – any material that you care to mention" (Law, 1992: 2). The analysis of ordering struggle is central to actor-network theory, with a focus on exploring and describing local processes of patterning, social composition, ordering and resistance. According to this theoretical lens organizations and institutions are also actors, tied into networks that participate and shape social processes of everyday life. In these organizations and institutions we find more or less patterned roles (bureaucracy, regulations, legislation, etc.) enacted by people, machines, texts – all of which may be complacent or may offer resistance. We usually do not detect network complexities in everyday business and activities, but according to Law (1992: 5) "all phenomena are the effect or the product of heterogeneous networks". Demystifying and uncovering network relations, for example, of the actors involved in solid waste management (from government, private business, 'informal' sector workers, cooperatives, associations and local entrepreneurs, to civil society), helps us understand existing dominant power structures, providing entries to deconstruct and innovate existing orders. A participatory research methodology provides opportunities to closely study the exertion and impacts of power.

2.3 Participatory methodology

Participatory research developed out of Marxist and critical social theory and is committed to social transformation and sustainability. It presupposes an inclusive research process, which creates new epistemologies, where knowledge is co-created and jointly validated and where the research process in itself is a major result situating and changing ontolog' s. This approach allows the bridging of gaps that often exist between research and practice, by addressing social and environmental justice and enabling people to gain control over determinants of their quality of life and working conditions. The value of this research methodology lies in engaging local community members or stakeholders in the research process, rather than including them only as passive subjects of the research. Participatory research means research with participants instead of on them. The individuals intended to be the beneficiaries, users and stakeholders of the research have a voice and participate in the research design, implementation and dissemination of results.

Paulo Freire, Orlando Fals Borda, João Francisco de Souza and later Carlos Rodrigues Brandão and Michel Thiollent, among many others, made important contributions to a Southern perspective of participatory research. Many different terms fall under participatory research approaches, such as participatory rural appraisal (Chambers, 1994), community-based research (Israel *et al.*, 2005; Minkler and Wallerstein, 2003), assets-based community development (Alison and Cunningham, 2003), empowerment evaluation (Fetterman and Wandersman, 2005), Participatory Action Research (Kemmis and McTaggart, 2000), appreciative inquiry (Cooperrider and Whitney, 2005), decolonizing methodologies (Smith, 1999) and other forms of action research taking on a participatory philosophy (Stringer and Dwyer, 2005). Participatory research approaches were first used to address public health issues (Cargo and Mercer 2008) and then developed for use in other disciplinary and thematic backgrounds.

Action research is a collaborative and transformative approach with joint focus on systematic data collection, knowledge generation, reflection and distinctive action elements that pursue practical solutions and change (Reason and Bradbury, 2008). Participation is one of the key characteristics. Scholars working in Participatory Action Research believe the oppressed and relatively powerless can develop agency by supporting them and making them aware of their own assets, by increasing their ability to solve problems and by helping them to become more self-reliant and less dependent (Fals Borda, 2001; Arieli *et al.*, 2009; Brandão, 1982; Thiollent, 2008).

The work with recycling cooperatives in the metropolitan region of São Paulo, which will be introduced in Chapter 3, has applied a Participatory Action Research framework. The research process, as well as some of the results (actions) achieved over the course of the *Participatory Sustainable Waste Management* (PSWM) programme, is discussed throughout this book.

2.4 Conclusion: situating waste into an everyday social and political context

Waste is inherently a trans-disciplinary problem that cannot be addressed by technology alone. Waste generation and how we deal with waste also requires social, economical, ecological and political lenses to fully comprehend the topic. For the analysis of everyday and multifaceted issues such as those associated with consumption and solid waste production, urban political ecology becomes a useful framework for understanding the connections between these apparently unconnected issues. The framework identifies relationships between consumers and households, the city and state regulators, 'informal' and organized recyclers as well as the relationships with industry, middlemen and other stakeholders who have an interest in waste (and in maintaining a clean city) in a broadly defined economy. The approach focuses in particular on the political forces involved and the power structures that keep the status quo (Foucault, 1982).

The urban political ecology approach allows for the identification of actors involved in waste collection services as well as the absence of these services. Actor-network theory is instrumental in mapping and highlighting the links between different actors and, in particular, in identifying missing links between them. Local governments are often unable to work with an inter-sectorial perspective, and these missing links between secretaries or other key stakeholders hinders the implementation of a city's public services and infrastructures. In solid waste management, for example, municipal secretaries and actors often do not talk to each other and don't collaborate in their programme implementations. As waste embodies and expresses social relations, it also represents the production and reproduction of power relations. With actor-network theory, power relations are uncovered, identifying the politics that lead to current waste dilemmas in many cities. Urban political ecology seeks for new approaches to human–environment interactions, such as those that are waste related. Deconstructing dominant discourses around waste generation, disposal and management, helps us to understand why there are disparities in waste collection services and different understandings about what to do with the increasing amounts of waste.

Analysing political discourse in effect on waste incineration, waste-to-energy, and also on resource recovery, waste picking and recycling, provides insights for dismantling the dominant paradigm in waste management. UPE links the analysis of specific urban environmental problems to larger socio-ecological alternatives. Solid waste links to wide-ranging challenges created by consumption/over consumption, resource depletion/environmental contamination, injustice and poverty. In political ecology, distributional and systemic inequities shaping social relationships and the socioeconomic order are studied at different levels from the global (North/South) to the local scale, and racism and colonial practices as a leading factors in environmental injustices are recognized.

A recent development of privatizing solid waste management is apparent in many countries of the global South, with the consequence of transforming solid waste – from common property good, being utilized particularly by the urban poor – into a privatized resource to be exploited by a few rich companies. These developments are part of a new wave of *accumulation by dispossession*. Similar trends have been described for water and sanitation, with water service provision shifting from the public to the private sector. Private investors are driven by full cost recovery, which often means investment in profitable neighbourhoods, while less wealthy neighbourhoods are left out or receive lower quality services (see, e.g. Smith and Hanson, 2003; Tan, 2012). Loftus (2012) argues that the violent appropriation of common resources marks not a brief and passing phase in the history of capitalism, but an ongoing process necessary for its survival (see also Swyngedouw, 2004).

Left wing theorists envision a wide range of new programmes, experiments and theories for a transition beyond capitalism. Supporters of a post-capitalist economy argue that the current capitalist economic system (which dominates production, distribution, consumption and discard) is approaching its end and will be replaced by a more dynamic system, reshaping the economy around new values and behaviours.

Some of the indicators for the weaknesses of modern capitalism are frequent economic and social crisis situations, as well as ecological impasses (climate change, biodiversity loss, natural resources over-exploitation, water crises, marine habitat destruction, overfishing, deforestation, etc.) culminating in those planetary changes recognized for having shifted the earth into a new geological era (the *Anthropocene*), characterized by the dominant, destructive influence of humans – primarily the political and economic elite – on the earth.

Given the urgency for fundamental changes in the way our economy is run to materialize, post-capitalists envision a transition that will be accelerated by external shocks and shaped by the emergence of a new kind of human being. They argue that this transformation process has already started. These new developments open up unlimited opportunities to reshape work, production, consumption, transportation and ways of addressing waste issues. With innovations in information technology and the spontaneous rise of the Social and Solidarity Economy in the fields of collaborative production and services, the market and the managerial hierarchy are no longer solely dictating the development path.

Still unnoticed in the mainstream media, alternative ways of engaging with the economy are emerging in different places. Parallel currencies, time banks, eco-banks, local exchange systems cooperatives, associations, social entrepreneurships and self-managed spaces are proliferating, often as a direct result of crisis situations. These mostly small-scale and local projects need to be nurtured, promoted and protected by fundamental changes in what governments usually do (Mason, 2015).

The collective work of waste pickers already contributes to the social and political transformation towards resource recovery, circular economy and a more inclusive, democratic and just society. The recyclers are important agents for that change, communicating with and educating the local population about resource recovery and *zero waste*. Collective forms of working and the sharing of assets, spaces and services are on the horizon. Cooperatives and social enterprises are bottom-up approaches in the waste management and recycling sectors that are already driving change in many parts of the global South and increasingly also in cities in the global North. These workers already contribute to building more resilient communities. They tackle what Nieman *et al.* (2009) and other authors have suggested in order to obtain more sustainable ways of dealing with waste; by minimizing material and energy consumption; closing product life-cycle loops through reuse, recycling and remanufacturing; as well as through dematerialization by offering services instead of physical products. Cooperative recycling is carving out new spaces of hope, and through praxis they embody the potential for democratic social and economic change.

3 Participatory community-based research

Theory and praxis

DOI: 10.4324/9781315686523-3
This chapter has been made available under a CC-BY-NC-ND 4.0 license.

Summary

Most empirical data presented in this book stems from participatory, action-oriented methodology embedded in a long-term international research collaboration: the *Participatory Sustainable Waste Management* (PSWM) project. This community–university partnership was conducted with recycling cooperatives in the metropolitan region of São Paulo, between 2005 and 2012. In this chapter I discuss the theoretical grounding of participatory, community-based research with reference to problem-based learning. I then present details about the project's history, objectives and implementation, followed by an analysis of key challenges that affected the project during its life. Finally, some lessons learned from the praxis in relation to the institutional and community rationale, contributing to theory, are shared.

3.1 Introduction: communities increasing research visibility

Universities are acknowledged places for innovative reflection, critical thinking and the generation and dissemination of knowledge for the enduring improvement of quality of life and the environment. Through teaching, learning and research, universities have a unique role to play in contributing to the advancement of society in a wide-ranging variety of fields (Toakley, 2004). Yet, there is often little transparency about the hurdles and challenges involved in community–university practices on an institutional level.

This chapter discusses the experience of the *Participatory Sustainable Waste Management* (PSWM) project, an action-oriented, participatory research collaboration between the University of Victoria, Canada, and the University of São Paulo, Brazil, realized with 32 recycling cooperatives in the metropolitan region of São Paulo between 2005 and 2012. The interactive qualitative research methodology applied to this project has allowed for the co-creation of valuable knowledge with the 'informal' and organized recycling sector, and for dissemination among the wider community, government, academia and agents working in solid waste management. The PSWM, originally conceived as a project, over time has evolved into a programme attending to a large additional spectrum of different research and outreach activities. Since funding for the project ended, the programme has continued with participatory and action-driven work between practitioners and recyclers, focusing on inclusive, selective waste collection and recycling, with objectives and work agendas adjusted to the current needs and interests prioritized by the recyclers.

I begin this chapter with a brief introduction to the theoretical context of Community–University partnerships and participatory, community-based research. The discussion touches on power-related challenges and barriers that can hinder universities in their quest to become more community oriented. Next, I describe the project's history, origins and development. I introduce the main objectives, long-term aims, and organizational structure of the project and, finally, present some of the lessons learned and contributions to theory and praxis.

3.2 Participatory community–university research

Universities are increasingly promoting the value of community engagement and there is a growing recognition of the importance of community-based research (CBR) in the academy (Armitage, 2005; Crowther *et al.* 2005; Israel *et al.* 2001, 1998). CBR arises out of a strong commitment between members from the community and from the university, meeting in dialogue and recognizing the knowledge that both sides can contribute. This means that the researcher has to get out of her or his comfort zone. It is research with, in, as well as, for the community, and is thus a form of participatory research that embodies a key to participatory development. In community-based research, partners contribute their knowledge to create a better understanding of a given phenomenon and then act on the problems identified to benefit the community involved. The paradigmatic difference to traditional research approaches is that CBR is done with the participants – academics work side by side with community members to define research questions and methods, and to analyse, disseminate and ultimately implement results. CBR derived out of social movement learning from the 1940s. In particular, Kurt Levin's insights on participatory and action-oriented research have further developed this revolutionizing, bottom-up, qualitative research methodology, which is now changing researchers, communities and institutions in many parts of the world.

There are key benefits to participatory CBR. This form of research tackles communities' real needs. Research questions are formulated with or by community members and leaders address their problems and bottlenecks, benefitting the wider society. CBR is more effective in explaining the complexity of everyday problems, taking a trans-disciplinary and often multi-sectorial approach. Because of its transparent and participatory nature, CBR has the potential to build trust and respect between university and community members and other organizations.

Israel and her colleagues have developed a set of key principles for participatory CBR (2001). First of all, CBR needs to recognize the community as a unit of social and cultural identity which has particular assets to build upon. CBR engages in the joint production of knowledge and needs to facilitate collaborative and equitable involvement of the partners during all phases of research. As in action research,

CBR has a cyclical and iterative nature, with phases of observing, reflecting and acting. CBR is a holistic method in the sense of including social, economic, cultural and environmental perspectives, knowledge and diverse ways of knowing in the research process. Finally, CBR does not mean parachuting into a research scenario, but rather builds trust and establishes long-term commitments with partners.

Participatory CBR is grounded in the experiences of the communities involved and aspires to generate research findings that have policy implications. It is not enough to just advocate for a CBR approach; the lessons learned need to be applied on a wider scale. Authors like Brandão (1987), Fals Borda and Rahman (1991), Hall (1981), Levine *et al.* (1994), Thiollent (2008) and many others have dedicated their work to developing inclusive, democratic and participatory research methodologies. Community–university partnerships, and specifically CBR initiatives, help in reducing disparities and finding appropriate pathways to our many current problems and unsustainable contexts. A Canada-wide survey confirmed that CBR "is rapidly gaining recognition as an important tool in addressing complex environmental, health and social problems" (Flicker *et al.*, 2007: 1). The study also found high levels of satisfaction with the processes and outcomes of CBR, including results in the form of policy changes. A recent study on global trends in support structures for community–university research partnerships sheds some light on the different types of institutional arrangements in place and on how research partnerships are initiated and supported (Tremblay *et al.*, 2014). The results emphasize the increasing international role of CBR. For a comprehensive overview of CBR see University of Washington (n.d.).

3.2.1   *Participatory CBR and power structures*

In some cases the trend of CBR may conflict with existing hegemonic roles within universities. Giddens (1997) identifies hegemony as the penetration throughout society of an entire system of values, attitudes, beliefs and morality that contribute to supporting the status quo, which also means maintaining existing power relations. For Giddens, hegemony is the "organising principle" that spreads with socialization into every area of daily life and becomes part of what is generally called common sense. Consequently the philosophy, culture and morality of the ruling elite appear as the prevailing natural order of things (Boggs, 1976). Gramsci sees the school system as just one part of the system of ideological hegemony in which individuals are socialized into maintaining the status quo. Crowther *et al.* (2005) hold a similarly critical view of the academy and its predominantly positivist and elitist attitudes.

Furthermore David Harvey (2001: 197) reminds us that:

> Foucault has again and again pointed out that discourses of power, attached to distinctive mediating institutions (such as the state apparatus or, more informally within the worlds of education, religion, knowledge production and the media) typically play their often overwhelming disciplinary and authoritarian role. Hegemony becomes the focus of political struggle. Imposing conceptions of the world and thereby limiting the ability to construe alternatives is always a central task of dominant institutions of power.

Knowledge co-generation on the basis of community-based and action-oriented research supports transparent, inclusive relations between participants and can become a threat to those in power who don't want a change in the status quo. Participatory education recognizes the importance of local and often indigenous knowledge and its complementary role in understanding processes and searching for appropriate solutions. Paulo Freire (1973) remembers the critical importance of community learners' own experience and knowledge in expanding capacities. Often participatory methodologies and epistemologies that are founded in the joint creation of knowledge challenge the existing power structures prevailing in communities and in formal institutions, including universities. As a consequence, these potential changes in paradigm question institutions and their administrators. Grassroots ontologies can generate conflict and produce disciplinary actions, repression and heightened bureaucracy, thus ultimately hindering the implementation of actions and activities for change.

3.2.2 Problem-based learning

Problem-based learning is a vehicle for involving students in research projects, giving them a practical learning experience as they contribute to participatory development. It is a radical alternative to mainstream academic work and teaching that is disconnected from "real life" and is thus not of direct benefit to local communities. Participation of different stakeholders in the research process is the fundamental ingredient of this approach (see also Blackburn *et al.*, 2001). Community–university research projects open up great opportunities for students to learn alongside community members about their specific, everyday problems that can be tackled in short-term studies or theses. Many universities support these transformative learning opportunities.

Problem-based learning is an effective approach applied within popular education. Crowther *et al.* (2005) define popular education as education that supports social interests and movements as they challenge inequality and discrimination. Popular education, which can be facilitated via partnerships between the university and the local communities, engages social interests and movements in knowledge generation and dissemination, particularly by helping people to connect their stories to global issues so that local experiences are understood as part of a larger context. Seen in this light, popular education incorporates community-based research by way of transforming research participants into key protagonists in the process of social change. The umbrella of CBR popular education and problem-based learning provides opportunities for sharing responsibilities and outcomes.

3.2.3 Participation

Participation is important for the achievement of durable results, because through participation the stakeholder has a sense of responsibility for the results. There are different forms in which people can participate and there are various levels of participation, as pointed out in Arnstein's *Ladder of Citizen Participation* (Arnstein, 1969). At the lowest level, community participation means providing data that is extracted from the community with no return. At the highest level, participants fully engage in decision-making related to all aspects of the research and the dissemination of results.

The participatory approach to education and research raises issues of agency and thus has the potential to promote power shifts (Tembo, 2003). It is in itself a form of participatory development particularly when it increases the involvement of socially and economically vulnerable people in decision-making over their own lives (Ericson, 2006; Guijt and Braden, 1999). As widely discussed for Participatory Action research, the research process itself has transformative power and is as important (or even more important) as achieving set results.

Finally, for popular education and participatory CBR to be effective, appropriate spaces for dialogue between university and community need to be created. Separation between academia and communities is often perpetuated through barriers of language (formalities, academic language or disciplinary jargon), bureaucracy, formal structures and lengthy procedures. Accessible, adequate, conducive spaces and access to the means required to bring people together are practical prerequisites for community–university partnerships to happen.

3.3 Aims, objectives and structure of the *Participatory Sustainable Waste Management* project

The vision that inspired the PSWM project was the goal of collectively transforming the life of waste pickers, improving their working conditions and their livelihood outcomes. The programme aims to expand participatory processes and strengthen the organization of 'informal' recyclers in order to increase existing capacities and to improve effectiveness and safety during the collection, separation, stocking and commercialization of recyclables. The understanding of the team involved in PSWM is that capacity building is concerned with social and political relationships and concentrates on enabling people to overcome discriminatory practices that limit their life-chances. It is a process of collective learning that enables people to determine and achieve livelihood improvements. This includes making information available, because information reduces uncertainty and widens decision-making options (Eade, 1997).

Another goal is to increase the awareness among governments and the public for waste co-management, acknowledging opportunities for employment creation with reuse and recycling. This, further, means recognizing and fairly remunerating the services provided by the recyclers. Inclusive forms of selective solid waste collection and recycling contribute overall to more sustainable forms of transitioning away from the current waste of resources via landfilling or incineration. In the long run, PSWM contributes to urban environmental sustainability, through promoting inclusive and environmentally pro-active actions related to solid waste avoidance, minimization, reuse and recycling (see Box 3.1).

BOX 3.1: Key goals under the PSWM project

1 improve the organization of 'informal' recyclers and strengthen their networking capabilities;
2 empower the recyclers to improve safety while handling recyclable materials (collection, separation, storage, and marketing);
3 promote the integration of recycling cooperatives for the collective commercialization of their recyclable materials;
4 promote discussion among government and civil society for the construction of public policies on solid waste management that are inclusive and supportive of community recycling initiatives;
5 improve overall environmental quality in cities and promote social and environmental sustainability.

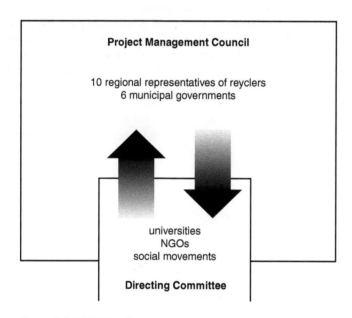

Figure 3.1 PSWM project management structure.

A significant differential of the PSWM project to other community–university collaborations is its deliberative and participatory management structure. The Management Council, composed of ten leaders representing the recycling cooperatives, six representatives from the local governments, and all members from the Directing Committee, embodies the heart of the PSWM project (Figure 3.1). The Directing Committee was composed of three university professors (USP, FSA, UVic), two leaders from the recycling cooperatives, two representatives from civil society organizations and a fluctuating number of graduate students from Canada and Brazil. Three of the participants of the Directing Committee were also engaged as field coordinators, responsible for maintaining a close contact with participants and stakeholders in two municipalities each.

The Management Council met three to four times per year, usually over a period of one to three days. Members from the Directing Committee who could not participate in person were present by way of teleconferencing. The meetings had the purpose of planning activities and discussing action strategies, informing results, and monitoring and evaluating outcomes. Research was combined with capacity building, designed to overcome knowledge gaps and deconstruct power relations. The use of interactive, participatory methods of capturing ideas and the voices of the participants made these meetings a rich learning experience. All Management Council meetings were audiotaped or videotaped and handwritten notes were generated. The meetings were also photographed. Reports on the previous meeting were handed to participants during the following meetings, keeping the participants informed and able to report back to their groups.

The overall methodology applied in the PSWM project was participatory and action oriented, inspired by Brandão (1987) and Thiollent (2008). Critical interdisciplinary literature on postcolonial and feminist theory, situated political economy and situated political ecology were some of the key frameworks that stimulated thinking and praxis. In the project design, participants had agreed unanimously to work with awareness-building processes in the sense of Paulo Freire's work on *conscientização*. Organized recyclers were considered the target group to benefit from this project. This meant prioritizing resources for actions/activities/training/ equipment that directly benefitted the recycling cooperatives. Continuous reflection on achievements, barriers, difficulties, and assets during the Management Council meetings provoked an unforeseen rich contribution to capacity development, which involved all participants. The concrete space created by the Management Council was fundamental for knowledge democratization and the collective creation of new ideas (Cahill, 2007; Hall, 2005).

3.4 Sharing a story: recyclers taking ownership of the project

Due to uneven development metropolitan regions in the global South suffer the complex social, economic and environmental consequences of increased waste generation, further augmented by the neglect of adequate solutions to the major environmental health concerns. At the same time, opportunities for generating livelihoods through resource recovery are apparent. The social and environmental intricacy of solid waste problems in the city, as well as the prospect for change, became the key motivator for the PSWM community–university engagement with the 'informal' and organized recycling sector.

A trustful partnership with a core group of Brazilian professionals (academics and grass-roots activists), most of whom I had previously known, enabled the formal development of the project idea on participatory sustainable waste management, which began to take shape in December 2003 during a workshop involving this group in the discussion of initial project ideas. We shared central notions and key principles on research and community extension methods linked to social and environmental justice as a fundamental prerequisite, enabling us to develop a deep collaborative and supportive relationship. In 2004, we submitted the Letter of Intent for the PSWM project to the funding agency (the Canadian International Development Agency), which was approved. During the following months, and particularly between July and September 2004, we created the original project documents in English and Portuguese. The project was approved in March 2005, giving rise to a long-term community–university partnership, co-creating the results described in this book.

A three-day workshop was held with all partners and collaborators during the inception phase of the project (June to October 2005), to adjust the strategic plan, redefine activities and time frames, establish the project's principles and form the Management Council. A social relations analysis with a *Venn diagram* was conducted to identify strengths and weaknesses of the relations among partner institutions, and to define and plan key procedures (such as timing of workshops, priority themes, numbers and characteristics of participants, etc.) and goals. The guiding principles agreed upon were: participation, co-management, partnership, continuity, sustainability, equity (which also includes gender equity), economic viability and *apropriação* (empowerment) (see Photograph 3.1).

Our strategy was to build on existing assets. Capacity building promotes not just isolated initiatives, but ongoing, socially constructed and negotiated processes involving a variety of stakeholders. It is not simply the execution of a plan of action; but it is also a process that touches political agendas, challenges existing power structures and facilitates previously excluded people to have a say in local

Photograph 3.1 Collective learning during a Management Council meeting.

development. In the context of PSWM, capacity building is understood as a reflective, agency-building process, allowing for leadership, inspiration and adaptation to flourish. Fostering communication, relationships, conflict resolution and improving the ability of dealing with differences are key characteristics in this process.

Interactive learning is central here, because learning is the process through which information becomes transformative, shifting perspectives. PSWM's participatory learning strategies promote learning from each other's learning, also known as *double-loop learning*. This kind of learning requires us to question and scrutinize fundamental assumptions and values. As Kooiman (2003) rightly identifies, such reflective and interactive learning exercises can be seen as intimidating to governing actors, who may be inclined to avoid or resist social change.

Given the hurdles and bottlenecks experienced over the first two years of the project, it was clear that this participatory endeavour posed an imminent threat to the conservative political spectrum of the administrators in the Brazilian project partner institution (*Fundação Universitária Santo André*) (FSA). Consequently, their bureaucrats severely constrained the implementation of the project during its initial phase. The fact that project activities would nurture the empowerment of waste pickers and allow them to enter spaces (e.g. the university) previously excluded to them, had intimidated the university administration, resulting in them generating an opposition to the PSWM project and its participants. The university administration made use of bureaucracy to delay and hinder project operations. Delays in signing the University Agreement and in opening a bank account hindered access to the project funds. This process peaked in the forced withdrawal of our Brazilian project director and the establishment of a token director by the university administration (who had no previous experience in participatory and community-based research or working with recyclers). Even when the University Agreement was finally signed in August 2006, key bottlenecks persisted, e.g. accessing project funds in Brazil, officially recognizing PSWM partnerships with local governments and NGOs and formalizing the contracts of staff employed by the project.

The democratic decision of the Management Council had granted the leader of the Recycling Forum in São Paulo (one of the PSWM members) a scholarship to enrol in an undergraduate university course at FSA. Given his active political leadership role in the student movement, the university president banned this student from classes. This caused the student movement at FSA to mobilize and produce a manifesto, which was then forcefully oppressed with military police force on campus. The recyclers negotiated a meeting with a group of councilors from Santo André, putting pressure on the mayor to address the conflict between the PSWM project and the university president of FSA (the FSA president is nominated by the mayor) (see Photograph 3.2).

In February 2007, ten local recycling cooperatives and their allies also organized a rally in front of FSA and at the city hall in Santo André. Their signs read: "o projeto é nosso" ("The project is ours"). A delegation of recyclers requested a meeting with the university president, which was not granted. These developments revealed a strong sense of ownership of the PSWM project by the waste pickers. The recyclers were also supported by the National Recyclers' Movement (*Movimento Nacional dos Catadores de Materiais Recicláveis*), *Forum Recicla São Paulo*, the

Vida Limpa selective waste collection programme in Diadema and many other allies. Soon after, FSA underwent a legal investigation of alleged corruption involving the university president, who was finally prosecuted. At the end of 2007, the PSWM transitioned into a new partnership with the Faculty of Education of the University of São Paulo (USP) (see Box 3.2). Although emotionally deeply troubling, this counter-hegemonic experience signified an important highlight in the process of empowering the waste pickers and their organizations. The shared emotions among all project participants created a political collective experience, offering a particular perspective on power and dissent. For our project these shared experiences in social mobilization and civil counteracting provided the necessary glue for the PSWM community partnership research endeavor.

3.5 Some of the achievements of the PSWM project

Outcomes of the Management Council meetings were translated into actions through the coordination and overview of the Directing Committee. During the weekly meetings of the Directing Committee, the implementation of the actions and sub-projects decided on during the Management Council meetings was planned in detail and put into practice with the participants that had agreed to become involved. Over the years, many different collaborators contributed their specific knowledge and methodologies, addressing particular challenges or implementing actions and activities.

New interdisciplinary knowledge was continuously collectively generated during these regular gatherings and during the various activities carried out by project members. The discussions, reflections and actions of the Management Council involved diverse solid waste policy and management issues, including challenges regarding participatory management, social inclusion, gender aspects, collective commercialization and microcredit, among others. We worked with participatory video, photo-voice and other arts-based research tools, helping capture perspectives and facts to address participatory sustainable waste management. Popular knowledge and the numerous elements that reference diverse experiences from the daily life as well as different readings and imaginations of the world became apparent during the Management Council meetings and workshops and were reflected on to guide actions and interventions. Interactive dynamic activities facilitated by members of the Directing Committee or by specific professionals (depending on the topic or theme to be addressed) were conducive to voicing challenges experienced by the recyclers and other members. The focus and research objectives were always defined with the knowledge and collective approval of all Management Council participants.

> The everyday practice and immersed knowledge of the political dimension of the cooperative members and supporters/researchers consolidated a commitment towards promoting empowerment, autonomy and the ability to overcome the oppression of the hegemonic power present in current capitalist modes of production. Respect for the knowledge of the participants, the co-construction of new knowledge and its systematization for collective ownership were fundamental principles in our methodology.
>
> (Gutberlet, 2013: 4612)

BOX 3.2: Voices from the grass-roots: "The project is ours"

Two recyclers, members of the Management Council reveal their commitment to the project and highlight the project's importance to their everyday realities.

> The impasse with the university president immediately harmed the recyclers. The purchase of equipment, an urgent necessity for the groups, was delayed by more than six months. The groups themselves had to reimburse lost earnings for their representatives who left their work to participate in meetings, as the project was unable to partially compensate lost wages as it normally would.
>
> (Interview conducted with Maria)

> But the groups that work with the Canadian project defended the project in this period, because they could already observe the important results that project meetings brought to their lives – organization of collective sales of recyclables allowed us to double the value of some of our materials, increasing workers' earnings, the creation of the micro-credit fund allowed groups to borrow money, and the purchase of equipment necessary to improve the processing of materials was about to begin. The recyclers had confidence in the Project because of these concrete results.
>
> (Interview conducted with Juliana)

Photograph 3.2 Council meeting in the city hall of Santo André with leaders from recycling cooperatives in the metropolitan region of São Paulo.

The results from PSWM were manifold and only some highlights, particularly those that demonstrate knowledge co-creation, are listed below:

1   Strong partnerships, forming a network among the recycling cooperatives involved in the PSWM project, resulted in the formation of two cooperative networks, with a focus on collective commercialization, one is called COOPCENT-ABC Cooperativa Central de Catadores e Catadoras de Materiais Recicláveis do Grande ABC and the other is called Rede Verde Sustentavel – Cooperativa Central de Trabalho de Catadores de Materiais Reciclaveis da Região Metropolitana de São Paulo. These networks continue to promote the ideas of PSWM in the region and beyond.

2   The establishment of continuous dialogue between local governments and recycling cooperatives to develop agreements guaranteeing the participation of cooperatives in solid waste management and related activities at the municipal level. The quality and strength of these collaborations vary. Currently Santana de Parnaíba, Mauá, Ribeirão Pires and Diadema have established strong partnerships, while the collaboration between the government in São Bernardo do Campo, Santo André and some sub-regions in São Paulo continue to struggle.

3   The organization of collection, separation and commercialization of recyclables with recycling cooperatives has expanded. Some of the cooperatives have upgraded their space and infrastructure, resulting in greater work safety.

4   The production of educational resources has been co-created with the recyclers through their praxis and dissemination in the region and outside.

5   Frequent meetings, seminars and workshops have contributed towards strengthening the autonomy and responsibility of individuals involved in cooperative work, fostering a process of emancipation, empowerment and self-management in the cooperatives (*autogestão*).

6   Many participants and leaders have received training on: project management, business administration, computer literacy, material composition and conflict resolution, among other themes, contributing to their professional and personal skills.

7   There has been a diverse and interdisciplinary production of academic products (theses, peer-reviewed articles, reports, books, book chapters) and research dissemination through videos, photographic essays, folders, banners, newspaper articles, participation in radio and TV shows, and other educational materials reaching far beyond the original geographical area of the project.

8   PSWM was also engaged in research and community activities on inclusive solid waste management in Victoria and Vancouver; working closely with the local communities of *binners* (term for 'informal' recyclers in North America). This research has also contributed to the empowerment of these workers and to building greater awareness about resource recovery and the role of recycling and inclusive forms of resource recovery in the global North. The following timeline of PSWM intervention was produced during a final seminar on project monitoring and evaluation (see Photograph 3.3).

Photograph 3.3 Mapping key events and project results during a PSWM evaluation meeting.

3.6 Final considerations

The PSWM project is a North–South, community–university collaboration, engaged in promoting social and environmental justice and involving organized recyclers; one of the most disenfranchised segments in society. The project has challenged the dominant development paradigm with increasing sustainability through participation in municipal solid waste management. The PSWM project has become a reference in co-creating knowledge based on inclusion, participation and democratic deliberation. The participatory project management approach has generated important learning outcomes, demonstrating the transformative potential embedded in the participants.

Our experience has shown that participatory development is an outcome of asset-building processes: procedures that involve transparency, capacity building and collective learning. By supporting recyclers and working with government agents, the project has fostered dialogue and tolerance, diminishing pre-conceived ideas and stigmatization. In the literature, these effects of capacity building are considered as a form of *bridging social capital*, which I like to call bridging social assets or goods (Chaskin *et al.*, 2006).

Participatory management is a lengthy and demanding process. However, over time, it builds the agency of its participants and provides them with tools for co-responsible decision-making. It is a critical ingredient of Solidarity Economy initiatives, including the formation of associations and cooperatives. It is important to remember that such forms of collective organization do not automatically evoke democratic processes (Kerstenetzky, 2003). We have learned that the praxis of democratic values needs to be understood as an ongoing challenging exercise.

The project has co-generated knowledge and has involved its participants in collective actions that have helped improve their quality of life. While corruption, opposing political agendas, and fear of changing existing local and regional power structures has at times seriously affected the project's implementation, the PSWM project has shown that transparent and participatory structures do encourage stakeholders to take ownership and co-responsibility for the project implementation, developing solidarity and collaborative relationships between themselves and their supporters.

The project experience also demonstrates that universities can actively engage in asset-building activities striving for more just and sustainable societies. The university has a responsibility to question and critically analyse societal processes and to propose appropriate system changing solutions. The student body needs to be involved in problem-solving, practice-oriented research projects. Empirical research through such projects, for example, leads to a better understanding of current social and political problems. As a result, students have real life experiences and are better prepared for their professional future. Furthermore, this experience revealed that student-led learning and grassroots pedagogical approaches have the potential for decolonization and radical learning (from the Latin *radix* meaning 'root').

There are a number of key lessons that have been learned through this project regarding community–university engagement through participatory development, pointing towards effective strategies for universities to proceed in the face of these opportunities and constraints.

- Institutional co-responsibility in setting and implementing development agendas is a process that requires patience, transparency and communication skills.
- Malfunctioning bureaucracy can create delays and be counter productive, taking away resources, time and energy. Formal procedures and regulations need to be streamlined and made more efficient.
- Changes in political leadership can result in unforeseen structural changes, new political agendas and the replacement of personnel. Related problems can be minimized through strong stakeholder involvement and the establishment of a robust and transparent support network.
- Participatory processes require time to be effective. Project participants are often overburdened with excessive workloads. University administrations need to recognize the significance of learning and knowledge creation through participatory, community-based research.
- There are deep and unsettling historical and cultural differences in project approaches and methodologies between the global North and the global South to be recognized and overcome in international development work.
- University administrations should thrive for a better understanding of the premises and constraints of community-based research and participatory

development which obviously transcend market oriented educational purposes that are usually the central focus in most North American universities.

- A trustful environment unfolds people's potential to participate and generates social assets. Indeed, a high level of trust is essential for the success of CBR.
- Transparency is fundamental in the establishment of trustful relationships.
- Involving project participants in monitoring and evaluation processes helps to avoid conflict.
- Good communication skills are essential. Listening and communicating in a non-aggressive way are central to maintaining an effective dialogue.

While much more case-based research needs to be done to understand the ways in which universities can best contribute to participatory development, the PSWM project exemplifies the struggles and challenges that can emerge in community–university partnerships. The experience discussed here identifies key requirements for engaging in pluralistic and heterodox community-based research. Having the skills and sensitivity to assess risks and being flexible to change direction if things go wrong is vital in participatory community-based research. In the case of the PSWM project, the effective democratic and transparent leadership by the Directing Committee and the collective management of the project with the Management Council were pivotal to the project. All individuals involved in the project, and particularly the leaders of the recycling associations and cooperatives, were always informed about the development of the project. An external evaluator termed the PSWM project as being "one of the most authentic, effective and in fact inspirational projects encountered since 1970". Another member of the evaluation mission wrote that the PSWM project was "very effective and productive at the grassroots point of delivery (which is often the weakest point in international research and development projects)". Universities have the potential to make important contributions, provided they embrace the participation ethos in their own praxis.

4 From hazardous 'informal' recycling to decent working conditions

DOI: 10.4324/9781315686523-4

Summary

Chapter four analyses various forms of 'informal' and organized recycling as performed by individuals and groups in different geographic contexts in the global South. To begin with, I define the informal economy and situate the recyclers and waste pickers within the context of 'informality'. Gathering recyclables can be done under different circumstances, from separating at waste dumps to working in cooperatives, performing selective household waste collection. Basic socioeconomic characteristics of recyclers are introduced. I then present social entrepreneurial initiatives related to recycling operations including recycling cooperatives, networks and social enterprises. In the second part of this chapter I describe the organization of recyclers into social movements, such as the Brazilian and the Latin American movements of recyclers. These new social movements have emerged in many parts of the world, objecting to the injustices committed on the waste pickers and demanding democratic deliberation on issues concerned with waste management. Finally, Brazil's pro-active legislation related to waste management is examined in this chapter and examples of tools to drive institutional change towards *decent work* situations for the recyclers are presented.

4.1 Introduction to the concept of 'informal' recycling

Historically, some people always made a living or complemented their livelihoods with the collection and the reuse of disposed reusable or recyclable waste. However, during the past three decades the number of individuals depending on this activity has grown significantly, primarily in the global South. The conditions under which most workers perform the collection, separation and commercialization of these materials are often hazardous and exploitive. They work unprotected by social and labour legislation, are mostly unrecognized by their governments, and are often socially excluded and thus considered as part of the informal sector. This chapter discusses what is known as the informal economy and introduces the International Labour Organization (ILO) appeal for transforming informal work into *decent work* conditions. According to the OECD the informal economy is more prominent than the formal economy worldwide, with 1.8 billion (60 per cent) workers compared to 1.2 billion (40 per cent) workers respectively (OECD, 2009).

Worldwide there are numerous different ways of doing this job, depending on the specific constraints recyclers face in accessing solid waste and depending on the quality and abundance of recyclable materials, gender and age of the workers, as well as specific political, cultural and geographic contexts. The resources available, creativity and whether recyclers receive external support further determines the levels of technology and tools employed in the activity. As a result there is a hybrid spectrum from informal to formal forms of organization, ranging from loose groupings, associations and cooperatives to social enterprises, all operating in the solid waste and recycling sector (Alter, 2006). According to the ILO, cooperatives that are formally established as legal entities are considered part of the formal sector and those that are not formally established are part of the informal sector (2013). Most recycling cooperatives are not established as legal entities, given the bureaucracies and costs involved in the process.

Brazil's experience with Solidarity Economy is an interesting case to observe and has been around for quite some time. It focuses on needs satisfaction and institutional innovations. Solidarity Economy crowns the re-emergence of alternative economic development and is gaining momentum in some parts of the global South, where concrete practical experiences and policies have been shaping economic and social landscapes since the 1990s. Solidarity Economy calls for societal and systemic transformations and centres on the agency of individuals and organizations through increased democratization.

Mostly, the organized recyclers are part of the Brazilian National recyclers' movement (*Movimento Nacional de Catadores(as) de Material Reciclável* – MNCR), and some of their leaders engage in the Latin American recyclers' movement and the emerging worldwide organization of waste pickers. These organizations have important voices, rejecting the unacceptable social and economic conditions under which informal recyclers work and requesting policies and structures for inclusive solid waste management. In Brazil some transformations have been reached, with institutional structures and specific legislations being created to assist the organization of the recyclers and support their operations under Solidarity Economy. Chapter 4 describes the recyclers' mobilization in Brazil and assesses the state's response in supporting the 'informal' and organized recyclers with institutional support and inclusive policies. Here, innovative laws have emerged to recognize the workers in the 'informal' recycling sector and to improve their organization and access to recyclable materials. It is yet to be seen whether current institutional and jurisdictive efforts are helping to widely transform 'informal' recycling into *decent work*.

4.2 'Informal' recycling inscribed within the informal economy

'Informal' recycling is about the thousands of *waste pickers, catadores, recuperadores, zabaleen, cartoneros, recicladores, mikhali, minadores, rag pickers, recyclers*, working in cities throughout the world under precarious and often hazardous conditions, recovering recyclables and reusable materials from disposed solid waste. Their work is mostly self-employed, labour intense, local and utilizes rudimentary equipment. Because waste pickers are part of the unregulated and unregistered economy, they do not have trading licenses, do not pay taxes and do not receive social benefits and welfare (Wilson *et al.*, 2006).

4.2.1 Informal economy concept

The term informal sector was first introduced by the ILO in the 1970s to refer to the "survival activities of those working in the marginal or peripheral segments of the economy and those who were not recognized, or protected by the public authorities" (ILO, 2002: 121). Debates over the past decades acknowledge the fact that the term *sector* does not really capture the complexity and heterogeneity which characterizes the many different actors and activities that have usually been situated under the umbrella of the informal sector. The notion informal economy better describes the diverse and multifaceted groups of individuals and enterprises that work outside of formality, in survival type activities (ILO, 2013).

The range of different occupations and services developed by 'informal' workers is large. There are some informal activities that are illegal. In this book I refer only to those that are considered legal. What characterizes 'informal' work forms is the fact that they all operate under a high degree of vulnerability. Their income is usually very low and unstable. Most of the workers are in the informal economy because they cannot find formal employment or are unable to set up their own business within the formal economy. In most cases these workers have no or very limited access to public resources and infrastructure. Often, they have to operate under exploitative arrangements and accept unfair conditions, depending on the attitude of the public authorities, ranging from support and tolerance to prohibition and repression.

Informal does not mean that these workers do not work without norms or rules regulating their operations. Indeed, they share public spaces (streets, beaches, parks, markets, trains, bus stations, waste dumps, etc.). They access common property resources, like disposed solid waste or discarded products. Informal arrangements are often in place to organize and uphold access to these resources and spaces. Sometimes even structures are set up for mutual support (e.g. sharing food or shelter, 'trap lines' to collect materials, or providing information and skills) and to enforce reciprocal obligations. Nevertheless, most 'informal' workers are struggling for survival on a daily basis, which also means competing amongst each other for resources.

According to a survey conducted by the not for profit organization *Women in Informal Employment Globalizing and Organizing* – WIEGO (2014) informal employment comprises more than 50 per cent of non-agricultural employment in most countries of the global South, particularly with 82 per cent in South Asia, 66 per cent in Sub-Saharan Africa, 65 per cent in East and Southeast Asia and 51 per cent in Latin America. In China, 33 per cent of non-agricultural employment is informal. This number might be under-represented, given the limited data currently available for China (and also due to language constraints).

Since many informal activities are run as small family enterprises (microenterprises), they offer job opportunities for women. Indeed in many parts of the world (South Asia, Sub-Saharan Africa and Latin America and the Caribbean) women are predominant in the non-agricultural informal sector (WIEGO, 2014). Nevertheless, as a study comparing data from six different cities in the global South and in transitional Europe shows, most women recyclers earn less than their fellow men. The study reports that even when doing the same kind of work, they tend to earn less and also are paid lower rates for materials sold to middlemen (CWG and GIZ, 2011).

The informal economy is growing. Economic restructuring with increased flexibility, decentralized forms of production, outsourcing, subcontracting and global competition, the prevailing efforts to reduce costs and to increase profits, as well as population growth in general, are among the root causes for informal work to be on the rise. As a consequence, high numbers of people work under precarious, unhealthy, unprotected and risk-laden conditions. 'Informal' recycling is one of the activities expanding worldwide and particularly in those regions where economic crisis prevents workers from getting formal employment.

4.2.2 From 'informal' to decent work

A key milestone in advancing the understanding and recognition of the multifaceted actors, activities and contexts in the informal economy was achieved in the 2002 International Labor Conference (ILC) *Resolution on Decent Work and the Informal Economy* where the goal to "promote decent work along the entire continuum from the informal to the formal end of the economy, and in development-oriented, poverty reduction-focused and gender-equitable ways" was affirmed (ILO, 2002: 4). *Decent work* was defined by the ILO and widely endorsed by academics and practitioners as being

> productive work for women and men in conditions of freedom, equity, security and human dignity. Decent work involves opportunities for work that is productive and delivers a fair income; provides security in the workplace and social protection for workers and their families; offers better prospects for personal development and encourages social integration; gives people the freedom to express their concerns, to organize and to participate in decisions that affect their lives; and guarantees equal opportunities and equal treatment for all.
>
> (ILO, 2007: vi)

In 2005, the target *decent and full productive work* was included under the First Millennium Development Goal, which aims to *eradicate extreme poverty and hunger*. The engagement with this target means creating employment and developing enterprises, guaranteeing social protection, standards and rights at work and a governance structure that fosters social dialogue. In order to move towards *decent work* conditions, the ILO has developed a framework of *seven essential securities*, which are often denied to informal workers (2002: 3). I have applied the framework to the working conditions of 'informal' recyclers in the global South, highlighting the main deficiencies and some solutions underway (at least for some parts of the world) (see Table 4.1). Most recyclers still live in situations where they are denied all of the listed seven securities. Identifying the deficiencies and

Table 4.1 Essential securities framework applied to the situation of 'informal' recyclers

Essential security	Examples for the denial of essential securities	Situation of 'informal' recyclers (IR)	Pathways towards 'informal' recyclers achieving essential securities
Labour market security	Unfair and lack of adequate employment opportunities, determined by macroeconomic policies.	Unrecognized contribution to solid waste management. Lack of participation in policy design, planning and implementation of SWM. Gender biases.	Recognizing and remunerating waste collection, separation and education services provided by organized recyclers (gender unbiased). Creating inclusive solid waste management policies and facilitating the organization of IR.
Employment security	Employment instability and vulnerability as a result of global economic dynamism.	Price fluctuations and low prices for recyclables. Dependency on middlemen. Economic restructuring and unemployment.	Municipalities engaging in partnerships with recyclers in waste management. Pro-active economic policies in support of the recycling sector. Job creation through inclusive solid waste management.
Work security	Legal workplace protection with safety and health regulations and limits on working time.	Lack of resources and institutional support to make workplaces safer. Lack of regulation prohibiting unsafe products and enforcing safe disposal.	Technical and financial support making the workplace safer, recognizing and considering the specific circumstances under which recycling cooperatives and associations operate.
Skill reproduction security	Lack of access to skill development and employment training.	Social exclusion preventing access to formal education or capacity development.	Popular and formal education, capacity development, e.g. digital inclusion.
Representation security	Political organization, protected collective voice, independent workers' organization (e.g. trade union).	Lack of organization. Lack of space for organization.	Strengthening of organizational forms (cooperatives, social movements, unions, etc.). Recognition of organized forms of representation.
Income security	Provision of fair and adequate income.	No remuneration for services provided by recyclers.	Fair remuneration for social and environmental services provision.
Decent work deficits	Inefficient, unproductive, poor quality and un- or low-remunerated work. Jobs not recognized, nor protected by law. Inadequate social protection and lack of representation and voice.	Work often inefficient, unhealthy and with low technology input. Very low pay for the materials sold to middlemen. Service mostly unpaid and unrecognized.	Appropriate technology. Fair trade for recyclables. Fair remuneration for social and environmental benefits of recycling (greenhouse gas emission reduction, energy savings). Collective commercialization for recycling associations and cooperatives.

Source: Based on ILO (2002).

focusing on strategies and policies that ensure *decent work* circumscribes the struggle of the diverse workers in the informal economy, as will be discussed further in this chapter.

The specific pathways towards *decent work*, outlined in Table 4.1, will be addressed throughout the book, but specifically within this chapter, when I refer to Social and Solidarity Economy (SSE) as an alternative concept to the current market and consumption-driven, capitalist economies. The SSE conceptualizes and provides practical instruments for the transformation of informal work into *decent working* conditions. In parts of Latin America, SSE has achieved constitutional and legal recognition. Here, national public organizations are responsible for the implementation of specific policies to support SSE and to facilitate the emergence of community-based social enterprises and cooperatives (Caruana and Srnec, 2013).

The recycling cooperative sector fits under this umbrella and has in some cases been able to benefit from specific institutional support, as for example in Brazil and Colombia. The reality of 'informal' recycling, however, demands significant structural changes from current informal work and livelihood conditions towards solidarity-driven, *decent work*.

4.3 Scope and character of 'informal' recycling

The ILO estimates that there are approximately 15–20 million 'informal' waste workers with very low incomes, often living below the poverty level. The working conditions pertaining to this sector conform to the characteristics described earlier for the informal economy. For Latin America and the Caribbean, estimates suggest that up to 3.8 million people are involved in 'informal' recycling, most of them working independently (Terraza and Sturzenegger, 2010). In India, at least 1.5 million people work in resource recovery (UNDP, 2011), while in China approximately ten million workers are reported to be involved in 'informal' recycling activities (UNEP, 2011). These numbers are significant and underline the fact that in most large cities in the global South, sometimes 5,000 to 10,000 'informal' recyclers are taking care of significant proportions of solid waste management in their city. Yet, they mostly are unrecognized by their government. In Brazil the numbers of 'informal' recyclers, *catadores*, are high and vary between 400,000 and 600,000, according to the source of information (IPEA, 2013). Because of the 'informal' nature of selective waste collection, the numbers are not exact. However, the 2010 Brazilian census data (IBGE, 2012; 2012a) provide the exact number of 387,910 self-declared *catadores* (69 per cent) and *catadoras* (31 per cent). Nevertheless, since these workers are highly stigmatized, not everybody declares themselves as pertaining to this professional grouping.

4.3.1 Informal recyclers' livelihoods

The detailed census data provide further socio-demographic insights to the circumstances in Brazil, where 38.6 per cent of recyclers are working in a formalized situation (cooperative, association or government-run recycling centres). The average age of these recyclers is 39.4 years. Of these, 66.1 per cent of recyclers declare themselves as being Afro-descendent and 20.5 per cent are illiterate, while 24.6 per cent have only completed the *ensino fundamental* (eight years of basic education). Most of the Brazilian recyclers (93.3 per cent) live in cities (IBGE, 2012a).

The vulnerable livelihood situations of 'informal' recyclers become evident in their housing conditions. While some live on or around the waste dumps – next to the places they work – and some are homeless, surviving in the streets, under bridges, and in abandoned buildings, the majority of the 'informal' recyclers live in informal settlements under dense and precarious conditions, often lacking basic infrastructure and services (water, sewage, electricity, waste collection). World-wide, only a very few waste pickers have benefitted from public housing programmes such as the social housing project implemented in Bogotá, Colombia (Photograph 4.1) or in Brazil, through the programme *Minha Casa Minha Vida* (Silva, 2012).

Uncountable waste pickers have worked in this sector for many years and decades, often since their childhood. Others mention being involved in the activity because of loss of formal employment and lack of formal alternatives (IBGE, 2012a). There are also some recyclers who work in this sector temporarily or during certain hours or days, complementing other income sources. The recyclers work in different environments. Some have fixed routes where they collect recyclables out of disposed garbage bags or they have established contacts with households or businesses to pick up their recyclables. Others work at landfills and dumps, sifting through disposed materials. More recently, recyclers also opt to working as employees in private or public recycling centres. In Latin America a growing number of municipalities establish contracts with cooperatives or associations for the service of selective waste collection; often employing door-to-door household collection. The cities provide different forms and levels of support, e.g. infrastructure, machinery, trucks, space, or they provide transportation or food aid. However, in very few cases does the municipality remunerate the recyclers for the service of collecting and diverting recyclables from the solid waste stream.

4.3.2 The work of informal recyclers

In many parts of the world, and particularly in informal settlements, waste collectors specialize in collecting the waste from unserviced households. Some of them also recover recyclables, while others only dispose the waste at official pick-up points (transfer stations) or at informal spaces, where garbage is occasionally incinerated (Zapata-Campos and Zapata, 2013). Research conducted in Kisumu, Kenya, identifies the existence of a wide-ranging hierarchy amongst informal recyclers and recycling entrepreneurs. These workers call themselves: *scavengers* when working at waste dumps, or *recyclers* and *waste pickers* when working in streets and communities, all of which collect recyclables. Then there are also *solid waste entrepreneurs* and community-based organizations (CBOs). Entrepreneurs can be well equipped and successful small-scale organizations in collecting waste

Photograph 4.1 Social housing programme benefitting waste pickers from the *Associación Cooperativa de Recicladores de Bogotá,* in Colombia.

and recyclables and are sometimes able to add value to the materials. In many cities CBOs are also collecting waste and/or recyclables. In addition these sometimes also pursue environmental education missions (Gutberlet *et al.* 2016).

Ali (2003) notes that CBOs ideally have no dependency on external resources and the ownership rests with the community members. Participation by the community and collective decision-making enhance the use of the service and improve cost recovery. Ali further records that CBOs allow for effective responses to complaints, as it is easy for them to access the providers of the service.

The monthly income of informal recyclers varies significantly, depending on the geographic region, level of organization, quality and quantity and prices paid for the materials. Research conducted with organized recyclers in different cities adjacent to the metropolis of São Paulo found a range of between US$ 0.84 and US$ 1.70[1] for the hourly income of the recyclers, which results in an average monthly income of between US$ 150 and US$ 290. The large variation reflects the differences in quality and quantity of work equipment, organization and logistics of the groups. The data are consistent with the Brazilian census data from 2010, with the average monthly income of waste pickers being R$ 571,56 (US$ 177 in March 2015), which is slightly above the Brazilian minimum wage (IPEA, 2013). Some of the well-established recycling groups supported by the municipality, as for example in the cities of Ourinhos and Londrina in Brazil, earn from R$1000 to 1500 (US$ 314 to 471) per month.

4.3.3 The collection of recyclable material from household waste

'Informal' recyclers and those who work in cooperatives or associations reclaim different forms of household and business waste, ranging from many varieties of plastics, papers, cardboard and metals to very special materials, like wood, cooking oil and other oils, electrical waste and electronic equipment (WEEE), and other specific packaging materials or discarded objects. Recyclers also separate by the specific quality of the material, for example, whether broken or intact, dirty or clean, coloured or uniform, etc. These materials form additional categories that obtain different prices on the market. The most impressive fact, however, is that in large metropolitan agglomerations, like São Paulo, for example, almost every material has a local market and is thus recyclable. Here only very few materials are considered unrecyclable. There are materials with very low (or no) market value, which are usually not collected by the waste pickers. Nevertheless, some cooperatives still separate and store these materials, awaiting the development of a specific market. Cooperpires in Ribeirão Pires, e.g. collects and stores styrofoam, separated by the households, arguing that they do not want these materials to end up in the landfill.

The contribution of 'informal' recyclers to recovering resources is significant although formally, very little is recognized. It is estimated that 'informal' and organized recyclers recover 60 per cent of the paper and cardboard that is recycled in Brazil and up to 90 per cent of all materials that feed the recycling industry in that country (Conceição, 2005). The author further underlines that 'informal' and organized recyclers recover up to 20 per cent of all municipal solid waste generated in urban Brazil, while the official recycling rate in most Brazilian cities still remains very low. For instance, only 1.3 per cent of the total 15,000 tons of solid waste generated daily in the megacity of São Paulo is officially collected for recycling purposes (Arini, 2012).

Resource recovery rates depend primarily on the quality of source separation. However, transportation mode, infrastructure equipment at the processing centre where separation, baling, and storage happens; topography; distances of the serviced neighbourhood; and level of training of the recyclers also matter. On average, a recycler carries up to 200 kg of recyclable material per day, which adds up to approximately 4 tons a month (Conceição, 2005). This number doubles when using an electric cart. Working hours are usually long, often 12 hours a day, pushing heavily loaded carts by foot or bicycle an average distance of 20 km per day. According to data from 2006 by the Brazilian recyclers movement (MNCR), there were only 24 highly organized and well equipped formalized cooperatives in the country. The same study identified 70 well-equipped cooperatives with an intermediate level of organization, and 80 groups with a low level of equipment and low level of organization, while 157 unrecognized groups of *catadores* were working under precarious and health threatening conditions on landfills (MNCR, 2006). We will see further within this chapter that better forms of organization are a way out of this dilemma.

4.4 Ways of organizing informal recycling

According to the ILO (2013) waste picker organizations fall under *autonomous membership-based organizations*. The ILO recognizes a significant growth in these organizations of informal economy actors and also mentions the strong participation of women workers, including those that are usually disadvantaged due to ethnicity or migrant status. The recent adoption of the 1996 ILO Homework Convention (No.177 and Recommendation No.184) is considered a milestone in bringing informal workers into formality, giving them visibility and legal protection (ILO, 2013).

4.4.1 Recycling cooperatives

Recyclers' cooperatives began to develop at the end of the twentieth century in Latin America, when some of the 'informal' workers began self-organizing to improve their visibility and power. According to the International Cooperative Alliance (ICA), a cooperative is

> an autonomous association of persons united voluntarily to meet their common economic, social, and cultural needs and aspirations through a jointly-owned and democratically-controlled enterprise.

While Gambina and Roffinelli (2013) note that cooperatives develop new and more humanitarian values and behaviours. The praxis of these values translates into: non-discrimination, self-management, democratic member participation, and equality in the decision-making. Many recycling cooperatives in Latin America have emerged as a strategic struggle for 'informal' workers to replace the vacuum under which many of them operate, often characterized by invisibility, voicelessness and lack of recognition. Cooperatives can represent alternative spaces for emancipation and empowerment that contest the states' inefficiency to support and include informal initiatives in public policy. Nevertheless, not all cooperatives are democratic and inclusive spaces. *Catadores* in Brazil refer to *false cooperatives*, where power is concentrated and where practice and decision-making are not transparent and collective. These cooperatives, in fact, may reproduce businesses that mock labour laws to avoid labour incumbencies and that do not respect the international principles of cooperatives (Gutberlet, 2013). Yet, overwhelmingly the recycling cooperatives represent the alternative economy (Gibson-Graham, 2008). They are emancipatory spaces of difference and creativity. Here thinking practices re-frame ontologies, often challenging politics with engagement and activism.

The administrative structure of most cooperatives includes a president, a vice-president, a secretary and a treasurer. The decisions are made during general assemblies, which take place regularly and can also be called in extraordinarily. Sometimes the groups receive financial support from development assistance programmes, grass-roots initiatives and not for profit organizations, universities and sometimes also from governmental institutions. Probably the most important result from the organization of the informal recyclers has been the empowerment of their members and the strengthening of their agency.

4.4.2 Cooperatives and women

Cooperatives are attractive for women workers, for this environment affirms collective female identities, allowing them to value themselves, develop self-esteem and provide opportunities for personal growth through leadership development. Many of the cooperative leaders in Brazil are now women and they have demonstrated extraordinary skills and sensibilities for key political issues.

Participating in a cooperative or association enables women, who are often excluded, to become part of a social grouping. Women work collectively in the same space, allowing for the exchange of ideas and discussions about their everyday lives. This sparks a feeling of collective belonging, which enhances the working atmosphere and the general wellbeing of the recyclers. In this sense the cooperative is a space that generates a collective consciousness.

The members of the cooperative generally value and cherish their work in terms of how they can contribute and are part of a collective effort. They value the social relations within the working space, which helps them to avoid alienation as described by Gambina and Roffinelli (2013). These authors say that frequently unhealthy relations between workers, bosses, employers and the products generate a sense of alienation for the employees, who then feel isolated, indifferent or hostile and sometimes do not see the utility of their work.

The self-management of the cooperatives changes the relation with work. In particular, women recyclers who have experienced leadership affirm how important collective working practice is for them. Collaborative practice and peer support are critical in politicizing the work of these women, empowering them to embrace emancipatory ways of knowing; a praxis of reflection and action.

The cooperative is a space where they can *escape* from the subordinated condition and where they grow awareness and discuss their rights. The absence of transparency, though, impedes the construction of social assets in the sense of Robert Putnam, who highlights that trust and reliability encourages links between people (Putnam, 2000). Recycling organizations have an enormous potential for creating social goods.

4.4.3 Organizing recyclers internationally

Internationally, recyclers have created trade unions, associations, cooperatives and cooperative networks, while others remain unconnected or are part of a loose network structure. As to the census survey in 2010, the number of organized recyclers is quite high in Brazil, with almost 40 per cent claiming to work in a *semi-formalized* situation (cooperative, association or government-run recycling centre) (IBGE, 2012a). A multi-country study recorded low levels of worker organizations in most countries. Only 7 per cent of the informal recyclers in Lima, Peru, and 2.5 per cent of the *zabbaleen* in Cairo, Egypt, belonged to an organization (Gunsilius *et al.*, 2011), while in Pune (Peru) and Quezon City (the Philippines) respectively, 60 per cent and 37 per cent of the waste pickers belonged to a sector organization (Gunsilius *et al.*, 2011).

Creating a cooperative can be a difficult ambition, given the complex legislation regulating the establishment of these organizations. The procedure to create a cooperative in Brazil is expensive, bureaucratic and time-consuming. Few groups have achieved the formal status of a cooperative, and even a smaller proportion is able to access the official microfinance and funding opportunities recently introduced specifically for recycling cooperatives by the federal government.

4.4.4 Social movements of informal recyclers and waste pickers

Although the organizing of *catadores* in Brazil dates back to the late 1980s, a national recyclers' movement (*Movimento Nacional de Catadores(as) de Material Reciclável* – MNCR) was created in Brazil only in 2004. Its goal is to expand inclusive solid waste management programmes throughout the country and to integrate the struggle of the *catadores* for self-determination (*autogestão*) and inclusion in the praxis of handling solid waste, which also means better access to funding and credit lines that can be used to expand the work infrastructure in cooperatives and associations. *Catadores* demand remuneration from the municipality for the public service of selective waste collection. Another struggle of the Brazilian recyclers' movement is the approval of the general Solidarity Economy legislation, which frames a legal policy instrument of support for cooperatives and other social enterprises at all government levels (Samson, 2009). The general societal changes proposed by the social economy and solidarity movement as described by Arruda (2008) match with the goal set declared by the recyclers' movement. On both local and individual levels, this means emancipation of the recyclers from subaltern social and economic situations, by expanding their capacities, thus providing working conditions that allow for the full development and use of human capacities, based on principles of reciprocity and solidarity.

Waste pickers organize worldwide. In the early 1990s, for example, the Trade Union of Waste Pickers was created in Pune (KKPKP). Also at the beginning of the 1990s, four recycling cooperatives that had been struggling against the closure of a waste dump in Bogotá, Colombia, decided to formalize their relationship and created the *Asociación de Recicladores de Bogotá* (ARB) (Samson, 2009). The ARB is now a leading voice of the 'informal' recyclers in Colombia. In early March 2008, the ARB hosted the *III. Latin American* and *I. World Waste Pickers* conference, bringing together recyclers from all continents. Norah Padilla, from the Colombian National Association of Waste Pickers, and at the time the chairperson for the World Conference shared her impressions about this event:

> The congress was super-important. At the first meeting of the Latin American network we resolve that we need to know about other parts of the world. This congress allowed us to bring together many people to know the conditions of recyclers in many parts of the world, and to discuss the need to sensitise governments about the problems of recyclers and the possibilities and alternatives for social inclusion.
>
> (Samson, 2009: 48)

The recycling leaders know that without agency waste pickers will remain unheard and excluded in policy measures, therefore they strive for organization and mobilization. The recyclers' social movement at regional and international levels, as well as local recyclers' organizations, play crucial roles in building agency to engage in transformative processes. In some cases these movements have been successful, with the waste pickers bringing their situation to international attention and developing partnerships to lobby for national and international instruments to support their progress towards *decent work*, globally.

4.5 Stepping up towards Social and Solidarity Economy

Social economy has roots going back to antiquity and medieval times, but, according to the academy, it was first conceptualized by French economist Charles Dunoyer, in 1830 (Moulaert and Ailenei, 2005). The significance, disappearance and re-emergence of social economy seemed to be closely related to episodes of crisis, acting as "a way to respond to the alienation and non-satisfaction of needs by the traditional private sector or the public sector" (Moulaert and Ailenei, 2005: 2041).

Polanyi's work (1944) has been influential in providing a foundation for defining social economy, which has regained importance with a focus on reciprocity. He differentiates between four ideal types of principles of economic behaviour to discuss the praxis of putting to work alternative economy initiatives, or re-embedding economy into society. These principles involve market, redistribution, reciprocity and householding. Polanyi recognizes the capacity of people to prompt change, which resonates with many social and environmental movements, including the cooperative sector and the social and Solidarity Economy.

Solidarity Economy is an emerging alternative strand that is re-capturing and re-shaping the social economy with a great variety of forms of economic activities, particularly situated within the context of the global South (Laville, 1992). Experiences with solidarity and popular economy in Latin America underline the specific Southern contexts. The use of the term Southern means to be reflexive and to "emphasize relations – authority, exclusion and inclusion, hegemony, partnership, sponsorship, appropriation – between intellectuals and institutions in the metropole and those in the world periphery" (Raewyn Connell, 2007, cited in Rosa, 2014: 859).

Solidarity Economy involves primarily bottom-up, grass-roots, community-based initiatives, which stress reciprocity and the social link to economy, producing a hybrid spectrum of market-inserted, redistributive and non-monetary economies, often operating within the conventional and market-driven economy. In order to honour the long-standing trajectory of the social economy, Moulaert and Ailenei (2005) suggest the use of the term Social and Solidarity Economy (SSE) to recognize the re-emergence of *old* social economy principles, but in current contexts. Thus, SSE is based on values of solidarity and cooperation, seeking autonomy and non-capitalistic economic relations or forms of organizations to transform hierarchical and authoritarian models and operations.

SSE is described as associative activities carried out by associations, cooperatives, mutual organizations, social enterprises and community-based organizations (Utting *et al.*, 2014; see also Moulaert and Nussbaumer, 2005). Operating as an SSE organization within the capitalist market – predominantly shaped by the private sector with firms and the public sector which is formed by a state – far from exercising deliberative democracy, translates into countless challenges.

Barkin and Lemus (2014) incorporate ecological sustainability into the definition for the key operational principles of SSE. This also reflects my own ideas on integrating Ecological Economy with SSE, recognizing the link between sustainability and just distribution (Daly, 1996). This more developed alternative economy concept takes a posthumanist approach and puts nature on the same level as humans and gives the same appreciation to environmental issues as to societal questions.

The following are the key values that Barkin and Lemus (2014) describe for SSE (the order has been changed by myself to reflect the level of urgency):

- sustainable natural resource management and protection of sensitive ecosystems;
- autonomy in governance (self-management) and participation in democratic decision-making;
- social goals and socialization of benefits, which means solidarity among community members and with other communities cooperating in a similar process;
- small-scale local solutions centered on self-sufficiency, given the resource endowment and ecological conditions;
- limited return on capital and yet productive diversification for trade with other communities and in the market;
- collective and individual empowerment.

SSE necessarily also requires Ecological Economy reasoning and principles, recognizing the utmost importance of caring for the natural environment in order to be able to care for societies. As of now most examples of Solidarity Economy, popular economy or social economy in the global South do not incorporate the ecological notion into economy and primarily focus on democracy and social justice. Here, there is a critically important innovation to be made. The discussions and reflections on the integration of the two economies have just begun.

In Brazil, the Solidarity Economy has been institutionalized and there are realistic opportunities for community-based, collective initiatives to excel. The following section introduces and discusses pieces of Brazilian legislation that have made a difference in promoting solidarity-based selective waste collection (*coleta seletiva solidaria*) in Brazil.

4.6 Translating actions into public policies

The conference proceedings of the *First International* and *Third Latin American Conference of Waste Pickers*, in Bogota, Colombia, in 2008 ("Waste Pickers without Frontiers"), recognize the following two key challenges for 'informal' recyclers:

- competition with multinational and large enterprises;
- existing prejudice against waste pickers.

The conference participants also highlight some steps to be taken for change towards *decent work*, including:

- training and building knowledge (e.g. training in digital inclusion);
- fair conditions, considering waste pickers as equal partners during tendering processes;
- implementation of and access to *social technology,* a concept used to describe the technologies that are applied for communication and specific social purposes;
- remuneration for services provided (collection, diversion and environmental education);
- opening up opportunities for waste pickers to add value to recyclable material and for collective commercialization.

Next to the required institutional transformations is the introduction of specific public policies to promote change towards *decent working* conditions. As highlighted at the beginning of this chapter, in Table 4.1, *decent work* for informal recyclers translates into (1) recognition of the work of 'informal' and organized recyclers and the remuneration for the public service and environmental benefits performed (for more details on the environmental services provided by recyclers, see Chapter 8; (2) access to appropriate infrastructure and technology; and (3) networking, for example collective commercialization for recycling associations and cooperatives and fair trade for recyclable materials. Taking the example of the Brazilian government, we observe advances and challenges as a consequence of the legal framework developed at the federal level.

4.6.1 Supportive legislation in Brazil

Over the past decade the federal government in Brazil has taken steps towards improving the working conditions of *catadores*. Since 2002, the profession of working as a *catador* has become legal. Several additional laws have been enacted since, in support of inclusive solid waste management and *decent working* conditions for 'informal' recyclers. Table 4.2 summarizes some of these public policies and actions, mostly from the federal government, which have become instrumental in changing the working conditions of *catadores* in Brazil, creating opportunities for cooperatives to be included in the recycling chain. The *Pro-Catador* programme aims to integrate and coordinate the actions of the federal government in support of recyclers' organizations, with actions to improve working conditions and expand selective waste collection, reuse and recycling through the inclusion of the 'informal' recycling sector in Brazil.

The fact that the federal law includes solid waste as part of sanitation furthermore extends funding opportunities for this sector. The federal solid waste management policy represents a landmark because it is based on integrated waste management, which means following the principles of prevention and precaution (reduction, reuse and recycling), in addition to applying environmentally appropriate final destination methods (except for the contradictory fact that the law allows waste-to-energy incineration when the municipality is unable to work with organized recyclers). The legislation further proposes shared responsibility for the product life cycle and the reduction of negative health impacts throughout the life cycle of products.

The Brazilian waste management legislation makes a strong case for defending selective waste collection of reusable and recyclable materials and supports the *catadores* in that activity. The new law encourages municipalities to hire cooperatives for selective waste collection. Nevertheless, with the advent of increased pressure to close landfills and quickly solve the surmounting problem of solid waste accumulation in large cities, conflicts have emerged in some municipalities,

Table 4.2 Brazilian legislation in support of *catadores*

Law/Decree/action	Main objectives
Federal Law No. 5,764 of December 1971	Establishes the National Policy on Cooperatives
In 2002, the Ministry of Labor and Employment creates the professional category: *catador* "collector of recyclable materials" and includes it in the Brazilian classification of occupations (CBOS), under the Code 5192-05 (MTE. Classificação Brasileira de Ocupações).	Legal and formal recognition of the occupation of collector of recyclable materials, setting parameters for the development of this activity.
Decree No. 5,940, 25 October 2006	Requires public institutions to separate and donate the recyclable fraction of their solid waste to recycling associations and cooperatives.
Federal Law No. 11,445 of 5 January 2007: National Policy on Basic Sanitation.	Authorizes the municipalities to hire recycling associations and cooperatives to collect, process and market recyclable or reusable municipal solid waste.
Federal Law No. 12,017 of 2 August 2009 and annex VII of 13 August 2009, published in the extra edition of the Diario Oficial da União (DOU).	Changes the law of the budget guidelines, allowing the direct transfer of resources to cooperatives, without intermediation of municipalities or social organizations of public interest.
Federal Law No. 12,305 of 2 August 2010 and its regulation through Decree No. 7,404 of 23 December 2010.	Establishes the National Solid Waste Policy and creates the Inter-ministerial Committee of the Brazilian solid waste Policy and the Steering Committee for the implementation of the reverse logistics systems.
Federal Decree No. 7,405 23 December 2010, published in DOU, 23 December 2010.	Institutes the *'Pro-Catador'* programme. It provides funding for capacity building, networking, research, acquisition of equipments and vehicles to waste picker organizations. Inter-ministerial Committee for social and economic inclusion of the collectors of reusable and recyclable material.
Federal Law No. 12,690 of 19 July 2012 published in DOU, 20 July 2012.	Rules on the organization and functioning of workers' cooperatives.

between *catadores* and local governments engaging in public–private partnerships for waste-to-energy (incineration).

Interesting developments happen on the municipal level regarding specific laws in support of *catadores*. The city of Diadema was the first example of implementing the remuneration of *catadores* for the service of collecting recyclable household waste (municipal law 2.336/2004 and Decree 5.984/2005). Other municipalities, such as the cities of Ourinhos, São Caetano do Sul, Ribeirão Preto, Guarulhos and Mauá, are now following that example. Similarly, some municipal governments in Bolivia, Argentina and Colombia are moving towards paying the 'informal' recyclers as public service providers in selective solid waste collection.

4.7 Final considerations

In this chapter I have discussed everyday work experiences of recyclers; from streets and waste dumps to recycling cooperatives and associations. Most of the workers that are part of the global waste picker community work under precarious, unsafe and exploitive work conditions. They are considered to be part of the unregulated and unprotected, informal economy. Despite the variety in the level of organization, these workers include thousands of *catadores* and *catadoras, zabaleen, recuperadores, recicladores* and waste pickers throughout the world who are struggling to become recognized as public service providers and remunerated for the benefits they generate for the city and the environment. Many challenges become apparent when trying to integrate these people into formal work relations, and often they continue as exploited and excluded as before. As for example, when municipal governments set up triage centres, employing trained recyclers who work under regulated and safer occupational conditions, but who have lost their autonomy and empowering self-regulating structure, which is present in many cooperatives, unions and associations.

The Social and Solidarity Economy provides some guidelines and practical experiences that demonstrate the potential for collective organization through cooperatives and associations. The spectrum between more and less market embedded SSE initiatives depends on the level of power sharing for decision-making of its members and ranges from community-based organizations and cooperatives to social and solidarity enterprises. There are differences between social enterprises, such as those where social programmes are incorporated in the enterprise activities, and those where the programmes are complementary to the activity.

The legal framework promoting inclusive and solidarity selective waste collection is at a very different stage in different parts of the world. Labour and social regulations of 'informal' recyclers are still deficient and, although the profession of recycler, for example, has now been recognized in Brazil, Argentina and Colombia, this category still suffers from widespread prejudice and stigmatization as well as poverty and exclusion. The current tendency in solid waste management is to move up the waste hierarchy, towards integrated solid waste management, valorizing resource recovery and recycling. Conflicts emerge when the informal sector is excluded from decision-making, resulting in the loss of access to waste resources. This has been the case at many landfill closures throughout the world or with threats from public private partnership acquisition of waste incineration technology (discussed in Chapter 9). In both cases the historical protagonists of resource recovery are locked outside, with their livelihoods in jeopardy. Waste pickers everywhere have a right to work and to be able to provide a service to the city, and particularly their community, which is valued and remunerated. Chapter 5 will examine details of the social conditions of the work done by 'informal' recyclers.

Note

1   Based on currency conversion from March 25th 2015.

5 The social aspects of waste

DOI: 10.4324/9781315686523-5

Summary

Waste pickers are not passively assisting the innumerous injustices committed against their category and a social movement is building up in many parts of the world, with waste pickers resisting and fighting for democracy and better working conditions. This chapter highlights persisting challenges such as social exclusion and the exploitation of 'informal' recyclers, manifest in stigmatization, lack of agency, disempowerment and poverty. I will discuss processes that have built agency, facilitating the empowerment of waste pickers. The social benefits from organized recycling are manifold. The generation of work, the recovery of citizenship and the potential for human development are some of the gains examined here. The chapter underlines the necessity for policies to safeguard the social dimensions involved in solid waste management. In Brazil, the national movement of *catadores* has had a significant role in writing the new federal solid waste legislation, which supports partnerships between governments and recycling cooperatives in waste management. Finally, I will discuss an assessment methodology that helps qualify and quantify the social impacts of informal and organized recycling operations. This knowledge is important for the elaboration of preventive and constructive policies, in different geographical contexts.

5.1 Introduction to the global social challenges of waste pickers

The previous chapter featured sections describing the livelihoods and unacceptable work conditions of recyclers in different parts of the world. Mostly poor, socially excluded, without access to education and formal housing, the majority of waste pickers worldwide remain in poverty and are subject to stigmatization. Emerging social movements of waste pickers struggle to change these aspects into enhanced livelihoods and *decent work* conditions for all recyclers.

Waste is perceived and treated as undesirable, useless, obsolete, dirty and messy. We don't like to see garbage and most of the times don't know where and how our waste is disposed of. Likewise, people working with waste are often framed as waste, made invisible, treated like waste, ignored and discriminated against. Stigmatization is widespread among people who work with waste and it deeply affects their lives. What does it mean to be stigmatized, to be ignored and treated with disrespect or aggression, because you make a living from waste, collecting and recovering resources? In this chapter I draw attention to persisting, global social challenges encountered by recyclers everywhere.

With their organization into associations, cooperatives, networks and social movements, waste pickers become visible; they have a more resilient voice which demands social change. These processes of collective work and organization generate personal growth and help develop skills, often resulting in a sense of empowerment for the participants. This chapter sheds light on what it means to build agency through work in a recycling cooperative, particularly for women recyclers. I provide examples of the social benefits generated within these spaces, referring to Putnam's and Coleman's theory of social capital[1] that helps us name and qualify these social benefits and assets.

Finally, the discussion focuses on the overall social contribution of inclusive solid waste management. Integrated solid waste management, with door-to-door source separated collection of recyclables by organized workers provides local employment particularly for individuals who are less easily employable. Inclusive selective waste collection generates many local benefits. It creates work locally, stimulates the local economy, and educates and generates more environmental awareness locally. Inclusive selective waste collection also produces other social benefits, usually not recognized by governments or expressed economically. For example, the regular presence of organized recyclers performing their work as environmental stewards helps placemaking and contributes towards the building of social cohesion in the neighbourhood. Recognizing the local environment as clean helps people to develop a sense of place and fosters a sense of belonging, making the street, and the neighbourhood a more desirable and respectful place. Door-to-door collection opens possibilities for environmental education, for example, on how and what to separate and how to store disposed materials at home, until they are collected (see Photograph 5.1). The recyclers disseminate information on how to avoid disease vectors, for example, related to the spread of dengue. Social Life Cycle Assessment is introduced as a method that helps put numbers and qualifiers to specific social indicators related to human rights, working conditions and socioeconomic livelihood repercussions.

As part of the Social and Solidarity Economy introduced in Chapter 4, organized recyclers become active agents in changing their own reality and are also part of the process of transforming current life-threatening, unsustainable consumption practices and lifestyles into life-supporting and more sustainable forms of living, working, production and consumption. The recyclers make communities and cities more resilient, by recovering resources and making them available for new production circuits. They support circular economy approaches, instead of the linear process where waste is discarded at landfills or incinerators. Resource recovery, as will be discussed in Chapter 8, reduces natural resources extraction and saves energy spending.

Photograph 5.1 Door-to-door selective household waste collection in Diadema.

5.2 Social stigma against informal recyclers

Social stigma and rejection is unfortunately a universal feature of social life. Stigma was first defined by Goffman (1963) as an "attribute that is deeply discrediting" and more specifically as involving characteristics that carry "a social identity that is devalued in a particular social context" (cited in Kurzban and Leary, 2001: 187). Humans seem to have a fundamental need to belong; social alienation and rejection can make people vulnerable to behavioral, emotional and physical problems. "Stigmatization occurs when an individual is negatively evaluated, be it conceptualized in terms of discrediting, negative attributions; perceived illegitimacy; or a devalued social identity" (Kurzban and Leary, 2001: 188).

Stigmatization and negative labelling of 'informal' recyclers and their activities are a contentious social problem, widely reported in different regional contexts (Ackerman and Mirza, 2001; Ali, 2006; Schamber and Suárez, 2007; GIZ, 2011; Gutberlet and Jayme, 2010). 'Informal' recyclers are frequently associated with filth and discard. They are stigmatized and harassed by officials and the general public, who feel justified by these close connotations. Alongside the wide array of titles the recyclers receive to describe their work, comes a catalogue of terms with negative meanings, such as in Argentina *cirujas*, translating to foraging birds, or *pepenadores*, meaning the garbage people (Schamber and Suárez, 2007). Demeaning language used in public discourse against these individuals re-produces stigmatization and reiterates social exclusion (Gutberlet and Jayme, 2010).

Waste pickers sometimes bring their collected recyclables to their home in order to separate or store the materials. Neighbours, concerned with sanitation issues related to waste, dislike these circumstances and react negatively; which can reinstate prejudice and stigma. These situations are prone to generate disrespect and apathy from neighbours, enforcing exclusion. Furthermore, the segregation may easily reiterate exploitive and dependent relationships with moneylenders, middlemen, or corrupted policemen (GIZ, 2011). The fact is that waste pickers, when working on their own, usually sell their day's work to middlemen, are dependant on the prices they dictate, and are also exposed to frequent price fluctuations. Unreliable income makes them more vulnerable and less confident.

The stigma attached to informal recyclers has profound and disempowering effects, often following a long history of exclusion and exploitation which is deeply entrenched in historically-rooted discrimination and subjugation. The stories waste pickers tell us often describe the circumstances of lifelong exclusion, for example working on waste dumps with their parents or grandparents since their childhood. It is not uncommon for recyclers to be harassed and shamed by members of the police force, the authorities or the general public. Sometimes recyclers hide their identity as 'informal' workers and avoid being seen by family members while picking recyclables.

As reported during the *First International and Third Latin American Conference of Waste Pickers* in Bogota in 2008, the struggle to end prejudice and stigmatization were considered the most important challenges to focus on (Conference Proceedings: *Waste Pickers without Frontiers*). Waste pickers from India reported the problem of caste and social hierarchy making everything more difficult in their country. In India, most waste pickers belong to the most economically marginalized and socially excluded caste, whose members are traditionally regarded as untouchables or outcasts. With better working conditions, for example, organizing groups of waste pickers to conduct door-to-door household collection – as has recently happened in Pune (India) – this work becomes more attractive. It was reported that members from other castes are now also interested in performing this work, which demonstrates a shift in perception of waste picking towards becoming a respectable service (SNDT Women's University and CHINTAN, n.d.).

Skin colour is another characteristic which, in combination with waste picking, generates discrimination and social stigma, as reported numerously by recyclers in many parts of the world (Samson, 2009). In Brazil, 66.1 per cent of 'informal' recyclers identify as black and in some regions, particularly the Northeast and the North, they are overwhelmingly African descendent and black, numbering 78.5 per cent and 82 per cent respectively (IPEA, 2013). Many of these workers are women, who are usually less empowered, have less access to education and professional training and are often doubly burdened with additional tasks such as keeping the household and caring for children and other dependents. In Brazil 31.1 per cent of the *catadores* are women.

Organization and collective work contributes to social learning and empowerment. There are many examples that demonstrate how stigmatization can be reduced through organizing recyclers, providing them with uniforms, adequate working tools, capacity development, improving their health and creating educational opportunities. Moving towards *decent work* diminishes the problems related to discrimination and social exclusion.

5.3 Cooperatives as life-transforming spaces

Communities capable of drawing on social capital are considered more resilient and participants seem to have a better quality of life (Putnam, 1995). Hanifan first mentions social capital in 1916 (Woolcock and Narayan, 2000), but the concept was popularized by Bourdieu (1986) and later by Coleman (1988), who defined it as "the structure of relations between actors and among actors that encourages productive activities" (cited in Pretty and Ward, 2001: 210–211). Putnam, from an Italian perspective, adds economics and collective action to this definition, stating that social capital consists of "features of social organization, such as trust, norms, and networks, that can improve the efficiency of society by facilitating coordinated actions. [He continues]. . . . Spontaneous cooperation is facilitated by social capital" (Putnam, 1993: 167). Pretty and Ward (2001: 211) identify four key aspects of social capital: "relations of trust; reciprocity and exchanges; common rules, norms and sanctions; connectedness, networks and groups".

Efficient networking brings about social cohesion (Emmett, 2000), a central aspect of social capital, involving bonding, bridging and linking among individuals (Woolcock and Narayan, 2000). In the context of the informal recyclers, bonding refers to close family and group networks, and happens within cooperatives; while bridging refers to the relations between different social groups – for example, between members from the recycling movement and the homeless movement or the local government. Linking social capital is defined as the "norms of respect and networks of trusting relationships between people who are interacting across explicit, formal or institutionalized power or authority gradients in society" (Szreter and Woolcock, 2004: 655). A good example for linking social capital is the declaration of principles and objectives produced by the national *catadores* movement in Brazil (MNCR, 2012). However, having social capital does not necessarily lead to social change (Emmett, 2000). That is precisely why the concept has also received criticism. Das (2004) underlines that social capital omits class struggles and economic redistribution issues, thus preventing collective action. I use the term social capital in the sense of social assets, where the concept evidences beneficial social results, emphasizing that these should be credited. Nevertheless, the concept helps account for these positive social impacts which usually are dismissed and not taken into account in economic assessments.

The cooperative is a space where members share experiences, problems and information, seek advice or support, articulate conflict and reflect. The process of separating and classifying recyclable materials allows for dialogue. While social bonds are strong within the cooperative, these relationships also extend beyond the cooperative into their communities. As Harrison (2000: 514) describes, "feelings, experience and sense are not owned individually, they pass through subjects, and become eminently telling of a wider collective context". This *passing through* can be interpreted as empowering emotions experienced by individuals and which transmit beyond the cooperative into the communities where they work. Organized recyclers perceive the cooperative as an emancipatory space that helps build social cohesion. When the recyclers who had participated in the PSWM project in the metropolitan region of São Paulo (see Chapter 3) were asked about what they value in a cooperative versus working autonomously, they frequently mentioned: trust, solidarity, reciprocity and connectedness as the key values created through the collective work approach (see Photograph 5.2).

The reasons why 'informal' recyclers associate with a cooperative is often not remuneration (the cooperative does not necessarily improve the income of the recyclers), but rather encountering autonomy, collective support and other forms of social security offered for those who are part of a cooperative. I have learned through my own experiences with cooperative recyclers that sentiments of trust and belonging are created in cooperatives and are central to re-defining the recyclers' identity. Common values as they are expressed, for example by the recyclers' social movement, are dedicated to achieving equity, justice and solidarity and are deeply connected with feelings of empowerment shared among the recyclers (see also: Ahmed, 2004; Ahmed and Ali, 2004). Shared identity and the collective support at work are major reasons why 'informal' recyclers work collectively, despite the cooperative often not being able to pay very well. The recyclers mention that feelings of honour, dignity and pride in their work justifies their dedication to this activity. It is precisely these attributes that are also indicated by cooperative

Photograph 5.2 Recyclers from the *Associação de Recicladores Reciclando Vida,* in Londrina, separating recyclables.

members as strengths and reasons why they identify with cooperative recycling, despite multifarious difficulties and challenges (Tremblay and Gutberlet, 2011). The cooperative builds trust in the ability for social change. Reciprocity and exchange in the sense of mutual support are decisive features of the cooperative, as norms and sanctions become collectively installed, questioning attitudes and behaviours of cooperative members. The human relations within the cooperative are not without conflict.

Women recyclers, who in Brazilian cooperatives are the majority, value the emotional benefits and flexibility at work the most. However, women recognize that working collectively is difficult, "because each one of us is a different mind" (Catadora Maria). Work can be stressful, as stated by another female recycler: "it gets on my nerves seeing the inefficiencies of my colleagues at work" (Catadora Magdalena). Nevertheless, several female recyclers reiterate the spirit of solidarity, present in moments where it was needed:

> I was having problems with my son who was in prison. My colleagues here understood and helped me out. All of them understood and I could take my vacation to sort things out. . . . We are accustomed to depend only on ourselves. During the recent economic crisis however, one helped the other with whatever was available.
>
> (Catadora Silvia)

For many female recyclers the cooperative fills an important space and provides what they can't find anywhere else, as expressed by one recycler: "here [cooperative] is our home, our family" (Catadora Elisa).

Recently, however, these assets are under jeopardy. Municipalities are increasingly transforming cooperatives into automatized recycling centres, with *catadores* becoming employees. Under pressure to be efficient and competitive, speedy conveyer belts are installed and recyclers have to work in record time. Formalizing these sector workers into city staff might put them into *more decent work* conditions; however, it takes away their autonomy, self-determination and maybe also their political action, the assets that come into play in Social and Solidarity Economy and citizenship building.

According to the Brazilian federal waste management legislation of 2010, municipalities have to give priority to recycling cooperatives in contracting out selective waste collection and recycling. However, most local governments still don't do this. Cooperatives are unable to generate sufficient income for a decent livelihood just by commercializing the collected and separated recyclable materials. Price fluctuations are high and income levels remain under the minimum salary. This has created extreme poverty levels among waste pickers, resulting in hunger for themselves and their families. This situation is also happening among those organized in recycling cooperatives. The following statement of a women recycler from the cooperative *Cooperpires*, in a small city next to São Paulo, tells the story of her struggle for recognition and, so far, waiting in vain for the situation to improve (see Box 5.1). The statement was presented during the opening ceremony of the public policy Seminar on *Experiences of Selective Waste Collection. Contributions to the Implementation of the National Solid Waste Policy*, held at the Federal University of the ABC, on 28 August 2015. Several local politicians, administrators and academics, as well as many recycling leaders were present at the seminar (to listen to the statement and other contributions during the seminar, visit the website of COOPCENT-ABC).

BOX 5.1: Desperation and hope expressed by a waste picker

My name is Joana and I am a waste picker of *Cooperpires*, a recycling cooperative in Ribeirão Pires, a city of 120,000 inhabitants, in the metropolitan region of São Paulo, the *greater ABC region*. I work as waste picker for over 11 years. Our cooperative is equipped with automatic conveyor belts, with presses, and other equipment (see Photograph 5.3).

There are now only 13 members who work from Monday to Friday from 8:00 to 17:00. We don't have any contract with the municipality for the waste management services we provide, as requested by the national solid waste legislation. We live from what we collect, separate and market.

As the market for recyclable materials is very unstable with fluctuating prices, our situation is dramatic. When prices decrease our income diminishes. For this reason, the turnover of the cooperative members is quite high.

Photograph 5.3 Joana D'Arc Pereira, member of the cooperative *Cooperpires*.

Many *catadores* leave the cooperative and will try their luck in another job, yet almost always they come back later. Between being hungry and eating a little and not eating anything and starving, they prefer the first option.

When I talk about starving, I am not exaggerating and I am not being dramatic. Just to give you an idea, in July, the salary for each member at *Cooperpires* was R$ 380.00 (US$ 111.49, 31 July 2015). Is it fair for someone who has ten years of work experience and is hard working to receive R$ 380.00 per month?

The Brazilian Constitution says that urban cleaning, waste collection, and proper disposal are duties of the municipality. We are providing a proper destination for part of the waste, the recyclable materials, thus we are doing the work of the city.

Here in the *greater ABC region* the municipalities have to pay about R$ 80.00/ton, only to deposit the household waste at the landfill. Besides the disposal costs there are about R$ 70.00/ton of transportation cost. This means that for each ton of separated materials the waste pickers should receive R$ 150.00 that the municipal government doesn't have to pay to the landfill operator. And yet the waste pickers get nothing from the municipality.

Everybody knows, even a child in elementary school, when recyclable materials are redirected into the recycling stream, the environment wins because it reduces the need to extract natural resources from nature, particularly the non-renewable resources; which generates air pollution, water contamination, and soil degradation. Without material recycling, for example of the packaging and post-consumer products, planet Earth is under serious risk. The future of humanity is at risk.

When we visit schools, city halls, town halls and other public spaces, everybody says that our work is important and that our actions are central and necessary for the sustainability of the planet. However, when we received our R$ 380.00 salary at the end of a month of work, that is not what we experience.

The national solid waste policy defines in article 36 that it is up to the public administration responsible for urban cleaning and waste management to prioritize cooperatives and waste picker associations, composed of low-income individuals, to perform the work related to separate waste collection. And the city must hire waste pickers to do this job.

Many public administrators still do not understand this law. Others don't know the procedures of hiring waste pickers without going through a bidding process. Others believe that the law is wrong, because of the differentiated treatment of waste pickers, and that's why they don't comply. And finally, some are struggling to understand the law and to abide it.

The fact is that in most municipalities, the cities are hiring companies instead of prioritizing waste pickers as the law says. And most of them deposit the recyclable material at landfills and dumps.

It is easy to see that fact. Brazil formally recycles less than 2 per cent.

Sometimes we hear from public administrators that we need to be patient, because the improvements are being implemented. It is only a matter of time. We can no longer wait for these conditions to change. We have been waiting for five years since the Brazilian solid waste policy was approved in 2010 and we are now in 2015. I can't ask our children and the children of other women recyclers, who often are close to starving, to have patience and to wait. Hunger doesn't wait. Only our children and we know about the losses caused by not implementing the law. We know it and feel it in our skin.

But, despite all that, we haven't lost hope. We hope that in all cities and regions in Brazil, the public administrators will meet with prosecutors, attorneys and public defenders, and with the waste pickers and women recyclers, and seek a solution according to the national solid waste policy, to improve the separation and collection so that it is actually sustainable, provides work to waste pickers, fair and *decent working* conditions and contributes to the building of a just and solidary society.

(*Joana D'Arc Pereira*)

5.3.1 Empowerment within the cooperative

The dictionary of Human Geography defines empowerment as:

A permanent increase in the capacities of relatively poor or marginalized individuals, households, and communities to shape their own lives and bring about social change. In development thinking, it can refer either to the increased autonomy of individuals to make choices or, from more critical perspectives, the shift in power from elites to non-elites, or from dominant to subordinate groups, such as from men to women.

(Castree *et al.*, 2013)

Empowerment is understood as an essential process for people to take control over their own development (Hjorth, 2003), meaning the increase of their social influence and political power through acquiring confidence in their own capacities and by using them (Wallerstein, 2006). It is "an intentional on-going process centred in the local community, involving mutual respect, critical reflection, caring, and group participation, through which people lacking an equal share of valued resources gain greater access to and control over those resources" (Speer *et al.*, 2001: 716). Empowerment translates into enhanced assets and capabilities of individuals and groups to engage, influence and hold accountable the institutions that affect them (Bennett, 2002). At the individual level empowering processes are those that provide opportunities for people to work with others, learn decision-making skills and manage resources (Schulz *et al.*, 1995; Zimmerman, 2000). Empowerment is often used to characterize approaches based on social mobilization. It does not refer to a single, one-time experience but is a process, which is continuous and can suffer interruptions. Bennett (2002) describes this process as "mobilization empowerment", which builds on the skills, information and linkages needed for livelihood empowerment: "Mobilization empowerment can lead to new self understanding, solidarity and capacity for collective action" (Bennett, 2002: 23). A key element in most social mobilization approaches is assisting vulnerable and socially excluded individuals to realize the power they can mobilize from collective action.

In the case of 'informal' recyclers, working in a cooperative and becoming part of a network or social movement has been a vital process, which has contributed towards changing the livelihoods of the recyclers. Cooperatives and associations often receive support from non-government sectors or from local government agencies, which promote collective learning and specific capacity building. Through these educational processes, the participants learn how to question and reflect on their conditions and they develop a better understanding of the structural and political reasons for their underprivileged situations. Activities developed under *Participatory Sustainable Waste Management* have evidenced different experiences with empowerment throughout the six years of the life of the PSWM project (see Chapter 3). While initially, even the term *empowerment* was new and unknown by many recyclers, over time the discussions on participatory project management and its praxis brought to light elements that helped deconstruct power, evidence the lack of it, and reconstruct their own power. During an evaluation session one of the recyclers puts it as follows: "I was a street collector [*catadora*], now I represent the recyclers' movement in Brazil and in other countries, I got this empowerment within the project" (Catadora Monica).

Another recycler highlights empowerment as a learning process: "So I learned to defend [the project], not screaming or anything, defend, with quality criteria. . . . [W]hen we were to decide as to how to spend the money it was us the recyclers who decided . . . we were empowered" (Catador João).

Inclusion and participation are key elements of empowerment (Laverack, 2001). Within the social policy context these two notions are indivisible; empowering people means promoting opportunities for inclusion and active citizens' participation (Sidorenko, 2006). Empowerment outcomes can influence policy choices and the implementation of agreed results. These impacts generate feedback loops, which may be positive, reinforcing the process of becoming empowered and gaining influence; or they may be negative if the achievements lead to resistance from other groups and even generate more conflicts (Walton and Smulovitz, 2003). Involving 'informal' recyclers in the planning and implementation of activities means opening spaces for them to participate in meetings with government and other stakeholders, to give talks at conferences and seminars, to be interviewed at public events and to participate in the analysis, evaluation and dissemination of research and project results. The PSWM, as discussed in Chapter 3, applied a participatory approach and its participants have benefitted from empowerment processes.

Empowerment and social inclusion are closely linked dimensions of the process of social change. While empowerment focuses on the individual level, social inclusion addresses the institutional or systems level. "Social inclusion is the removal of institutional barriers and enhancement of incentives (through good policies) to increase the access of poor men and women and other excluded groups to assets and development opportunities" (Bennett, 2002: 23). Like the social mobilization aspect of empowerment, social inclusion seeks to provide agency for excluded individuals to change the overall system within which the needs of disenfranchised people are satisfied. Empowerment has a contested and varied nature, translating into both power over others and power to do something individually or collectively for oneself, or for others. In the context of community development power can exert pressure on public and private sector institutions – for example, to improve quality of life (Saegert, 2006). Nevertheless, empowerment can also reiterate certain agendas in which only the voices of the more powerful are heard and exclusion is further reiterated.

5.3.2 Empowerment for political action

The recyclers' movement in Brazil has been influential in the formulation of the national solid waste policy (*Política Nacional de Resíduos Sólidos – PNRS*), law No. 12,305/2010, to implement integrated and environmentally sound solid waste management. The participation of organized *catadores* in the policy design reflects in the outcome of the final legislation, where at 11 different sections in the law, specific reference is made to inclusive solid waste management with *catadores* (see Table 5.1). These are signs of empowerment for the informal recycling sector. Shortly before approving this law, however, a significant change was made in altering the solid waste hierarchy by allowing incineration with waste-for-energy as a final destination, which defeats the cause of inclusive selective waste management and demonstrates the fact that other more powerful stakeholders are capable of reverting previous victories. The example illustrates the difficulties in changing existing power structures. Empowerment may provide more access to previously excluded voices, however, their inclusion does not necessarily guarantee participatory praxis towards deliberative democracy.

The articles mentioned under the federal law in Table 5.1 have allowed for extensive training and capacity building of *catadores*, and have made available specific funding for infrastructure improvements, from which many cooperatives have benefitted. Some municipalities involve recycling cooperatives in their selective waste collection programme and support the groups anchored in policy (e.g. remunerating the service), guaranteeing working space and machinery or through specific educational and health-promoting strategies.

5.3.3 Empowerment and participation

Participatory approaches in development aim for empowering outcomes for participants, including increased community capacities, broader stakeholder participation in decision-making (Lennie, 2005), and promoting social justice (Gutberlet, 2008a). There is a substantial amount of literature reinforcing theories of empowerment through participation, particularly as an approach to address inequalities

Table 5.1 Specific references to *catadores* in Brazil's federal solid waste legislation (*Política Nacional de Resíduos Sólidos, Lei 12,305/2010*)

Articles	Content referring to waste pickers
Art. 7	XII – integration of *catadores* in fulfilling the shared responsibility between producers and consumers for the life cycle of products.
Art. 8	IV – incentives to create and develop cooperatives or other forms of organizations of *catadores*.
Art. 15	V – goals for the elimination and remediation of waste dumps, associated with social inclusion and economic emancipation of waste pickers.
Art. 18	II – implementation of selective waste collection with the participation of cooperatives or other forms of organizations of *catadores* formed by individuals from low-income families.
Art. 19	I – programmes and actions for the participation of interested groups, particularly cooperatives or other forms of organizations of *catadores* formed by individuals from low-income families.
Art. 21, § 3.	I – rules on the enforcement and content of the solid waste management plan with respect to performance of cooperatives or other forms of organizations of *catadores*.
Art. 33, § 3.	II – acting in partnership with cooperatives or other forms of associations of *catadores*, in the cases contemplated in § 1.
Art. 36, VI	§ 1. For the compliance with the provisions laid out in sections I to IV of the caput, the holder of public services of urban cleaning and solid waste management will prioritize the organization and functioning of cooperatives or other forms of organizations of *catadores* formed by individuals from low-income families.
Art. 42	III – implementation of physical infrastructure and acquisition of equipment for cooperatives or other forms of organizations of *catadores* formed by individuals from low-income families.
Art. 44	II – projects related to responsibility for the life cycle of products, primarily in partnership with cooperatives or other forms of organizations of *catadores* formed by individuals from low-income.
Art. 50	The absence of the regulation provided under § 3 of art. 21 shall not preclude the actions under this Law, of co–operatives or other forms of organizations of *catadores*.

and exclusion (Sreberny, 2006; Itzhaky, and York, 2000). Empowerment and dis-empowerment are a concomitant result of social and political negotiation. Nevertheless, only with increased participation can real social change happen.

Participatory approaches provide a platform to reduce and circumvent power relations and provide a voice for excluded populations by facilitating their involvement in educational or development programmes. Individuals involved in participatory learning processes are the agents of change, rather than merely the recipients. Empowerment is not an end state to be achieved in a systematic way. Essentially, it is about challenging existing power structures and enabling new political and economic relations to emerge. Non-violent conflict can sometimes be a needed step in the empowerment process. It is therefore necessary to critically engage in the understanding that the process of empowerment is political and by nature non-linear, often controversial and subjective. Empowerment can be *generated* inasmuch as it can be potentially reversible; it is an unstable and unpredictable process that makes it problematic both practically and theoretically.

Despite the increasing use of empowerment in monitoring and evaluation, it is a controversial approach and it is not possible to measure or quantify levels of empowerment. Qualitative methods can capture the subjective sense of empowerment expressed by participants. Miller and Campbell (2006) highlight concerns about empowerment evaluation, including conceptual ambiguity, a lack of unanimity in practice and limited documented evidence of success. Since empowerment is a process, its results should also be captured through the process, involving participants in monitoring and evaluating their perception of empowerment as has been done in some research with members of recycling cooperatives (Tremblay and Gutberlet, 2011).

5.3.4 Gender-specific empowerment

Like all social spaces, recycling cooperatives also have complex and contradictory meanings. On the one hand, the cooperative redefines the common ideology about gender roles, while on the other hand these spaces also conform to hegemonies ascribed to neoliberal and capitalist values. Despite the recognition of structural causes for being excluded and systemic sources of oppression that exist in the lives of the recyclers, female cooperative members generally agree that working in a cooperative offers them more personal dignity than other low-income jobs that are typically performed by women. Women have expressed a preference for working in the cooperative over paid domestic labour because of the sense of autonomy they gain with their work in the cooperative (Nunn and Gutberlet, 2013).

Cooperatives proclaim the absence of hierarchical structures, with everybody being an equal member, a situation different from other forms of employment that are typically performed by women (maid services, food hospitality, childcare, health care). Autonomy is an important component in shaping feelings of empowerment among female recyclers. Within the cooperatives women are given the chance to overcome hegemonic obstacles and they experience feelings of empowerment, particularly when achieving leadership positions that are generally reserved for men. A fascinating and notable feature of the group of cooperatives involved in the PSWM programme is the female leadership in these cooperatives. Currently the majority of leadership positions in cooperatives in Brazil are filled by women and even within the Brazilian recyclers movement, which until recently had an exclusively male leadership, women are taking up more prominent positions (Nunn and Gutberlet, 2013). The phenomenal representation of women leaders reflects a unique culture that exists among cooperative recyclers and demonstrates how emotions – specifically in this case confidence, composure, and courage – in relation to specific gendered codes of conduct can define how a space can be either conducive or non-conducive to social change. In previous research (Tremblay and Gutberlet, 2011: 9) we found that cooperative members commonly expressed empowerment in relation to "leadership skills, collective autonomy . . . and political participation." This unique social context and the emotions and subjectivities that are produced in the cooperative space serves to disrupt the status quo and has the potential to shape the conventional idea of which individuals are best fit to serve as institutional leaders – offering women the power to serve in a position that allows them the opportunity to affect institutions that are central to their lives. Women recyclers are still subject to moments of masculine oppression inside and outside the cooperative. However, despite these asymmetrical gender roles and hyper-patriarchal systems of domination within the cooperative, these spaces provide many opportunities for women to take up leadership. The feelings of empowerment also create a sense of pride and accomplishment, particularly when put to proof at occasions of resistance and manifestation. The cooperative offers social recognition and dignity to the recyclers, "The prejudice of seeing us as waste bins is over. We are *catadoras*. We have a name and we are recognized. We are, entrepreneurs" (Catadora Amelia).

Many of the female recyclers are single mothers. In trustful situations and safe environments female recyclers admit the scale of domestic violence,

> I tried many times . . . it took a while for me to make a decision. . . . But when he treated me so badly, humiliating me in front of my children, then I thought; what kind of an example am I setting for my children! . . . I left him and I don't want him to know where I am.
>
> (Catadora Ruth)

For many of the women the reality is as expressed here: "Sunday is the worst day of the week. Because that's when I wash the cloths, clean the house. That's when we fight with everybody, because nobody is helping, just being in my way" (Catadora Cibele).

5.4 Other social contributions of inclusive solid waste management

5.4.1 Generating employment

Unemployment is a global challenge, and is a central feature in countries in the global South, where the population pyramid has a wide basis, reflecting a young and still rapidly growing population. Brazil as a transition country (BRIC country) with a mostly urban population showcases the problematic related to high youth unemployment.

The official rate of people out of work in Brazil, according to the ILO (2014), shows an increase in unemployment from 2012 (6.3 per cent) to 2013 (6.5 per cent) to 2014 (6.6 per cent). The official number of women out of formal employment is higher than the number of men (11.1 per cent and 6.2 per cent respectively). Unemployment is concentrated mostly among youth (15 to 24-years-old, neither in school nor in formal work) and African descendent, particularly black individuals (IBGE, 2010). Coincidently the map of violence for Brazil also illustrates that the highest rate of homicides is among black people (Waiselfisz, 2012).

The overall youth unemployment rate in Latin America is between 2.3 and 5.5 times higher than the rate for adults (ECLAC/ILO, 2012). According to UNICEF (n.d.) between 25 per cent and 32 per cent of youths in the region are suffering the consequences of at least one of the following behaviours, considered socially risky: "they dropped out of school, are young parents, are not employed, are addicted to drugs, or have been arrested". Latin America and the Caribbean are considered particularly violent regions, presenting the highest rates of armed violence, with 42 per cent of global homicides happening here (UNICEF, n.d.). In Latin America most victims of homicide are young males between the ages of 15 and 24 years and of lower income levels (Briceño-León *et al.*, 2008). The same study informs that young men have committed most homicides in Latin America. The authors demonstrate that the numbers fluctuate over the years, according to stronger or weaker efforts to control violence. Homicides cost lives and also impact directly on healthcare and other institutional budgets, as well as private insurance expenses, material losses and many other costs related to the loss of quality of life and community wellbeing (UNDP, 2006). UNDP stipulated that approximately 1.4 per cent of Brazil's gross domestic product (GDP) was lost in 1999 due to homicidal violence (UNDP, 2006: 22).

Lack of *decent work* corrodes the wellbeing of the present and future society as a whole. The ILO recognizes that youth employment is particularly strategic on the public policy agenda, given its importance to producing social cohesion and safeguarding the collective wellbeing (ECLAC/ILO, 2012). The facts displayed earlier support the argument that social policies demand a focus on generating employment, especially for youth of African descent and of lower income levels. So far, macroeconomic policies have been largely detached from the social goal of generating employment, and focus instead on reducing public debt and containing inflation. Employment should be at the core of economic policies. Heintz and Razavi remember that, "employment and social policies are intrinsically linked and inseparable" (2012: 1). Of course, access to formal employment does not necessarily guarantee a pathway towards improved welfare or out of income poverty. Social policies thus need to act in tandem with economic policies.

Selective waste collection and recycling as performed in the global South is extremely labour intensive and creates more employment than landfilling and waste incineration. As argued earlier, there are immediate social benefits to be gained from pro-actively organizing recycling groups and integrating them into selective waste collection. These gains translate into providing employment opportunities, particularly for young people and those who suffer most from social exclusion, finally reflecting also in the overall social wellbeing and quality of community cohesion. Organizing and formalizing the recyclers with public support does not mean cooperatives or associations losing their autonomy or rights for self-determination, usually highly valued by most organized recyclers. Working with organized recyclers (cooperatives or associations) and implementing inclusive solid waste management requires a multifaceted approach, which integrates policies among different sectors of the public administration, tackling the various areas that need support. In Brazil the situation is gradually changing, with more municipalities recognizing the advantages of investing in organized resource recovery. In these few cases the recyclers are remunerated for the contribution of selective waste collection, separation and recycling, as also suggested by IPEA (2010). These types of solid waste co-production or partnership will be discussed in Chapter 9.

5.4.2 Socio-environmental stewards

While many 'informal' recyclers perform this activity due to lack of formal work opportunities, many of them confirm that they want to be *catadores*. The adaptable work schedule, the absence of a boss and the satisfaction of being able to contribute to the community and to improve the environment for future generations are some of the motivations of the recyclers captured in the study by Ramos *et al.* (2013). These authors reiterate that independent recyclers are able to choose when to work and what materials to collect, valuing the freedom and flexibility of this job. They also mention that so far, there has always been work because so much waste is being generated. The recyclers perceive waste as common property and as a good that generates income.

With regards to those recyclers that have organized in recycling associations and cooperatives, Ramos *et al.* (2013) confirmed frequently reported prejudice against recyclers. Society at large seems to be ignorant about the social, environmental and economic contributions of waste pickers. The general public mostly does not recognize the value of the work of resource recovery and has no understanding of the role of the recyclers as socio-environmental stewards. One of the direct forms of recognition would be for households to provide clean and properly separated materials during the door-to-door selective waste collection of recyclables (Ramos *et al.*, 2013). So far, recyclable material still arrives mostly dirty and contaminated with organic waste into the hands of the recyclers.

In order to evaluate the social side of recycling operations, and particularly the organized groups, a recent case study from Peru applied a Social Life Cycle Assessment (SLCA) method to evaluate the social impacts of informal and formalized recycling operations (Aparcana and Salhofer, 2013). The study developed a methodology to classify and evaluate positive and negative indicators, based on three categories and a number of subcategories: human rights (child labour, discrimination, freedom of association and collective bargaining); working conditions (working hours, income, recognized employment relationships, fulfilment of legal social benefits, physical and psychological working conditions) and socio-economic repercussions (education, including access to education for children from recyclers' families). Although not every social condition can be captured in a quantifiable form, this method helps identify key areas that need to be tackled with specific strategies and preventive policies. In the process of providing an enabling environment for 'informal' and formalized recyclers, change has to be monitored and verified and measured against the key objectives and goals. The method has not yet been applied to unorganized recyclers, whose social impacts are more difficult to capture.

5.5 Final considerations

It is important to refine methods to capture the social facets of the prevailing working conditions and livelihood circumstances of 'informal' and organized recyclers, to see the things unseen before and to highlight assets and failures. It is unfortunate that worldwide waste pickers experience discrimination, stigmatization and often aggression or violence. Being stigmatized seriously affects the life of these workers, who for that reason also suffer from low self-esteem. The social movement of waste pickers globally seeks to change these circumstances. These networks struggle for policy and legal changes in favour of waste pickers, recognizing the social and environmental service the waste pickers provide to the community. Since the beginning of the 1990s, waste pickers have begun to organize in India and other parts of Asia, and since 2004 the waste pickers have created a network in Latin America. In 2008, during the Third Conference of the Latin American network, held in Bogotá, Colombia, the realization of a World Conference of Waste Pickers was brought into existence. This global network describes itself as "a 'movement' that operates with minimum bureaucracy and with rotating secretariat responsibilities" (WIEGO, n.d.). As a movement, these recyclers' organizations pursue adaptation to constantly arising new challenges. In many cases their collective approaches have built agency and generated processes that have empowered recyclers collectively and individually, depending on their level of participation.

Organized recycling operations provide meaningful work and generate social goods, for example, by incorporating individuals who are not formally employable, due to long-term unemployment, lack of skills, physical or mental handicaps or drug dependencies. Especially for women, the cooperative embodies a space that supports agency building and helps them develop their capacities and leadership skills. The cooperative is a safe space where stories can be told and heard, reflecting on the wellbeing and emancipation of the workers.

Through door-to-door selective household waste collection, the recyclers perform socio-environmental services that are not recognized by the government, nor remunerated. Their presence in the neighbourhood improves the environment, be it by informing households about waste and recycling or by cleaning up littered waste while collecting recyclables. A clean neighbourhood is more valued by its inhabitants, and thus the clean up activity of recyclers also creates opportunities for greater community cohesion.

Innovative policies can make a difference. In Brazil the new federal solid waste legislation (Law No. 12,305, 2 August 2010) provides new opportunities for municipalities to collaborate with recycling groups in waste diversion and recycling. The law requires municipalities to adopt selective waste collection and composting. It supports the involvement of *catadores* in actions for shared responsibility for product life cycles and prioritizes recycling cooperatives in formal recycling programmes. Nevertheless, political will is the most important prerequisite for inclusive solid waste management. Governments often favour corporate waste management solutions or do not remunerate the recyclers for their service, which consequently delays the opportunity to recover the livelihoods of these recyclers.

Capacity building for effective and efficient resource recovery, adaptive policy design and public awareness building for efficient stakeholder collaboration in source separation are all critical. As socio-environmental stewards, recyclers can help disseminate information about selective waste collection, waste reduction, resource recovery and the many other social and environmental benefits of organized, selective waste collection. Finally, the organized activity of *catadores* is also an important catalyst for waste reduction and the creation of a more equitable and responsible society.

Note

1   I prefer the term "asset" over the term "capital" to express the social gain without using the hegemonic economic lens.

6 Health and risk factors for waste pickers

DOI: 10.4324/9781315686523-6

Summary

The health of 'informal' and organized recyclers is at risk because of unsafe working conditions and drivers for socioeconomic exclusion. This chapter helps understand specific health problems and occupational risk factors that affect the workers in this sector. I draw on secondary sources and my own qualitative, empirical, action research. General body pain, injuries and accidents are very frequent among 'informal' recyclers. Working in recycling cooperatives can also be precarious and unsafe. Here the workers report chemical and biological hazards, musculoskeletal damage, mechanical trauma, and poor emotional wellbeing. Ergonomically organized workspaces, better source separation at the household, appropriate technology, education and supportive policies can all make the difference to reduce risk factors and to improve the health of recyclers.

6.1 Introduction

This chapter examines the health conditions and risk factors affecting 'informal' and organized recyclers in cities in the global South while they perform the activity of collecting recyclables from disposed solid waste. The discussion draws on secondary data sources related to occupational health in the informal solid waste sector and on empirical research conducted by myself and colleagues from Brazil, in collaboration with *catadores* from recycling cooperatives in the metropolitan region of São Paulo over the past ten years. In our first study (Gutberlet and Baeder, 2008) we applied a survey and conducted interviews with *catadores* working in the streets of Santo André to find out about the health and risk factors they are exposed to. The second study, conducted with members from six recycling cooperatives in São Paulo, São Bernardo do Campo and Diadema, using a participatory, action-oriented methodology, focused on health issues the recyclers were facing under organized working conditions (Gutberlet *et al.*, 2013).

In this chapter I will first briefly present the most common health hazards and risk factors 'informal' and organized recyclers are exposed to all over the world. These impacts are usually classified into biological, chemical, musculoskeletal damage, mechanical trauma, stress and poor emotional wellbeing. The intensity and type of risk factors varies according to the work location (recycling centre, depot, the street or dumpsites) and the working conditions ('informal' or in organized groups). As outlined here, working on landfills and in dumpsters is unsanitary and bears severe health risks, particularly due to the mixed exposure of household and hazardous waste. Increasingly, recyclers are also involved in separating valuable materials from electronic and electrical waste (*e-waste/WEEE*). The dismantling of these products generates high concentrations of heavy metals in the surface dust, contaminating the workers, as well as the environment and the population living nearby e-waste recycling sites. I introduce these and other emerging health-related challenges and discuss solutions and measures to prevent unhealthy and risk-prone work conditions in resource recovery.

6.2 Livelihood conditions and health of informal recyclers

Working with solid waste is a health hazardous and risk-prone activity, particularly when conducted informally: sorting through trash on landfills and dumps, or garbage left at the curbside in city streets or drainage systems. Research confirms the many negative impacts from this activity on the workers' health, their quality of life and life expectancy. Informal recyclers at a dumpsite in Mexico City, for example, were reported to have an average life expectancy of merely 39 years, whereas the typical Mexican life expectancy at birth was on average 72 years for males and 77 for females (Medina, 2000).

There are also other variables that affect the health of 'informal' recyclers, particularly the fact that they are mostly poor and live in precarious housing conditions, without reliable water, sewage or energy access and sometimes even adjacent to the dumpsite. Recyclers sometimes spend the night on the streets guarding their collected materials, or they bring the recyclables into their homes, thus exposing themselves and family members to pathogens (Da Silva *et al.*, 2005).

During one of the interactive workshops my colleagues and I conducted under the PSWM programme, members from recycling cooperatives identified the following levels of need satisfaction, based on *Maslow's hierarchy of needs* (Maslow, 1970). Maslow's framework is based on the reasoning that human beings are motivated by unsatisfied needs, and that certain lower needs must be met before higher needs can be fulfilled. When re-defining Maslows pyramid according to waste pickers' livelihood perspectives, they recognized that for some of them the most basic needs, including shelter and food requirements, were not satisfied (see Figure 6.1 and Photograph 6.1).

6.2.1 Working on the dumpsite

Often, women of childbearing age, pregnant women and young children can be found working on open dumps. Children are particularly vulnerable to toxins, given that they ingest more water, food and air per unit of body weight and their metabolism is less developed to detoxify harmful substances. Impacting their growth development can ultimately disrupt the development of their organs, nervous, immune,

Figure 6.1 Maslow's pyramid according to waste pickers' livelihood perspectives.

Source: Based on Maslow (1970) and redefined during workshop with recyclers (PSWM Management Committee) and Sonia M. N. Felipone (Mestre em Gestão Integrada em Saúde do Trabalho e Meio Ambiente pelo Centro Universitário SENAC).

Photograph 6.1 Workshop on the state of health of *catadores*.

endocrine and reproductive systems (Cointreau, 2006). The same reference also indicated that women recyclers working on dumpsites were much more likely to lose a child. The author references a study conducted in Bangalore, Manohar, and New Delhi, India, where 38 per cent of the women recyclers had lost one child and

10 per cent had lost three or more children in their lifespan until the interview. The main self-reported causes of these infant deaths were diarrhoea, tetanus, smallpox, bronchitis and viral infections (Henriksen *et al.*, 1993, cited in Cointreau, 2006: 14).

Because many of the waste pickers have lived in lifelong exclusion, most of them did not access formal education or were unable to finish primary school. Lack of formal education comes alongside reduced access to professional skill development and training, locking these individuals into conditions of social and economic exclusion. This lack of education and access to information and knowledge reinforces unhealthy and dangerous behaviours, putting the workers, and often their families, at risk. Limited opportunities to earn a decent income also affect their capability to access regular, nutritious meals, and this translates into malnourishment and undernourishment. These restraining factors affect the overall health of the workers. I have witnessed repeatedly, and in different cities and countries, recyclers consuming products out of garbage bags or directly from dumpsters, exposing themselves to risks of intoxication, stomach infections and parasites from expired and contaminated food and drinks, and putting them in danger of developing bacterial or fungal infections through being in touch with dirty products. However, simply restraining the 'informal' recyclers from accessing solid waste is not a solution. Closing dumpsites and landfills to these workers does not tackle the health issues. On the contrary, sometimes the health-risk factors increase or affect a wider public. In Managua, for example, at *La Chureca* I have witnessed waste pickers being banned from the landfill, which has caused them to access the dump illegally having to climb over the bordering wall with their handcarts and bags and to sort their material near the landfill, resulting in littering and often the development of hazardous micro dumps in the vicinity. Often, the leftover waste is set on fire, causing additional air pollution impacts in these neighbourhoods.

6.3 Social stigma and emotional wellbeing of the recycler

It is widely known that 'informal' recyclers suffer from stigmatization by the general public and authorities, which often perceive them as dirty, worthless and invisible. The recyclers frequently report being harassed, robbed and bullied. Insecurity, coupled with social exclusion, shame and humiliation, leads to a higher self-assessed degree of vulnerability (Cavalcante and Franco, 2007; Martin *et al.*, 2007). As a *catador* in Diadema puts it:

> You need audacity and good will and not to be ashamed. A lot of people don't work in the street because they are ashamed. For this reason sometimes people go hungry, a lot of times even . . . they become a criminal, or something else, what for?
>
> (Catador Marcelo)

The precariousness of their work, the social stigmatization and the lack of financial security all lead to stressful livelihood situations. Stress-related symptoms, such as ulcers, high blood pressure and stomach problems were, for example, also self-assessed by informal *catadores* in Santo André (Gutberlet and Baeder, 2008) and street recyclers in New Delhi (Sarkar, 2003).

Social marginalization can also lead to conflict, as informed in studies with *cartoneros* in Buenos Aires, Argentina, by Parizeau (2013, 2015). Her research demonstrates that of the 397 *cartoneros* surveyed in the streets of Buenos Aires, more than half had already experienced aggression or conflict during their work and one-third of the respondents had been involved in conflict with the police force, which sometimes became violent.

Organizing the informal sector in cooperatives helps address the particular health issues related to stigmatization and discrimination, from which recyclers often suffer (Ezeah *et al.*, 2013). Cooperative members have the opportunity to participate in training and group activities, which has the effect of empowering them, enhancing their voices and giving them greater visibility. The cooperative also provides a chance to work with the wider community and to raise awareness of the recyclers' work as service providers and socio-environmental stewards in the solid waste management sector. Especially for women, the cooperative provides a chance to work more safely in resource recovery. This is one of the reasons explaining why the number of female workers is typically larger than male in organized recycling. Work life is more structured in the cooperative, in terms of work hours and regular intake of water and meals, which helps maintain health.

6.4 Physical health impacts

Many different physical impacts from the occupation of collecting, transporting, separating and manipulating recyclable materials from solid waste have been described in the literature, where they are characterized as chemical and biological hazards, infections, ergonomic and musculoskeletal damage, as well as mechanical trauma. Typically working without adequate protection, recyclers inadvertently come into contact with a variety of biological and chemical byproducts of waste.

6.4.1 Chemical and biological pollutants and pathogens

Chemical and biological exposure is associated with poisoning, infections, skin injuries (such as burns), allergies and respiratory illnesses. Contact with funguses and bacteria accumulating in contaminated packaging and food scraps mixed with recyclable materials is frequent. Decaying waste growing in bottles and on unclean discarded packaging can contain measurable inhalable particulate matter, including funguses and endotoxins, which are associated with many ailments, such as nasal infections and acute chest symptoms (Malmros *et al.*, 1997). These toxic reactions are thought to be caused by endotoxins and substances excreted by Gram-positive and Gram-negative bacteria (Van Eerd, 1997). Plastics, glass and discarded user goods carry the danger of biological and chemical contamination. The *catadores* in Brazil reported that it was not uncommon to find urine-filled bottles, toilet paper or dirty diapers mixed with recyclable materials, sometimes even in the selective household waste collection. The study by Kennedy *et al.*

(2004) reiterates the perceived risk factors from biological contamination, as modelled by other studies which cite respiratory ailments as being a leading complaint perceived by 'informal' recyclers (Nguyen *et al.*, 2003).

Stomach infections are common, as recyclers inadvertently come into contact with human and animal excreta (Gutberlet and Baeder, 2008; Nguyen *et al.*, 2003; Gomez-Correa *et al.*, 2008). Working in the streets or on landfills means having restricted access to sanitary and toilet facilities. A study conducted in several middle- and low-income countries detected acute diarrhoea more frequently in 'informal' recyclers than in the general population (Cointreau, 2006). Similarly, in Durango City, Mexico, researchers discovered that waste pickers tested with *Toxoplasma gondii* antibodies at higher rates than city waste workers and other populations less exposed to direct contact with solid waste (Alvarado-Esquivel *et al.*, 2008). Proximity and contact with flies, as it frequently happens with workers at dumpsites and landfills, causes infestations that often also lead to diarrhoea. Structural poverty is at the core of these health and sanitation hazards.

The presence of hazardous pollutants in liquid and gaseous emissions from landfills and dumps is well documented. A number of potentially toxic and carcinogenic trace volatile organic compounds are released that can have serious health impacts (e.g. affecting kidney functions or causing leukemia). Exposure to airborne particles of biological origin (bio-aerosols) also intensifies allergic and asthmatic pulmonary diseases. Evidence from an epidemiological survey conducted on 400 dumpsite recyclers in Calcutta, India, compared with a control group of 50, indicates an increased incidence of respiratory diseases among those waste pickers, with a 71 per cent incidence of respiratory disease, compared to only 34 per cent in the control group (Van Eerd, 1997).

Residues in packaging, including toxic cleaning products or leftover cement in the packaging bags pose severe health hazards to the recyclers when they manipulate these materials. Infections due to disease vectors such as rats or insects are also common biological health-risk factors on dumps, in recycling depots and in recycling centres. In some cooperatives pigeons pose a threat to the workers by putting them in contact with their excreta. These animals are transmitters for severe diseases, such as the Bubonic Plague and Leptospirosis, transmitted through the rodents' urine. Infections may also occur by direct contact with biological pathogens, such as Hepatitis-B. Mishandling solid waste, such as medical waste and syringes, or contact with sharp objects like glass, paper, metal or wood that produce cuts are some of the higher occupational threats perceived by the recyclers (Martin *et al.*, 2007; Patwary *et al.*, 2011).

There have also been numerous self-reported respiratory ailments, such as decreased lung function, lung infections and eye irritation, resulting from exposure to diesel fuel exhaust gases from the machinery at the dump and fumes from burning waste (Gomez-Correa *et al.*, 2008; Ray *et al.*, 2004). The latter is very common on landfill sites and surrounding areas, where garbage is often illegally deposited and burned. Sometimes 'informal' recyclers work in the proximity of these dumpsters. Respiratory diseases range from tuberculosis, pneumonia, asthma, and bronchitis (Porto *et al.*, 2004).

6.4.2 Ergonometric problems and risks of accidents

Working on the landfill and at dumpsites is particularly health hazardous. The material is dirty and is sometimes mixed in with hospital waste or sharp and broken objects. The recyclers have to compete with heavy machinery: trucks and bulldozers which are accommodating and layering the waste and which, in addition, contaminate the air with diesel fumes. A recycler from Gramacho landfill in Rio de Janeiro commented: "The recyclers have to be quick and alert to not get run over. Almost every week there is an accident caused by the interaction between humans and machines. This goes on day and night, 24 hours every day" (Interview conducted on 22 April 2008) (see Photograph 6.2). Although the Gramacho landfill is now closed, similar working conditions still remain in countless landfills and illegal dumps in the periphery of cities throughout the global South.

The activity is done under all kinds of weather conditions, exposing the workers to sun, rain, wind and extreme temperatures. Recyclers usually work long hours, more than five days a week and often also during the night. As one worker commented: "[T]here are people that work 16 hours according to how much money they want to make, so they work more . . . if they are satisfied they work, one, two, or three hours . . . according to his/her own needs" (Interview conducted on 22 April 2008).

Working in the business of collection and separation of recyclable materials involves carrying and lifting heavy loads. Moving material by loading it on the back or in hand-pushed carts may lead to sprains, fatigue, muscle pain and back problems. The work often requires repetitive movement and recyclers have to

Photograph 6.2 Everyday work practices at the landfill.

squat or remain in awkward postures for a long time. Frequent kneeling occurs while sorting and collecting recyclables and is thus associated with lower extremity pain. In our study, all 'informal' recyclers that were interviewed reported some sort of pain or discomfort in their limbs and back (Gutberlet and Baeder, 2008). Long days, repetitive movements, heavy lifting and loading present themselves as short-term pain and discomfort. The long-term musculoskeletal physical effects on the body over a lifetime of such manual labour have not yet been studied.

'Informal' recyclers frequently collect and separate their material on landfills, dumpsites or in the streets. Often the material is separated and stocked at their homes. The workers push their carts with heavy loads through busy streets and heavy traffic for long distances to finally sell the material to small merchants. Consequently, traffic accidents are perceived as high risk to the recyclers, according to a study conducted in Brazil and Argentina by Cavalcante and Franco (2007).

Hand selecting the recyclable materials from garbage is a risky task, as the material often comes mixed together with broken glass, construction materials, or even hospital waste, including syringes. Recyclers often claim to prefer working barehanded, as it allows for greater tactility, which is necessary for quickly sorting paper and plastics out of the garbage bag. Speed is important, particularly when working at the landfill in competition with other recyclers and trucks or bulldozers. It is also a widespread opinion among the recyclers that gloves are useless in preventing needle punctures or cuts from glass. Dall'Agnol and Fernandes (2007) found that sometimes recyclers acquire discarded gloves from hospitals, which they wash for reuse, in an ineffective attempt to remove the risk of infection. In tropical areas, recyclers might wear sandals, shorts and T-shirts, thus having little to no protection for their feet, arms or legs.

The absence of safety equipment leads to the common occurrence of lacerations to the hands, arms, legs and feet. The detailed studies of Martin *et al.* (2007) enquired as to how waste workers dealt with injuries, typically lacerations. The interviews conducted with recyclers in Buenos Aires highlighted the fact that they were unwilling to pursue professional medical care, even if it was free of charge. Seeking out public healthcare can mean long waiting periods, translating in loss of income.

Only 32 per cent of the recyclers in Colombia went to see the doctor when they were ill, citing lack of health coverage as the issue (Gomez-Correa *et al.*, 2008). Further answers ranged from doing nothing about the injury, finding rags in the trash to wrap around cuts, using lemon juice to clean wounds or even licking the dirt out of the wound. Nevertheless, it is a fact that waiting too long for adequate healthcare increases the risk of infection.

6.5 Health implications from separating e-waste

Electric and electronic waste, in short, e-waste, is the term used to describe "old, end-of-life or discarded appliances using electricity" (e-wasteguide.info). It is among the fastest growing solid waste streams in the world. The category ranges from large household appliances, like refrigerators, air conditioners, computers, printers, televisions, stereo systems, or fluorescent lamps, to small digital apparatuses like power tools, toys, iPads or cell phones. E-waste accounts for over 5 per cent of all municipal solid waste and is growing steadily (Schwarzer *et al.*, 2005). Projections for the near future estimate an exponential increase of discarded e-devices, particularly in transition economies like China, Brazil, South Africa and India (Heart and Agamuthu, 2012). The notion of *planned obsolescence* and Joseph Schumpeter's concept of *creative destruction* characterized by rapid innovation and quick disposal fit the e-consumer good production line. These two concepts are at the heart of capitalism and its essence growth, stimulated by incessantly destroying the old and creating the new.

E-waste causes a particular threat to the environment and to human health because of its toxic components, including organic pollutants and heavy metals, such as lead, nickel, chromium, cadmium, arsenic and mercury. While many countries in the global North have special collection points and recycling methods in place for discarded electric and electronic devices, in the global South these e-products mostly still end up on landfills or in dumpsters (Pérez-Belis *et al.*, 2014). Trans-boundary movement of e-waste is another major issue, with disposed e-waste being transferred to countries in the global South where environmental and health legislation for this specific waste is still non-existent or not practiced (Mckenna, 2007). Among the favourite destinations for e-waste are Bangladesh, China, Hong Kong, India, Indonesia, Malaysia, Nigeria, Pakistan, the Philippines, Sri Lanka and Vietnam (Heart and Agamuthu, 2012). Recently, many countries in the global South have also emerged as significant generators of e-waste themselves.

Informal workers recover some of the more valuable and easily identifiable components of e-waste, through backyard recycling, mostly applying inadequate methods and low-efficiency processes. Open burning of plastics to reduce e-waste volumes and to expose valuable copper wires and other metals, or acid leaching to recover precious metals from PCBs (Polychlorinated Biphenyls) are common practices, releasing toxic leachate and fumes to which the recyclers are exposed. BCPs are highly toxic synthetic organic chemicals, which are classified as persistent pollutants. The leftovers from these operations often accumulate in open dumps or are disposed of in surface water bodies, generating severe environmental health problems.

Such informal recycling practices pose enormous challenges because of the lack of proper training and infrastructure for environmentally sound handling of these products. Current literature draws particular attention to Brominated Flame Retardants (BFRs), which have negative environmental and health effects. BFRs are used in PCBs, connectors, covers and cables. Informal e-waste recycling practices expose the workers to heavy metals. Studies from China, for example, confirm the significantly higher concentrations of these metals among the workers, compared with control sites (Ma *et al.*, 2011; Wang *et al.*, 2009). Heart and Agamuthu (2012) have compiled evidence from recent research worldwide on the health effects of exposure to BFRs and heavy metals of personnel working in e-waste recycling facilities and of people living in surrounding areas.

Even so, given the critical environmental and health implications, public policies preventing illegal e-waste transportation and promoting proper e-waste recycling still have to be developed in most countries in the global South. In India, for example, e-waste is not yet regulated, however, since 2012 the *e-waste rule of 2011* clearly outlines extended producer responsibility to fund the collection and recycling of these products (Heart and Agamuthu, 2012). Yet, poverty, lack of education and lack of access to funding are additional barriers to the implementation of safety measures in this sector (Widmer *et al.*, 2005).

6.6 Cooperative recycling and health

Worldwide, 'informal' recyclers have begun organize in cooperatives and associations (discussed in detail in Chapter 4). Organized recyclers are able to create advantageous situations and legitimatize and formalize their work, empowering their members with participatory decision-making opportunities, and generating collective actions. A recent research project was aimed at identifying key health aspects of workers in cooperatives and confirming whether the general benefits of collective work also extend to the occupational health situation in the cooperatives (Gutberlet *et al.*, 2013).

Our research involved the following six cooperatives/associations within the metropolitan region of São Paulo, Brazil: (1) *Vila Popular e*; (2) *Nova Conquista*, of the city's *Vida Limpa* (Clean Life) programme, in Diadema; (3) *Associação de Catadores de Papel, Papelão e Materiais Recicláveis do Bairro Assunção e Adjacências (Refazendo)*; (4) *Associação dos Catadores de Papel, Papelão e Materiais Recicláveis (Raio de Luz)*, in São Bernardo do Campo; (5) *Cooperativa de Trabalhadores da Coleta, Triagem e Comercialização de Materiais Recicláveis e Prestadores de Serviços (Coopercose)*; and (6) *Cooperativa União Ambiental e Artesanal Mofarreje*, in São Paulo.

The research process was organized into three phases: mobilization, workshops and feedback sessions. During the mobilization phase, the researchers presented the idea and objectives of the action-oriented study to the six recycling groups and invited cooperative members to choose two representatives each to participate in the workshops and to act as knowledge transmitters between the research group and their cooperative. The workshops involved brainstorming and active learning, applying collective mapping, acting and drawing methods focusing on possible risk factors and health hazards, as well as respective strategies to overcome these during the work phases of collecting, separating and manipulating recyclable materials. After having completed the workshops, the systematized data was presented at the cooperatives. These feedback sessions provided insights to the main occupational health issues and discussed some of the proposed solutions with all cooperative members.

The research confirmed the existence of a number of serious occupational risk factors for cooperative recyclers (see Box 6.1).

BOX 6.1: Voices from *catadores* in Brazil

Working in cooperatives: "Stress is a very large problem at our recycling center. There is a lot of stress because of the lack of cooperation and understanding between the people within the cooperative."

(*Catador* João)

"The daily workload is 8 hours, but people work more, because there is a lot of work and because people need the money. Usually we work 10 hours or more per day."

(*Catadora* Helena)

"The trash comes all mixed and therefore contains many risks."

(*Catadora* Paula)

Working 'informally' at landfills: "The major health problems among the recyclers at the landfill Gramacho are: diarrhoea and malnutrition, particularly among the children, as well as Tuberculosis and Leprosy among adults."

(*Catador* José)

"Fatal accidents are very frequent, falls and collisions with trucks at the landfill. It all happens based on improvisation."

(*Catadora* Maria)

"Cuts are frequent. There is a great dispute for material. During the fight you forget your hand. It happens almost daily, the loss of fingers or even the whole hand. Such accidents are not reported. The rush of everyday life at the landfill increases the risks."

(*Catadora* Joana)

Most of these impacts are related to chemical and biological hazards from handling dirty packaging material; infections, due to cuts from glass, paper, metal or other sharp objects; muscoskeletal damage due to carrying heavy loads or performing the separation under inadequate ergonometric and organizational conditions; mechanical trauma from accidents in the street or at the workplace; and poor emotional wellbeing due to stress, lack of illumination and lack of air circulation at the recycling facility. In some cooperatives, frustration and dissatisfaction were the results of a lack of transparency and participation in the cooperatives' decision-making. Some participants raised stressful work relations amongst cooperative members as a key health issue and we learned that these were often related to leaders who were emulating hegemonic and oppressive social structures, including unequal gender relations. Furthermore, the presence of rats, pigeons and insects were mentioned as key problems in many of the cooperatives. Local health authorities are aware and regularly spray the cooperatives to reduce these infestations. However, the root causes of badly organized work conditions within the cooperative and poor material separation at the household level are not yet tackled sufficiently.

Although conflicts and stress related to working collectively were mentioned, several participants also underlined the opportunities for empowerment and personal growth via the cooperative: "Now I live in my own house, when I was a street collector, I lived on the street, and I used to drink" (Catador Beto); "Solidarity and collective work are important. While people are working, they're off drugs. We have to take care of social health" (Catador Murilo).

Acute issues related to social exclusion and homelessness surfaced repeatedly during the workshops, escalating alongside the problems created by alcohol and drug abuse among recyclers, who usually do not receive professional treatment (see Box 6.2).

One cooperative member revealed the stress experienced recently due to pressure exerted by the local drug lord and dealers who, for a short period, used the cooperative space to hide from the police. The study further revealed the emotional health impacts caused by stigmatization and prejudice against those who work in selective waste collection. The recyclers expressed the need to generate more awareness about their work to help them become recognized as socio-environmental stewards. They reiterated that first of all the government (and particularly the local governments) should recognize and address the vulnerable working conditions of recyclers, not through prohibition (e.g. closing down cooperatives because of the lack of sanitation and non-compliance with safety regulations), but by providing the means to improve recycling operations, making them safer and less health impacting.

BOX 6.2: Perception of a health practitioner

Alcohol ends up being a calorie supplement, and many people think that drinking feeds you, ... you take some shots of a drink . . . . a couple of glasses of beer and you feel full, and why do you feel full? Because of the amount of calories each type of drink, mostly distilled drinks, contains. But this is an empty calorie the person doesn't take in any protein or vitamin, quite the contrary, the drink sucks some types of proteins out of your body, ..., over time the alcohol dependent also suffers from a deficiency, for example a deficiency of vitamin B. It is absurd.

(Interview conducted with Tereza Luiza Ferreira dos Santos,
FUNDACENTRO, São Paulo, 7 April 2005)

6.7 Final considerations

Unorganized and informal recycling activities expose the workers to a wide variety of hazards and dangers on a daily basis. The recyclers are vulnerable to accidents and health-risk factors while working at open dumpsites, and when they are exposed to trucks and bulldozers, and toxic, hazardous and infectious materials contained in the waste. Women, children and elderly individuals working with waste are the most susceptible group. As a result of recent dumpsite closures in many parts of the world (Brazil, Nicaragua, Peru, etc.), 'informal' recyclers are prohibited from working on landfill sites. As a consequence, they access these areas illegally, sometimes creating new dumpsters in the vicinity of the landfill, where they sort through the garbage, seriously affecting not only their own health but also the environment and the health of nearby residents.

Some of the health hazards discussed in this chapter are common for 'informal' as well as organized recyclers. These include ergonometric issues related to lifting and carrying heavy loads of recyclables, generating body pain and back problems. Another key health hazard experienced by waste pickers comes from chemical and biological contamination. Even with formalized selective waste collection involving recycling cooperatives, the material is often mixed and dirty. The use of compacting garbage trucks, as used in the city of São Paulo, for example, affects the quality of the material by crushing glass and metals, which often produces sharp objects, posing the risk of perforating skin and creating an infection. Chemical and biological injures are preventable and happen because of a failure in policy enforcement regarding commercial and industrial regulation and lack of residential awareness in source separation. Without *continuous* environmental education, the level of awareness in the community remains low, which is reflected in the poor quality of source separation.

Recently, in many countries in the global South, informal resource recovery of e-waste has evolved into yet another critical environmental and health hazard and the absence and/or insufficient implementation of regulations to prevent occupational risk factors urgently needs to be rectified, particularly given the exponential growth of the discard of these products in the global South. Extended producer responsibility (EPR) is the most important tool to pro-actively reduce unregulated and unhealthy practices. EPR charges the producer that designs products and places them on the market with the responsibility for the end-of-life treatment of those products. EPR obliges producers to cover the cost of collection, recycling and disposal, which could benefit the recyclers. Businesses are compelled to be responsible and use designs that are beneficial to reuse and recycling, for example, choosing non-toxic, non-hazardous substances and recyclable materials. Policies are urgently needed to prevent the illegal trafficking of waste, improper recycling activities and the dumping of residues.

Overall, poverty and its related health-risk factors still seem to be the number one cause of unhealthy and risk-laden work conditions for the 'informal' and organized recycling sector. Usually recyclers live in precarious housing (or are homeless) and do not regularly access nutritious food. Action research with cooperative members confirmed the very low level of needs satisfaction of the recyclers; often, these workers do not even achieve the basic level of physiological requirements (basic needs and food) of *Maslow's hierarchy of needs.*

A difference that can be significant in terms of the occupational health of these workers is related to the benefits of organizing into associations, cooperatives and wider networks uniting interest groups. These initiatives are powerful means of promoting better working and livelihood conditions. Organizing the 'informal' sector dignifies the workers in the labour market and provides opportunities for education and organization, which is reflected in higher visibility and bargaining power to improve their living and working conditions and access to public healthcare. The workers are more able to access infrastructure (adequate sorting equipment, hygienic sanitary facilities, kitchen and change rooms, storage areas, battery-driven hand-carts, etc.), social services and training or skill building as well as access to personal protective equipment (PPE), uniforms and information on safety and risk prevention. It is widely recognized that wearing uniforms and carrying ID cards changes the perception of the recyclers, making them visible and recognized as environmental agents, empowering them and adding to their emotional wellbeing. These simple measures help to build self-confidence and reduce the stigmatization and marginalization of recyclers. Organized recycling helps limit the physical strain a worker is exposed to on a daily basis, for example, by controlling the number of working hours and by facilitating separation and manipulation processes with adequate equipment and ergonometric planning.

In order to generate the funding required for capacity development (including funding for the acquisition of proper technology and training) and the implementation of minimum health, safety and environmental standards, a *recycling fund* fed by the financial contributions of producers and importers has already been suggested by many scholars and practitioners (Akenji *et al.*, 2011). This would allow the recyclers to access and purchase appropriate technology. A certification scheme preparing skilled recyclers for specific tasks in resource recovery (e.g. e-waste, organic waste, specific industrial/business waste) would be instrumental in this context. These recyclers would be trained to avoid health-risk factors and could disseminate this acquired knowledge within their cooperative.

In order to enhance safety measures during collection and separation, states and organizations should monitor both the public and private sectors, making sure they adhere to sustainable solid waste management practices and policies. Health promoting policies must be addressed and enforced at all government levels. In many cases governments have already moved forward to creating branches that work with recyclers, (e.g. the municipal administrations in Buenos Aires, Argentina or Londrina, São José do Rio Preto, Ribeirão Pires in Brazil). Educating the public on waste separation and on the work of waste pickers and educating the recyclers on pro-active, hazard-preventing working procedures could certainly cut down on injuries associated with manipulating recyclables.

7 Recycling the organic fraction of household waste

DOI: 10.4324/9781315686523-7

Summary

Municipal solid waste in the global South often contains more than 70 per cent organic matter. In most cases this material is landfilled or dumped mixed in with inorganic waste. Under these circumstances the organic fraction generates liquid leachate, methane and other greenhouse gases, thus compromising environmental and human health. These materials can be recovered for the production of compost to fertilize the soil or to generate energy for heating and electricity. This chapter presents data on the scope of organic waste generation, briefly describes key environmental challenges related to landfilling organic waste and introduces some methods of capturing and recycling these resources. The debate is supported by sustainability and resilience theory. Different projects of organic waste recovery are presented, particularly the composting of household waste for food production in urban gardens. Recovering the organic fraction of source separated solid waste contributes towards tackling some of the planetary challenges we face today. Remaining questions involve the redesign of city spaces for decentralized composting and bio-digestion, as well as the re-education of society for responsible consumption and quality source separation. Reclaiming the organic fraction of municipal solid waste (MSW) is a sensible form of making urban environments more resilient; this already happens in some cities also in the global South.

7.1 Introduction

The composition of MSW in Southern cities is predominantly organic and is mostly not recovered. Given the magnitude of the environmental and health-related challenges attributed to the generation of solid waste, it is of paramount importance to not only advance inorganic material recycling but to also reclaim the organic fraction in waste. However, as solid waste is most often not perceived as a key obstacle to urban sustainability, investments into projects for infrastructure and treatment of organic waste, other than landfilling as well as necessary environmental education measures for source separation, are yet to become municipal priorities. Furthermore, city budgets for solid waste management are usually limited and pressure to collect and dispose of waste in rapidly expanding urban and peri-urban areas is high.

Chapter 7 introduces the generation of municipal solid waste as a global environmental challenge, given the scope of its generation and the deposition rate of mixed waste at landfills and dumps, despite the possibility of recovering the organic fraction. The two basic forms of reuse and recycling for organic waste are aerobic composting and anaerobic digestion. These two processes involve source separation and selective collection, which are important steps in guaranteeing high quality fertilizer for cultivating food and ensuring a sustainable recovery.

Landfills and waste dumps are major sources for greenhouse gas (GHG) emissions, including carbon dioxide (CO_2), methane (CH_4) and nitrous oxide (N_2O). All three gases are produced during the management and disposal of waste. Methane gas is also responsible for global warming and generates local hazards such as fires and explosions at waste dumps. For several months, for instance, the dump in remote Iqaluit, Nunavut, Canada, was on fire and the municipality was facing severe difficulties with putting out the dump fire and had to pay a high price in order to control the situation (News: Nunavut, 2014). Examples involving expensive landfill remediation in the global South are common, but sometimes the necessary measures are not taken due to the high costs involved, in which case water pollution (leachate) and gas emissions cause dangerous environmental hazards.

Some carbon compounds may be retained in landfills for long periods and are therefore not returned to the atmosphere as CO_2. In addition, landfills emit odour and liquid leachate, formed as waste decomposes (Smith *et al.*, 2001). For all these reasons, perceiving organic waste as a natural resource signifies an important paradigm shift that is yet to happen on a wide scale. From a big picture perspective, it is not landfilling, but recovering organic waste for composting and bio-digestion that creates many benefits and addresses some key planetary challenges. The top challenge relates to reducing GHG emissions, which are a cause of climate change. The reintroduction of natural fertilizer into unproductive land helps reduce the pressure to expand agricultural land, thus addressing the environmental problems related to land system change and biodiversity loss. Substituting industrial fertilizer with compost also reduces human interference in the global phosphorus and nitrogen cycles, cutting out the impacts from industrial fertilizers and their production.

Besides the environmental benefits, this chapter also discusses the potential of generating work with composting and urban agriculture. The ideas are discussed from a systems-oriented, sustainability framework, supported by concepts from Ecological Economy and Social and Solidarity Economy. The concept of urban metabolism is helpful in order to understand the cyclical nature of waste as output from production and consumption and input for local fertilizer and energy production. Also, from the resilience perspective, we will see that reclaiming organic waste contributes towards long-term sustainable and less vulnerable cities.

The second part of the chapter analyses specific examples and case studies that showcase the diversion of organic waste for compost production and bio-digestion in some Southern cities. The literature describes many benefits and challenges linked to these methods. The installation of anaerobic digesters for energy generation, for example, can become a viable alternative, particularly for the population in peri-urban and low-income settlements. We find inspiring cases and pilot studies from many parts of the world, beyond the famous examples for small-scale, decentralized organic waste diversion, composting and urban agriculture in La Habana and other cities in Cuba (Altieri and Funes-Monzote, 2012), and in Rosario, Argentina (Piacentini *et al.*, 2014). These cases demonstrate the capacity of low-income neighbourhoods to engage in grass-roots organization for the collection, separation and composting of household waste for food production. A pilot study from Diadema, Brazil, discusses some of the difficulties and institutional hurdles involved in the introduction of bottom-up community innovations. Finally, the chapter revisits some of the requirements for a governance environment that enables the use of the full renewable resource potential embedded in organic waste.

7.2 Sustainability – resilience framework

Cities, suburban and peri-urban areas are dense spaces of material consumption and waste generation. Yet, most of the resources that are consumed come from afar, involving the depletion of resources and natural environments somewhere else (Satterthwaite, 2009). After World War II, in particular, the intensity of material consumption has drastically increased in the global North and is increasing more recently also in the rest of the world. "Human population on the planet has increased fourfold over the last hundred years, while—in the same time period—material and energy use has increased tenfold" (Lehmann, 2011: 156). Urban populations are the main consumers of materials, energy, water, and food and consequently are also the principal generators of GHG emissions associated with climate change. However, there are significant variations in the use of resources based on income levels. Higher incomes are associated with using up more resources and with generating larger *ecological footprints*. This situation portrays primarily the conditions found in the global North and among the elites in the global South.

Urban ecology (Marcotullio and Boyle, 2003) sees the city as the urban metabolism within the ecosystem, recognizing it as a process of metabolically transformed nature, a socio-natural hybrid (Gandy, 2004). From a complex systems theory perspective, the notion of circularity in urban resources use is being challenged by the argument that rather than optimizing a single set of supposedly ideal circumstances, the goal should be that of achieving greater resilience to the inevitable internal and external shocks that will impact urban areas (Alberti, 2008). Ecological economists like Daly (1996) suggest a steady-state-economy, based on stability without growth in consumption (*de-growth*), to counter the serious environmental impacts humans have created (primarily) over the past century.

The depth of the urban crisis related to wasteful production and consumption patterns is too obvious to be ignored and yet unsustainable development patterns still persist. The identification of pathways for transformation towards sustainability in social ecological systems has not yet received sufficient attention (Pelling, 2011; Pelling *et al.*, 2011). Among major challenges to be addressed are the issues of energy and resource/material efficiency and more radical strategies to promote and apply the concept of sufficiency. Resource effectiveness and recovery are central to this emerging discussion. Resource recovery is crucial in order to make our cities more resilient and, ultimately, more sustainable. However, sufficiency addresses moral and ethical questions of reducing consumption for the collective good.

Resilience is the ability of a social or ecological system to absorb disturbances while retaining the same basic structure and ways of functioning, the capacity for self-organization and the capacity to adapt to stress and change. The concept builds on the premise of strong social ecological connections and takes a co-evolutionary systems perspective (Walker *et al.*, 2004). The concept is complementary to the various theories on Ecological Economy as well as on Social and Solidarity Economy and urban metabolism introduced in other parts of the book.

A resilient city supports the development of greater resilience in its institutions, infrastructure, and social and economic life. Resilient cities reduce their vulnerability to extreme events and respond creatively to economic, social and environmental change in order to increase long-term sustainability. Vulnerability is defined as "insecurity and sensitivity in the well-being of individuals, households and communities in the face of a changing environment and implicit in this, their responsiveness and resilience to risks that they face during such negative changes" (Moser, 1998: 3). People are recognized as active agents, with their own voice and able to engage in transformative community building. The concept of resilience has been used to characterize "a system's ability to bounce back to a reference state after a disturbance and the capacity of a system to maintain certain structures and functions despite disturbance" (Turner *et al.*, 2003: 8075).

From a resilient city perspective, development is sensitive to distinctive unique local conditions and origins, thus focusing on *the local* and *the community*, encompassing long-term perspectives; much longer than the four- or five-year legislative periods that usually prescribe urban development. Similar to the idea of sustainability, building resilience is one of the big challenges of our time and requires unprecedented collaboration between different civil, government and business actors to safeguard the present and a future for next generations.

Efforts undertaken to prevent crisis or disaster in one area should be designed in such a way as to advance the community resilience and sustainable development in a number of other areas as well. As such, resilient cities define a comprehensive *urban resilience* concept and policy agenda with implications to urban governance, infrastructure, finance, design, social and economic development, and environmental as well as resource management.

Resilience studies focus on change and transition events – certain sorts of tipping points. Solid waste generation is reaching a tipping point and current prevailing waste management methods are clearly not taking care of the problem. Pritchard and Sanders (2002) remind us about the important role power plays in shaping the outcomes of interactions produced by the agency of individual social actors under specific structures. Perceiving how power is held and used by individuals or groups is pivotal in fully understanding the outcomes of these interactions, either resulting in the facilitation of change, or in the blocking of it (Pelling *et al.*, 2011).

If we apply the resilience discussion to solid waste, we can identify concrete opportunities nested in some forms of waste management. The separate collection of organic waste for composting, for example, is a pro-active measure which helps to reduce the amount of waste that has to be landfilled and can support food production. Organic waste recycling diminishes people's vulnerability by generating work and a product that can generate revenue (electricity, cooking gas, compost, nutrients, etc.). When conducted as community-based, collective, grass-roots initiative the activity additionally generates social goods, which also make the community and city more resilient.

The chapter continues with a practical approach, discussing how cities, communities and individuals can increase their resilience and ultimately their sustainability by altering current solid waste management processes. Many cities in the global South are challenged by high poverty and unemployment rates. Hazardous waste accumulation is particularly an issue in informal settlements. These neighbourhoods often lack basic infrastructure and services, and many of their residents suffer from hunger and malnourishment. Only 20 per cent of the 200,000 inhabitants in the informal neighbourhood of *Kibera* in Nairobi, for example, have access to electricity. The lack of a stable electricity supply can be tackled with the use of alternative energy sources, such as organic waste. 40 per cent (262,800 tonnes) of the annually generated waste in Nairobi is not collected but illegally dumped. Informal settlements are most affected by the lack of waste collection. Only 1 per cent of the total 567,648 tonnes of organic waste generated yearly in Nairobi goes to composting and land application (UN-Habitat, 2010). Examples also highlight the fact that food security can be improved with composting and urban farming. These ideas are discussed by a wide range of different disciplines, for example under the topics of *livable* or *green urbanism* (Lehmann, 2010).

7.3 Resource potential: organic waste

A comparison of municipal waste composition in 20 cities around the world confirms the high level of organic matter in household waste in middle- to low-income countries in the global South, with an average of 67 per cent (ranging from 48 per cent to 81 per cent), compared to an average of 28 per cent (ranging from 24 per cent to 34 per cent) of organic waste content reported for cities in the global North (Wilson *et al.*, 2012: 244). The organic fraction in municipal waste can vary significantly between one neighbourhood and another. In low-income residential areas, household waste tends to be composed of primarily organic matter, as demonstrated by the example of Ghana's dense capital city Accra, where the organic waste portion ranges from households with 60 per cent to 90 per cent organic waste content (Asomani-Boateng, 2007). The differences in waste content are often explained by the claim that populations in lower income countries and in low-income areas consume more fresh fruit and vegetables and less packaged items or disposable goods, which are more likely to be reused and recycled as a resource. However, in peri-urban areas, households often feed organic waste to animals (pigs, chickens, goats) or use it in composting for vegetable gardens. Due to (on average) higher temperatures, higher rainfall, and greater humidity, the water content of municipal solid waste in the global South is also usually higher. This fact has critical implications for waste management practices.

Previous chapters have already highlighted the fact that in many cities in the global South, part of the population is not serviced with solid waste collection. It is surprising how much waste is not collected in these cities, given the severe public

Table 7.1 Average municipal solid waste collection in
urban areas

Country	Average (%) population not covered by MSW collection	Data year
Colombia	2.8	2005
Bolivia	20.1	2004
Peru	29.2	1991
Nicaragua	35.3	2001
Senegal	37.4	1997
South Africa*	39.0	2007
Guatemala	43.5	1998
Ghana	60.4	2003
Ethiopia	61.0	2005
Kenya	71.5	2003
Benin	72.5	2001

Sources: UN Habitat (2010: 96); *Greben and Oelofse (2009).

health consequences (see Table 7.1). Waste collection coverage varies from almost 100 per cent, as is the case for cities in Colombia, to situations where most of the population has no access to solid waste collection, as in the case of Benin, West Africa, where only 27.5 per cent of the country's population receives this service (UN-Habitat, 2010). Usually the population living in informal settlements is excluded from formal MSW collection.

Lack of waste collection generates dumping and illegal waste disposal sites, which are often visited by waste pickers in order to recover recyclables (Greben and Oelofse, 2009). Uncollected organic waste creates breeding grounds for disease vectors and blocks waterways, causing flooding during rainy periods. Proper solid waste management practices can avoid such health hazards and sanitation problems. Low-cost, appropriate technology solutions are essential, specifically in poor and neglected neighbourhoods.

7.3.1 Composting organic MSW

Composting and bio-digestion of animal manure for the production of fertilizer has been practiced for thousands of years in China, India and other parts of the world (Nayono, 2010). Compost is produced to improve soil productivity, while the process of anaerobic digestion primarily generates energy, as heat or electricity (Greben and Oelofse, 2009). Both methods require the separation of the organic from the inorganic fraction of waste. To safeguard the quality of both the process and the product, this is best done at the source, with households having a special container for their organic materials. Composting treats organic material as a result of the action of aerobic bacteria, funguses, and other organisms. Vermicomposting specifically involves different species of worms to create a heterogeneous mixture of decomposing material. Recovering organic waste can encompass different scales, requiring diverse levels of technology, energy and labour input. It ranges from small-scale (bin composting) to large-scale approaches, including passive and active windrow composting and in-vessel composting. Worldwide, large-scale composting is used to divert agricultural waste, sewage sludge and organic waste from landfills (Greben and Oelofse, 2009).

The advantage of using compost is that it brings nutrients back into the soil and reduces the environmental impacts generated by the use of industrial fertiliser and peat (Premakumara, 2012). Applying compost diminishes the need for irrigation and reduces soil erosion rates. Indirectly, the use of compost is also more environmentally sound because it does not generate air contamination during its production, as fertilizer industries do. Composting also bears the potential for carbon sequestration by increasing organic matter storage. Nevertheless, the composting process needs to be carefully controlled to avoid the creation of bio-aerosols, because of their potential impact on both occupational health and the health of nearby residents. There is still a major lack of knowledge concerning the dispersal of the airborne microorganisms (funguses, bacteria, endotoxins, etc.) emitted by composting plants (Wéry, 2014).

Formal MSW management operations involve collection, transportation, intermediate treatment and final disposal of the waste. The reduction of landfilled waste as a result of organic waste diversion diminishes municipal spending in waste collection, transportation and landfill management. Premakumara (2012) discusses how composting as a solid waste management practice has helped reduce municipal expenditures and GHG emissions in Cebu City in the Philippines. The city was facing a significant increase in the generation of municipal waste from 212 tons/day in 1982 to 470 tons/day in 2010, turning solid waste into a serious environmental issue. The introduction of waste separation at the source, recycling and composting activities contributed to 30 per cent less waste landfilled in 2012, which also translated into the reduction of approximately 12,000 tons of CO_2 equivalent not generated in Cebu City (Premakumara, 2012: 12).

7.3.2 Anaerobic digestion of organic MSW

The first confirmed historical evidence of harvesting biogas dates back to 3,000 BC, in Assyria when the gas was used for heating bath water (Botheju and Bakke, 2011). During the eighteenth century, methane gas was captured from natural anaerobic habitats for the purpose of producing light. An anaerobic digestion plant for wastewater and solid waste treatment was first installed in Bombay, India, in 1859 and by the end of the nineteenth century, the technology was also widely applied in the UK and, later, in other parts of Europe (Gijzen, 2002).

Anaerobic digestion creates the possibility of energy recovery in the form of methane, involving microorganisms that break down organic material in the absence of oxygen (Greben and Oelofse, 2009); the result is an almost complete conversion into methane (CH_4), carbon dioxide (CO_2), hydrogen sulphide (H_2S), ammonia (NH_3) and new bacterial biomass (Nayono, 2010). Biogas is used for cooking, heating or electricity and can also be compressed for alternative uses. As a byproduct, it creates a nutrient-rich sludge, which can be applied as fertilizer, but is dependent on the quality of the materials being digested. The energy generated in this way can replace fossil fuels and avoid emissions of CO_2 (Smith *et al.*, 2001). Thus, "the recovery of biogas as well as the recovery of nutrients makes anaerobic digestion of organic waste a sustainable waste treatment concept" (Hartmann and Ahring, 2006, cited in Greben and Oelofse, 2009: 676).

Anaerobic digestion has the advantage of requiring less space and generating less emission of bad odour and greenhouse gases (Baldasano and Soriano, 2000). Food waste produces the highest biogas yield. The gas content decreases with increasing amounts of garden waste added. Anaerobic digestion is also used to reduce the amount of organic matter produced at sewage plants, generating more biogas and a better quality of sludge (Greben and Oelofse, 2009). Gebreegziabher *et al.*, (2014), however, highlights the fact that sewage entering the bio-digester plant can negatively affect the anaerobic digestion process and the author only supports co-digestion when combining food waste with sewage sludge. In terms of energy recovery, anaerobic digestion is reported to be the best practicable option for municipal organic solid waste related to diminishing environmental impacts, improving human health as well generating positive technical, economic and social outcomes.

7.4 Experiences with organic waste recovery

Today, most formal solid waste collection systems in place in the global South do not separate organic matter and the vast majority of this material is deposited mixed in with inorganic fractions on dumps and landfills. In North America as well, only a relatively small number of cities divert all organic household waste other than gardening waste. The number of projects focusing on organic waste diversion in North America is now growing, mostly involving the composting of food and garden waste (Yoshida *et al.*, 2012). Data from the EU demonstrate that between 2001 and 2010, recycling rates for organic materials have increased less than for inorganic materials, with most countries still sustaining a very low level of bio-waste recycling (0–10 per cent of the municipal waste generated) (EEA, 2013: 16). The data demonstrate that in rich countries, the potential of organic waste as a sustainable energy and fertilizer resource also has not yet been fully put into practice.

In the global South the largest contribution in recovering organic waste comes from 'informal' recyclers and encompasses many different forms of organization and purpose in their work. These workers treat and view organic solid waste as a valuable resource. They work as small businesses or are organized as cooperatives or associations, in the collection of source separated or mixed household waste. They do the sorting of the compostable material and work in the preparation of the compost and sometimes in farming activities. In some cities there are also private-sector composting firms, operating on a larger scale and often employing workers from the informal sector to collect the organic material (UN Habitat, 2010).

Engaging the private sector in waste management requires municipal authorities to create access to, and rights over, solid waste, which also means restricting the access of some to the same resource. Disputes have been documented, primarily over accessing inorganic recyclable materials. In most cities, once garbage is placed in the street or in municipal bins and skips, the solid waste belongs to the municipal authority and, based on the prevailing legislation, it is generally their responsibility and right to collect and dispose of it. Involving private operators can generate conflict when these compete with waste pickers over the access to waste.

These circumstances related to disputes over access to waste have been discussed in the case of Melbourne, Australia (Lane, 2011), Victoria, Canada (Gutberlet and Jayme, 2010) and Vitoria, in southeastern Brazil (Cavé 2014). In some cases the appropriation of urban waste has resulted in the forceful implementation of policies and projects and the consequent exclusion of workers or their animals, preventing them from accessing these resources on waste dumps or in streets, and sometimes contradicting long-established patterns. The 65,000 *zabaleen* working in Cairo exemplify the struggle and resistance of disenfranchised 'informal' recyclers who have long been the target of repressive policies, stigmatization and violence (Fahmi, 2005). Farmers living in peri-urban areas often depend on organic municipal solid waste. The *zabaleen*, Egypt's 'informal' recyclers, have for decades successfully recovered recyclables and have collected organic waste to feed their animals (Fahmi and Sutton, 2006). Recently, their livelihoods had been jeopardized by the privatization of solid waste management in Cairo, which has excluded them from accessing household waste (Kuppinger, 2013). After having been sidelined for more than a decade, the government has recently started to attempt to re-integrate the *zabaleen* into the city's services.

Similar challenges have been reported for Hubli-Dharwad, India, where the increasing role of the private sector in the collection and disposal of solid waste has caused the eviction of livestock from urban areas, affecting the urban poor (Nunan, 2000). In some cities in the global South urban farming (or urban agriculture) is a common local food production practice: "Urban farming includes the cultivation of crops and trees, raising of livestock, and fisheries within and in peri-urban locations of cities" (Asomani-Boateng, 2007: 134). Urban agriculture is defined as, "food and fuel grown within the daily rhythm of the city or town, produced directly for the market and frequently processed and marketed by the farmers or their close associates" (Smit and Nasr, 1992: 141). Urban farming also provides an opportunity to generate or supplement livelihoods (Smit *et al.*, 1996).

7.4.1 Composting in Accra, Ghana

In Accra, soils are naturally salty and poorly drained and fertility has significantly decreased as a result of intensive cultivation (Asomani-Boateng, 2007). To cultivate on a continuous basis, soil fertility needs to be enriched regularly. Adding organic matter in the form of compost is therefore vital to guarantee future urban agriculture activities (Smit *et al.*, 1996). Action research conducted in a poor, high-density neighbourhood in Accra, with a population of approximately 2,500, involved major actors (households, urban farmers, community groups, women and youth groups, as well as local leaders) in source separation and composting activities (Asomani-Boateng, 2007). In this pilot project, participants developed the techniques and skills for recycling organic household waste into compost for urban cultivation. The study demonstrates the feasibility of transforming organic solid waste into compost for urban gardening, thus, reducing the amount of waste to be managed.

The biggest challenges identified by this study were related to overcoming issues of land availability for composting and motivating the participants and other stakeholders to initiate and sustain the project. The author concludes that there need to be tangible benefits for the individuals involved; otherwise it will be difficult to sustain projects like these (Asomani-Boateng, 2007). Other studies also underline the technical feasibility of local composting projects. Results indicate that, at present, the biggest hurdle in Quezon City (Metro Manila, the Philippines) is securing buyers for the compost. Therefore, most compost is still distributed to large neighbouring farm villages (Hara *et al.*, 2011). The research also reiterates the necessity for further studies on the social relationships among stakeholders (e.g. lot users or caretakers, lot owners) and on the institutional framework supporting organic waste recovery and urban agriculture.

7.4.2 Food production in Dar-es-Salam, Tanzania

Several lessons can be learned from a study on the assets and barriers of bottom-up composting initiatives in Dar-es-Salaam (Oberlin and Szántó, 2011; Oberlin, 2012). Since 1999, when municipal solid waste collection and street cleaning became privatized in Dar-es-Salaam, many new jobs were created in small-scale, private enterprises and community-based organizations working with waste collection. As such, the community initiative *Kisutu Women Development Trust* (KIWODET) became officially in charge of municipal solid waste collection, initially in three sub-wards. By 2007, KIWODET collected the household waste from more than 3,500 households and the women also became involved in the service provision of street sweeping. Some members of this group started a first composting operation in Dar-es-Salaam, with organic material collected from hotels and local markets. Yet, this particular group did not receive sufficient support from the local community and even experienced hostility, as some individuals repeatedly sabotaged the composting site. The major claim against this operation was that odours from the organic material would concentrate on the site, which was located within the densely inhabited settlement of *Hananasifu*. This turned out to be the major barrier to the acceptance of this project by the community (Oberlin and Szántó, 2011). Community-based composting projects require continuous community outreach in environmental education, maintaining an open dialogue with community members and with the local government to sustain acceptance and support. This pilot experience from Dar-es-Salaam on setting up a door-to-door collection of organic waste reiterates the requirement of environmental education and dialogue with key stakeholders and the community to guarantee their support.

7.4.3 Organic household waste collection for composting and food production in community gardens

The story told in Box 7.1 reveals some of the monumental hurdles waste pickers in Diadema, Brazil had to overcome in order to become officially supported for their work in resource recovery. It is logical to involve the experienced, organized 'informal' recyclers who are already conducting the door-to-door collection of recyclables in the recovery of organic household waste and yet they are often sabotaged, discriminated against and simply ignored in the design and implementation of waste management programs.

BOX 7.1: Insights from a pilot study on organic household waste collection for food production in the city of Diadema, Brazil

In 2008, a pilot study conducted in Diadema involved *catadores* from the recyclers' association *Pacto Ambiental*, as well as community gardeners, local residents, and municipal government representatives. The main objective was to explore the social and political feasibility of collecting organic waste for composting and urban gardening. The *catadores* and local health agents were involved in the research design and participated throughout the implementation of the project. As an initial step, educational material (folder) was produced on how and what material to separate, providing information on the collection details and benefits from organic waste recycling. These folders were distributed to the households, inviting them to participate in a pilot study involving household visits and dialogues. The recyclers collected food waste from 41 households on a twice-weekly basis for three months and transported it to the composting site where the gardeners processed the material. As one of the gardeners noted: "the organic waste is practically clean, there is no meat leftovers, no salt, no plastic . . . practically, a clean thing that will provide healthy vegetables and healthy vegetable gardens". The gardeners were working in a municipal urban agriculture project and were thus familiar with composting.

The pilot study included a survey, applied to all residents in that neighborhood, as well as in-depth interviews with key informants from the government, residents and *catadores*, to help understand the level of institutional and community support for such an initiative. The survey indicated a high environmental consciousness among participant community members. Nevertheless, several practical and social constraints also became apparent. Some residents were unsatisfied with the collection frequency, given the fact that food waste attracts insects and rodents, and they had difficulties with in-home storage. Residents also mentioned that they were already using food waste to feed their animals and plants. Some residents refused to provide material because they did not want to be associated with *catadores*; these residents held a low opinion of the recyclers due to their waste-related work and, thus, perceived lower socioeconomic status. As a result, *catadores* only visited those households that they knew were sympathetic to the cause. The findings indicated the need for constant educational activities to address stigmatization, prejudice, and knowledge gaps within the community. Yet the most difficult hurdle evidenced through this pilot project was getting the local government on board with real and long-term commitment, recognizing the value of waste as a resource for livelihood sustainability (organic waste to food) (Yates and Gutberlet, 2011a, 2011b) (Photograph 7.1 and Photograph 7.2).

Photograph 7.1 Composting organic household waste collected by *catadores* in Diadema.

Photograph 7.2 Cooperation between community gardeners and *catadores*.

The term *deliberative truncation*, coined by Darbas, captures "the process by which discussion of what would constitute the most productive ecological institutional designs and policy settings was sabotaged by unyielding understandings of efficiency, success and progress" (2004: 2). The concept fits the situation described in the pilot study (see Box 7.1) in Diadema, where *catadores* and gardeners experienced this form of 'informal exclusion', where they were invited to discuss inclusive solid waste management with government and yet their ideas were sabotaged and ignored. Deliberative truncation emerges from routine politics that consists of "mutually reinforcing and institutionally hardened constellations of beliefs and practices that constitute fronts of resistance to novel ideas" (Darbas, 2008: 1467). The deliberative struggles of the recyclers have done little to change hierarchical political structures and patronage, resembling what Swyngedouw calls the *placebo-politicalness* of formal politics (2009: 615).

Many municipal representatives remain unaware of the fact that compost possesses economic value. The study reminds us that there is always the threat of community gardeners and waste pickers literally doing the dirty work of capitalism in providing an under-remunerated ecological fix to the challenges of waste accumulation, despite all the attempts to equitably re-circulate the value inherent in organic waste (Yates and Gutberlet, 2011a). Finally, this case study evidenced the need for more research into the economic viability of community-based enterprises related to composting household waste to support such a shift. Paternalistic relations will only perpetuate exploitation and poverty. Fair remuneration for the service is what these workers demand (Lavalle *et al.*, 2005).

7.4.4 Anaerobic digestion of organic waste

There is no abundant academic literature about successful Southern city examples using the organic fraction of municipal waste for energy production. Most studies analyse the use of animal manure to produce energy in countryside areas, where the principle raw material is widely available. Singh and Sooch (2004) for instance, describe the successful use of cow dung, in India and other Asian countries, to generate biogas as supplementary cooking fuel. Although the majority of case studies focus on rural energy production, Gebreegziabher *et al.* (2014) refer to biogas production from organic municipal solid waste to produce electricity for street lighting in Pune, India. The non-academic literature provides many more examples on successful small to large-scale projects in cities in the global South.

In South Africa 18.5 per cent of households are not connected to electricity (Greben and Oelofse, 2009). Given the increase in informal settlements in this country (from 12.7 per cent in 2002 to 15.4 per cent, in 2007), with rising demand for electricity, the authors analysed the potential for anaerobic digestion of organic waste for heat and electricity generation. This technology also produces a positive health benefit by avoiding energy sources such as gas, paraffin, wood or coal for heating and cooking purposes, which are known to cause respiratory diseases, particularly in the young, elderly or weakened (e.g. individuals with immunodeficiency) (Greben and Oelofse, 2009). The study confirmed many positive environmental impacts from using organic waste for bio-digestion. Biogas installations help reduce the need for firewood consumption and thus also create positive environmental impacts, by avoiding deforestation and consequent erosion and soil degradation. In the African context it is believed that firewood consumption could be reduced to such an extent that a gradual regeneration of forests would be possible (Gebreegziabher *et al.*, 2014).

The remaining challenges for co-digestion plants in South Africa are mostly related to the operation and maintenance of the infrastructure (Snyman *et al.*, 2006). Technology failures are often ascribed to low levels of professional preparation of the plant operators. Greben and Oelofse point out that "maintenance problems with complex and expensive systems/equipment; technical and financial constraints; social considerations and infrastructure requirements" were all hindering factors that held up the development of anaerobic digestion technology in the general context of many countries in Africa (2009: 677).

According to the literature, cost recovery remains a key challenge in most anaerobic digestion projects (Gebreegziabher *et al.*, 2014). A comparative study focusing on the economic aspects of different models of family-size biogas plants in the state of Punjab, India, calculated the payback period for different bio-digesters (Singh and Sooch, 2004). For all three models it was true that the larger the biogas plant capacity (varying from 1 m³ to 6 m³), the quicker the cost recovery. Cost recovery under the three models, for the 1 m³ biogas plant varied between 4.7 and 26.66 years, while for the 6 m³ biogas plants, the variation was between 1.62 to 3.71 years on average (Singh and Sooch, 2004: 1337–1338). Thus, from an economic perspective, it is most viable to set up a reasonably sized facility for volumes around approximately 6 m³.

Municipalities often have trouble funding waste recovery projects and have to find ways of recovering the expenses by charging residents household waste management fees. Besides cost, several other crucial factors are to be pondered when planning a biogas operation for municipal waste digestion. Longevity and space are also important considerations when deciding the most appropriate biogas technology for urban applications. Different models for bio-digestion are available, based on scale, location, geography (climate in particular), technology or quality of the refuse material. In addition, a reliable, cost-effective and appropriate form of organic waste collection needs to be in place. Many new jobs can be created with the collection, involving appropriate technology, such as bicycle trailers, hand-pushed carts, electric carts, among other forms.

Finally, political will and social acceptance are crucial in maintaining a flourishing organic waste collection, composting, or biogas production service in the city. Cultural and religious taboos can also be potential hindrances. Hence, governments and non-governmental organizations involved in this form of resource recovery need to be creative to maintain an informative dialogue with the community, which needs to be on board for such an endeavour to become successful.

7.5 Final considerations: assets and barriers for the implementation of organic waste recovery

Organic material is ubiquitous and is generated in large quantities in Southern cities. It is potentially rich in nutrients and energy and thus can become an abundant resource for composting and/or bio-digestion. Yet organic waste is mostly not collected separately, nor used for resource recovery purposes. Composting as a practical solution for managing organic household waste has not yet been sufficiently explored in the current global context of waste generation and recovery (Asomani-Boateng, 2007). Not salvaging organic waste constitutes an environmental hazard, adding to global warming and climate change.

Difficulties in sustaining composting operations have been reported from many parts of the world. In India, for example, it is reported that many of the large-scale, national government-initiated composting plants had to close due to high production costs, inappropriate technology, inadequate maintenance and poor marketing of the compost (Nunan, 2000). The author reports that countless community-based neighbourhood composting schemes, which have been more successful, have developed in response across India. In Bangalore, for instance, a number of neighbourhood schemes supported by non-governmental organizations work with waste pickers to collect household waste on a door-to-door basis, sell or dispose of the inorganic part and use the organic part in local vermicomposting pits (Nunan, 2000).

Funding shortage and lack of municipal support still represent significant barriers in the implementation of composting projects, often impeding the success of community-based solid waste management, composting and urban farming initiatives. This has been documented for many different parts of the world. The initial investment of an anaerobic digestion plant is usually high, followed by ongoing operation and maintenance costs. However, the input materials are often free of charge and comprise mainly collection and transportation costs. Cost recovery is important for the sustainability of these projects, which means finding outlets for the resulting compost and energy.

The contamination of municipal solid waste remains a significant problem, and, as noted by Furedy and Whitney (1997), the separation of different types of waste at source is recommended as the most efficient way of producing good quality compost. Such schemes require considerable support from authorities, supporting their implementation and promoting citizens' education for best practices in source separation. Despite the prominent role that non-governmental organizations play in the implementation of waste recovery, the government needs to demonstrate financial backing to these projects. The pilot study from Diadema, Brazil, confirms the fact that without political will and support from the local government, such initiatives have a hard time surviving.

Finding an adequate and low-priced location for composting operations or bio-digestion is often difficult and involves continuous dialogue with the local community to assure their support and acceptance to locate the facility close to their 'backyard' (as is also true for any other waste management facility, e.g. recycling centres). Receiving municipal support with infrastructure, technical and/or financial assistance is essential because it is nearly impossible for composting businesses to be economically sustainable: "Composting, as with any form of waste processing, is often a break-even or just marginally profitable business" (Oberlin and Szántó, 2011: 1076). This statement is based on a purely economic perspective and does not value the social and environmental components of work related to organic waste recovery. 'Informal' recycling generates social and human goods, which need to be valued and paid for by local governments. 'Informal' and organized recycling generates meaningful, community-oriented work, which contributes to the wellbeing of the community and even reduces greenhouse gas emissions and improves environmental health. Composting of organic waste is a strategy with job creation, environmental advantages and long-term economic benefits. Labour-intensive practices, rather than processes depending on expensive technology, help cut costs and expand the job market (Nunan, 2000). By diverting organic material from landfills, less leachate and greenhouse gas emissions (CH_4 and CO_2) are generated and the landfill's lifespan is expanded. These aspects also reflect in lower waste management costs (Yoshida *et al.*, 2012).

Taking care of the organic fraction – in addition to the inorganic, recyclable part of waste – is overdue if we are to address the critical planetary challenges humankind is facing. We still mostly waste the opportunity of reducing greenhouse gas emissions by not depositing organic waste on landfills or dumps, and we miss the opportunity of composting food and garden waste for urban farming. Recycling organic waste into compost or energy through aerobic and anaerobic digestion indirectly helps fight biodiversity losses linked to land system changes by bringing food production closer to the consumer (urban agriculture). This measure also has the potential to reduce human interference in global phosphorus and nitrogen cycles, by producing organic fertilizer and reducing the need for the industrial production of synthetic fertilizer. Local urban agriculture helps shorten the distances that food has to travel, thereybe reducing transportation emissions and helping to reduce the food losses that inevitably happen with long travelling times.

A realistic challenge for practicing organic resource recovery is the need to redesign city spaces and remodel public solid waste management infrastructure and services. Community support for composting and urban agriculture and access to land for those who want to be involved are paramount. For these initiatives to be sustainable, they need to be anchored in local policies and they require participatory approaches to land-use planning, particularly to solid waste management

For cities to become transformed into green, liveable and sustainable spaces with more resilience and less vulnerability, *good governance* is a fundamental requirement. This also means political support for integrated municipal waste management, taking care of the organic waste and using the final products deriving from composting and bio-digestion processes. Finally, the strategies proposed here empower and enable communities and individuals to become actively involved in framing new quality standards for city life, including the creation of new, local jobs and combating climate change with local action. A systems perspective and understanding of the city as a form of urban metabolism evidences the resource flows related to solid waste and helps reshape cities into cleaner spaces, making use of the abundant organic waste they generate. In many countries, waste pickers are already collecting these resources for composting or for use as animal feed. As discussed earlier in Rosario but also other cities in

Argentina (e.g. Mar del Plata, Mendoza, Cordoba and Chubut) organized waste pickers are trained to perform door-to-door pick-up of organic municipal waste redirected into composting. The city benefits from the local knowledge in selective waste collection operations accumulated by these workers. First of all, fair pay for the work; second, *decent work* conditions; and third, recognition by way of inclusive solid waste management policies are key demands for consolidating the involvement of 'informal' and organized recyclers in the recovery of municipal organic solid waste.

8 Contributions to climate change mitigation

Environmental benefits from the work of waste pickers

DOI: 10.4324/9781315686523-8

Summary

Selective waste collection and recycling generate many environmental benefits, which are usually not accounted for. This chapter begins with a discussion on how consumption and production have radically changed, at the expense of nature. Mass consumption-driven lifestyles – symbolized by plastic wrapping everything, from food to suitcases – and the practice of quickly discarding what has become useless, have left traces in distant spaces, engulfing their populations and nature alike. In its lifetime every product possibly has generated multiple environmental impacts: from natural resource extraction, resource transformation, to production processes and transportation to consumer markets and final disposal. When a product is discarded after consumption, it turns into 'waste', generating additional environmental impacts through disintegration, entanglement with nature (e.g. animals eating discarded plastic, bio-accumulation of toxins from degrading discard), waste management and recycling. Parts of our waste enter the food chain and thus also enter our bodies through water and food ingestion. Contaminating the environment means ultimately also poisoning our own bodies.

Some of the main environmental concerns stemming from solid waste management are introduced in this chapter. Solid waste and recyclable materials travel far and globally. Recycling processes require energy, water, or additional virgin raw materials, as well as fossil fuels for transportation. Recycling processes can be polluting and pose risks (e.g. the transatlantic transportation of recyclable materials such as plastic pellets shipped to China). However, if compared to other forms of waste management (incineration and waste-to-energy, landfilling) recycling overall has a better environmental performance. Upstream emissions are avoided when recycled resources replace virgin materials in the fabrication of new products. The development of a method to calculate greenhouse gas emission reductions and energy savings related to materials recycling is introduced as a way for recyclers to account for the environmental gains generated by their work.

8.1 Introduction: what's the link between consumption and climate change?

Rising consumption goes along with increased generation of waste, causing climate change and exacerbating global environmental problems. Recovering the resources from the waste stream can mitigate these effects. The chapter begins by outlining the dimensions and characters of the environmental impacts created by our transformed lifestyles, forms of production and consumer habits. Solid waste is a final leftover of consumption. Current rapid climate change, in the dimension and timescales we are talking about today, is linked to human activity. Thus, how we deal with waste can have diverse impacts on the environment and the climate.

Solid waste generation has grown exponentially with expanding resource extraction and highly diversified industrial and agricultural production. Mass consumption is being dispersed throughout the world, and its leftovers affect land and oceans alike. Landfills and waste dumps are only the visible tip of the iceberg, denoting a much larger problem that is affecting all layers of the biosphere. In terms of the scale of human history, the profound changes that production and consumption have undergone are very recent and older generations are able to still recall ways of life before modernization, which is characterized by mass consumption, suburbia and creative destruction.

A closer look at the end point of waste generation identifies different forms of environmental impacts, linked to the way we treat solid waste. Landfilling is still the standard form of solid waste management worldwide. However, landfill technologies differ from open dumping to sanitary landfills, with methane capturing. Solid waste incineration resurfaces as waste-to-energy and comes with different technological innovations, primarily found in the global North. In developing countries, the uncontrolled burning of waste is common, particularly in and around informal settlements and in rural areas. Informal collection of recyclable and reusable materials is widespread in the global South and significant amounts are recovered with this system. Here, formal recycling programmes are still rare and insignificant in terms of the percentage of recovered materials. There are environmental and health impacts of various degrees involved in the act of collecting, separating, redirecting and recycling materials contained in waste.

With a changed perception of waste, by recognizing the resources embedded in every piece of what is termed garbage, profound transformations that produce environmental benefits are possible. Debates emerging out of Ecological Economy theory provide us with fresh systems perspectives, which help us to understand the current global environmental challenges and identify radical proposals for change, therebye addressing human and systems failures. There is no ready answer, but there are important questions we must ask in order to address the alarming concerns that impact life-supporting systems and jeopardize the long-term survival of our species and other life forms. After providing an overview of global waste generation, the main forms of waste management and possible impacts from these methods are outlined. Next, this section introduces the theoretical concept of Ecological Economy. In combination with Social and Solidarity Economy – a framework previously introduced in Chapter 4 – Ecological Economy provides a practical approach to understanding and tackling these challenges in realistic, everyday contexts.

The fact that 'informal' recycling does reduce environmental impacts is no news and by now is widely recognized, even by conservative bodies like the World Bank (and other banks), along with most international technical cooperation agencies and also by the international solid waste association (ISWA). These agencies, however, concomitantly promote growth-oriented, top-down, large-scale 'technological fixes' that reiterate the neoliberal politics. This chapter provides insights to the dimension of environmental contributions coming from 'informal' and organized recycling. A case study conducted with a recycling cooperative in Brazil highlights how *catadores* contribute to greenhouse gas emission reduction and energy savings along with a large spectrum of social gains (the latter are discussed in Chapter 6).

Finally, door-to-door selective waste collection embodies an opportunity for environmental education in the community; shifting attitudes and values away from current consumption patterns and wasteful habits, towards reuse and informed/educated consumption. Chapter 8 argues that recovering resources for reuse and recycling is a transitional solution, which helps to immediately diminish environmental impacts. A change in perspective is needed, promoting a paradigm shift from wastefulness to closed-loop solutions, tackling producers and consumers alike and thus ultimately also addressing climate change. Ecological Economy can help us construct a path towards that direction. There is not just one way out of the current waste dilemma and multiple, creative solutions are possible. Here, I will focus on experiences from developing countries that can teach inspiring lessons to the global North.

8.2 Ecological Economy a framework proposing radical societal change

McNeill (cited in: Daly and Farley, 2011: xx) stresses, "The overarching priority of economic growth was easily the most important idea of the twentieth century". Based on Joseph Schumpeter's concept of "creative destruction", capitalist economy builds on the continuous destruction of the old and the incessant creation of new consumer goods, new businesses, new technologies and new markets, without asking whether we need these and what will be their impacts (see also Chapter 6). At present, this idea is more clearly perceived as mistaken, given the existing limits to our planet and the extent to which we have already compromised the future survival of the human race and other species. Increased mass consumption, planned obsolescence and reinforced throwaway attitudes in modern society have expanded the scramble for mineral, biological and fossil resources worldwide. The wastefulness of current lifestyles, linked to the economic growth paradigm, contributes to continuous resource extraction. Solid waste is just a visible fraction of the overarching problematic. The current economic development model has produced a society based on a perception of unlimited quantitative growth and unrestricted natural resource availability through an economy and society that is detached from the ecosphere (see Figure 8.1).

An economy based primarily on growth, resource depletion and market expansion, however, is incompatible with environmental protection, healthy communities and overall, long-term sustainability. Economic growth presumes continuous and expanding consumption, which requires resources and energy. Social and environmental costs are externalized, which makes production profitable and consumption accessible. Another of the unbalanced outcomes of the current economic world system is uneven development, with unequal concentration of wealth as a result.

Critical economic theory (Ecological Economy and Social and Solidarity Economy) proposes a radical change in how and what to pursue with economic activity.

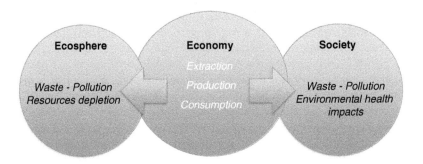

Figure 8.1 Mainstream understanding of our economy as separated from the ecosphere and society.

Critical economic theorists place ecology (including humans) at the centre of their analysis on economic activity and suggest an orientation towards sufficiency and collaboration (Røpke, 2005). Ecological Economy proposes a trans-disciplinary approach to economics, which seeks

> the maintenance of ecological life-support systems far from the edge of collapse (which requires an end to material growth of the economy) and healthy, satisfied human populations free to work together in the pursuit and clarification of a still vague ultimate end—for a long, long time.
>
> (Daly and Farley, 2011: 58)

Several key assumptions distinguish Ecological Economy from mainstream economics: (1) the economy is part of a larger human–environment system; (2) bio-physical principles also determine economic models and have to be respected; (3) there are limits to the ability of technology to substitute natural resources and the environment, primarily due to: thermodynamics (to transform matter minimum amounts of energy are required) and the fact that essential natural capital is required for planetary life support; (4) economic policy needs to consider economic efficiency together with equity and *strong sustainability* (Costanza, 1991; Pezzey, 1992). These principles underline the fact that there are limits to growth (Stern, 1997). The following figure (Figure 8.2) presents the understanding of an economy embedded in the biosphere, depending on biophysical principles and planetary limits. Attention is given to the avoidance of waste through preventive measures, and recovery for reuse and recycling. The economy in transition towards ecological and social/solidarity principals tends to diminish the portion of final discard, prioritizing waste prevention, altering the use of waste and regaining materials. Overall the tendency is towards reduced extraction of new resources (particularly of non-renewable resources).

Following the principle of conservation of matter and energy, as determined in the first law of thermodynamics, we cannot create or destroy matter or energy. Economic processes "absorb, qualitatively transform low entropy and release it outside the economic system in the form of high entropy" (Fuks, 2012: 105).

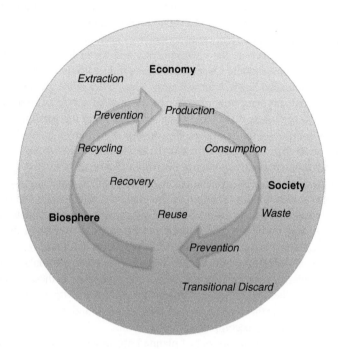

Figure 8.2 Integrated ecological and social economy understanding.

High entropy means greater levels of disorder and less availability of a system's energy to do work. As Georgescu-Roegen has pointed out, the economic system exists as a subsystem of a finite global ecosystem, on which it depends to extract resources and release waste and other outputs, in the form of higher entropy (1971).

Social and environmental justice concerns are key when transitioning into de-accelerated growth and building sustainability in community development as a pathway to reshape our current economy into an ecological economy (see Callari and Ruccio, 2008). From this perspective, recovering resources for reuse and recycling becomes an essential strategy which has the potential to make distinct social and environmental contributions when taking a collective, inclusive and participatory approach to waste management. As has been argued in Chapter 6, Social and Solidarity Economy creates positive synergies between actors from different interest groups (government authorities, private enterprises, non governmental organizations, citizens), resulting in the generation of workplaces, and a commitment to social and ecological wellbeing. In the long run, the participatory approach to waste management aims to alter consumer behaviours towards ethical and sustainable consumption.

8.2.1 Cultural and ethical change

The responsibility for driving change is not only in the hands of governments or business, but lies also with each citizen by way of decisions taken regarding lifestyles and consumption habits. The prevailing disconnection between products and their embedded resource value, energy or labour input generates a purely utilitarian relation between consumer and product. The decision about which product to purchase usually depends on necessity, price, appearance, function, fashion, peer pressure and also ethical considerations such as the environmental and social footprint created during production and consumption. Overall, once the product life is considered to be over, it usually gets handed down or thrown away. Many cities in the global North have established formal recycling programmes and the level of public awareness is rising about reuse. Nevertheless, too much waste still ends up in the garbage. This attitude of humans consuming far more than the available *bio-capacity* on earth (the capacity to generate an ongoing supply of resources and to absorb the wastes generated) is responsible for creating the *ecological overshoot* (Schor, 2010).

The aspects of human culture being anchored in the body or daily practices of individuals, groups and societies show a pattern of disconnection that enables the consumer to discard unwanted products. Current waste management options facilitate this behaviour by taking away from both the consumer and the producer the responsibility for the environmental impacts caused by waste. Most producers don't take responsibility for what happens with their products after discard. They place materials on the market, without considering appropriate forms of recycling and reuse of these materials. Education and awareness building are fundamental in the social transformation, generating the understanding that *there is no such thing as waste* and that every cause has an effect and every action is accompanied by a reaction.

Consumers have a hard time to opt out of planned obsolescence. Nevertheless, diverse forms of alternative living are emerging following concepts of voluntary simplicity and sufficiency. Sufficiency rejects the unrestricted pursuit of consumption, growth and the perception of unlimited resource availability. The preservation of natural environments for perpetuity is non-negotiable and human activities need to accommodate to this precedence. This means accepting the rights of nature, of other species to co-exist and it means to question human-centric views.

Consumption drives our economy. Applied sufficiency translates into changes in lifestyles and habits, resulting in conscious consumption, which incorporates social and environmental ethics in product choices. The direct consequence of this could be reduced consumption and less need for new products. Living sufficiently and simply could spark the critical, necessary threshold, provoking the needed qualitative change into a low-carbon energy system. Recovering the materials embedded in solid waste helps reduce the carbon footprint, has the potential to educate for responsible consumption and suggests new creative forms of living and of development. Ecological Economy promotes steady state economy, which is an economy with a stable or mildly fluctuating size, and it is aiming for stable or mildly fluctuating levels in populations and in the consumption of energy and materials. Steady state translates into birth rates equaling to death rates and production rates equaling to depreciation rates.

8.2.2 *Urban metabolism*

Cities are urban metabolisms with complex sets of processes, flows, interdependencies and new formations affecting both nature and society (Marcotullio and

Boyle, 2003). This adapted metaphor emphasizes the goal of circularity in material flows. Determining inflow and outflow rates and their qualities to show material fluxes in cities sheds light on hidden externalities, for example waste, heat or sewage. The approach thus helps direct attention towards system-wide imbalances and the impacts of consumption and waste within urban environments. The urban metabolism perspective takes into consideration human and material interchanges with the environment and notes that no process or phenomenon happens in a vacuum. Environmental services, material inputs and energy are extracted from the natural environment and eventually return as waste, surplus heat or pollution.

Wackernagel and Rees (1996) further build on the idea of cities as metabolism by devising the *ecological footprint*, a spatial tool to measure consumption and to visualize the impacts of humans in urban systems. A major critique of these methods is the fact that they aim at achieving greater resilience of urban areas so that inevitable internal and external shocks from human activities can be better absorbed (Alberti, 2008). As much as the urban metabolism and the *ecological footprint* help shed light on deficiencies and weaknesses in the system, optimizing and focusing on efficiency in the processes, this is not enough given the current environmental and social predicaments many cities, particularly megacities, are facing.

8.3 The challenge: environmental impacts from solid waste

8.3.1 Solid waste generation

Waste generation is an almost unavoidable consequence of human activity. Humans generate more waste than ever before, not only because of the dramatic population increase since the past century, but also because of the changed nature of consumption and the different composition of solid waste. Per capita consumption of packaged goods and consumer products skyrocketed after World War II, along with the rapidly expanding adoption of the growth-oriented economic development model. This is when material consumption gained momentum on a global scale (UN-HABITAT, 2010).

Municipal solid waste (MSW) is the visible leftover from consumption and involves every citizen on a daily basis. Post-consumer waste generation has more than doubled worldwide between 1971 and 2002. Particularly from the 1980s onwards, growth has been exponential in most parts of the global South, and continues to steadily grow in most of the global North, except for Central and Eastern Europe and the former Soviet Union (Bogner *et al.*, 2007). While Western Europe and North America have, on average, already experienced MSW rates between 1.4 and 1.8 kg/capita/day over the past decade, the population in many large cities in developing countries is now also reaching MSW values of between 1 and 1.4 kg/capita/day (Vergara and Tchobanoglous, 2012). In 2012, urban residents generated about 1.2 kg/capita/day of MSW globally, compared to 0.64 kg in 2002 (Hoornweg and Bhada-Tata, 2012). In Brazil the average daily quantity of MSW generated per person is currently about 1.1 kg. Generation rates for major cities in Africa are estimated to range from 0.3 to 1.4 kg/capita/day (Achankeng, 2003). Differences in solid waste generation can be large, as demonstrate the data for the cities Bamenda and Yaounde in Cameroon, which generate between 0.5 and 0.8 kg/capita/day, respectively (Achankeng, 2003). The author draws the attention to the factor population size that influences municipal solid waste management and states that there is a positive correlation between population size and both the rate of waste removed and the percentage of households enjoying regular waste collection. Rapidly growing cities have a hard time providing regular waste collection services.

In the current era, industrial production is characterized by a reduction in product life-span, growing product variety, material component diversity and increased packaging. All these characteristics are drivers for the increased use of natural resources and are responsible for generating waste and producing water, soil and air contaminants. The rise in solid waste is linked to increased levels of urbanization and wealth. Between 1997 and 2007, the gross domestic product (GDP) in India has increased by 7 per cent, while estimates indicate a rise in municipal solid waste over these ten years by 45 per cent, from a total of 48 million to 70 million tons (UNEP, 2010). The figures for Brazil demonstrate a similar correlation between increased wealth and solid waste generation. From 2009 to 2010, GDP rose by 7.5 per cent, while MSW increased by 6.8 per cent, during that period. In the following year, GDP slowed down to an increase of 2.7 per cent, and MSW generation also increased only by a smaller rate of 1.8 per cent (BNDS, 2012).

Population growth implies an increase in consumption and waste. More affluent segments of the population consume more and their consumption generates a larger environmental impact. China, India and Brazil alone have added another 509 million new consumers during the 1990s until 2000, with an average purchasing power of US$ 839 billion (Myers and Kent, 2003). New consumers are defined as

> people within typically four member households with purchasing power of at least PPP $10,000 per year, i.e., at least PPP $2,500 per person . . . (PPP dollars are between 1.3 and 5.3 times higher than conventional dollars in 20 countries [17 developing and 3 transitional countries])
>
> (Myers and Kent, 2003: 4963)

Increased income enables consumers to purchase household appliances, electronics, cars and other items that mark affluent lifestyles, including the consumption of more packaged food items and meat. The increase in consumption and the differentiated lifestyle drives solid waste generation.

8.3.2 Waste composition and waste management

Waste composition reflects cultural and technological trends and varies greatly between different continents and regions over time. While ashes from heating and cooking, for example, were reported as large components of household waste in North America until the middle of the last century, plastic appears only since the 1970s as a separately recorded substance (Walsh, 2002). Urban waste in the global North currently contains more recyclable goods and electronics, while municipal waste in the global South has a larger biodegradable fraction and less recyclable material content; often because these have already been reclaimed by household members for reuse or by waste pickers for commercialization. The average waste composition in Brazil is still typical for the global South, with large fractions of organic (51.4 per cent) and recyclable (31.9 per cent) materials (metals, paper and cardboard, plastics, and glass), and a small proportion classified as other materials (16.7 per cent) (ABRELPE, 2011). The organic content of solid waste in African cities is identified as being as high as 70 per cent (Achankeng, 2003).

Seventy per cent of the municipal solid waste generated worldwide is still deposited at landfills and waste dumps, 11 per cent is incinerated and 19 per cent is officially recycled or treated by mechanical or biological treatments (ISWA, 2012). Although, worldwide, many countries are upgrading their landfills to sanitary landfills, as happened in South Africa, Uganda, Ghana and Egypt a decade ago, Achankeng (2003: 17) at the time raised the concern that most landfills in Africa are "owned and operated by the very body that is supposed to enforce standards. The philosophy of getting waste out of sight and consequently out of mind seems to be the overriding consideration of these authorities". As a consequence, limited resources are spent on the removal of waste, particularly in formal neighbourhoods, and little investment is made in infrastructure for more sustainable waste management.

Currently, approximately 80 per cent of the household waste generated in Brazil is regularly collected; of which 17.7 per cent is deposited at open waste dumps, 24.2 per cent at controlled landfills and 58.1 per cent at sanitary landfills, which are not always environmentally safe (ABRELPE, 2011). Only 28 per cent of municipalities have some sort of official selective waste collection in Brazil. Only 1.4 per cent of all MSW generated in Brazil is officially recycled. In Brazil, as in most countries in the global South, selective waste collection happens primarily through *catadores*.

8.3.3 Environmental impacts from waste management

Landfills are still necessary, but they are a source for environmental impacts on soil, water and air. Landfills and dumps generate significant greenhouse gases (GHGs), primarily methane (5–10 per cent of global methane is emitted by landfills) and carbon dioxide, as microbial communities decompose the organic matter contained in the waste (Matthews and Themelis, 2007). Converting open dumping and burning to sanitary landfills implies "control of waste placement, compaction, the use of cover materials, implementation of surface water diversion and drainage, and management of leachate and gas" (Bogner *et al.*, 2007: 595). Ironically, the landfill upgrading process now creates a shift from mostly CO_2 emissions – from aerobic decomposition and burning – to CH_4 emissions, which continue for several decades after waste disposal. Nevertheless, methane emissions from landfills can be stabilized with gas recovery technology, as is already widely implemented in the global North. Landfills further impact the soil and groundwater with leachate produced as water percolates intermittently through the refuse pile. Leachate can contain high levels of nutrients (nitrogen, phosphorous, potassium) heavy metals, toxins (such as cyanide) and dissolved organic compounds. One of the big challenges is to ensure that all operating landfills are designed properly and are monitored once they are closed.

Mismanaged and uncollected waste, which mostly accumulates in the urban periphery and in informal settlements in cities in the global South, is a public health hazard. Abandoned waste attracts disease vectors (including rats and mosquitoes) and if carried into waterways, leads to clogged drains and creeks, causing inundations. When burned, a number of toxic substances are emitted, impacting the population and the environment of local neighbourhoods (see also Chapter 6).

Waste incineration and other thermal processes are local sources of air pollution, constituting a health-risk factor for nearby communities. These installations produce CO_2 from fossil carbon sources and generate other contaminants such as dioxins, furans, polycyclic aromatic hydrocarbons (PAHs), volatile organic compounds (VOCs), mercury (Hg) and many other GHGs. Particularly, the fly ashes and slags become a hazardous output (Porta *et al.*, 2009; Vergara and Tchobanoglous, 2012). Nowadays, waste-to-energy incineration technology is widely sold as the solution to increased solid waste accumulation and energy shortage in the global South. The number one waste technology corporation worldwide, called *Veolia*, generates 9 billion euros in revenue every year. They are present in 33 countries and have recently accelerated the organization's international growth, particularly in Asia.

According to Morris (1996), recycling mixed solid waste saves more energy than is generated by waste-to-energy facilities. His findings underline that recycling conserves energy that would be used in extracting natural resources and transforming them to produce goods that can also be manufactured with less energy from recycled materials. Mining, extraction, transportation and transformation of natural resources generates environmental impacts (often in pristine environments) and also emits greenhouse gases (GHG), thus affecting the global climate.

Recycling values the resources and energy incorporated in the making of these products, often allowing for new goods to be manufactured from the recovered materials. It is global consensus that "the climate benefits of waste avoidance [reuse] and recycling far outweigh the benefits from any waste treatment technology, even where energy is recovered during the process" (UNEP, 2010: 1). With well-designed and functioning recycling operations, all resources can be recovered from the waste stream for reuse and up-cycling and for down-cycling in the generation of new products. These operations generate multiple environmental benefits, including: (1) displacing the use of virgin materials spares the environment (e.g. in the case of paper recycling, trees are kept alive as CHC sinks); (2) in many processes recycling requires less energy than production from virgin materials (e.g. recycled aluminium compared to the transformation of bauxite into aluminium); (3) emissions from MSW transport to transfer stations and disposal sites are prevented. Waste and recyclable materials can travel long distances and is sometimes exported into faraway continents. De-regulation and globalization under neoliberal capitalist market economy are reshaping the movement of waste. Worldwide, half of all plastics, paper and scrap metals are exported to Southeast Asia. China is the largest importer of recyclable material, with yearly imports of over 7.4 million tons of plastic waste, 28 million tons of waste paper and 5.8 million tons of steel scrap; mostly treated in backyard shops or small-scale industries (ISWA, 2012). In 2006, Korea, Malaysia and the Philippines were the main importers, while Singapore and Japan were considered the largest exporters of MSW in the region (ISWA, 2012). More recently, the transcontinental shipping of Waste Electrical and Electronic Equipment (WEEE) has become a serious challenge, especially as it is shipped to Asian countries such as India and Pakistan, and also West African countries including Nigeria. Seventy per cent of global WEEE ends up in China (Bartl, 2014a). Waste trafficking is mostly illegal but "has become institutionalized practice among certain corporations that pollute, dump toxic waste and make environmental crime victims of various global minorities" (Simon, 2000: 103). Large amounts of plastic materials (e.g. pellets) are shipped long distances. Due to stormy oceans, negligence and accidents part of the materials end up in the oceans' food chains, ingested by fish, sea turtles and seabirds (Kühn *et al.*, 2015).

Lack of down-cycling alternatives for many waste materials and waste flows poses additional challenges. In addition the collection, transportation and processing of waste and recyclables generates fossil-derived carbon dioxide and other pollutants from the fuel used in transportation, and therefore also need to enter the equation, when evaluating the impacts of waste management and recycling.

8.4 Benefits from 'informal' waste recovery

Most of the material recovery in the global South is 'informal' and comprises a wide spectrum of domestic reuse of bottles, cans, plastics, paper, cardboard and many other discarded materials. Occasionally, as e.g. in many countries in Africa the lack of local markets for recyclables is still a prevailing limitation (Achankeng, 2003). The informal recycling sector makes a significant contribution to resource recovery. Yet its role is largely unrecognized in waste management by city authorities. In Delhi, India, 15–20 per cent of the MSW is collected by waste pickers. Here the recyclers also redirect 200 tons of separated organic material to a large-scale composting plant. They also collect from households in the affluent neighbourhood called *Defence Colony*, where they compost it in a series of neighbourhood composting pits (CHINTAN, 2009).

In most cities in the global South, the informal sector recovers far more resources from MSW than the formal recycling system. A well-known example is the work of the *zabaleen* in Cairo, who recover 66 per cent of the material entering the solid waste system, compared to 11 per cent recovered by formal recycling. The city of Lima, Peru, has no formal recycling and approximately 17,643 local *recicladores* (ranging from informal service providers, street collectors to dump pickers) divert 20 per cent of the MSW into recycling (GIZ/CWG cited in UN-HABITAT, 2010). These two examples illustrate a very common situation in the global South, where a large number of workers recover significant quantities of recyclable material from the waste stream, generating savings of around 20 per cent or more for the municipal waste management budget, which in large cities can represent many millions of dollars per year (Wilson *et al.*, 2006).

A study by GIZ/CWG has translated the environmental benefits associated with material recovery into reduced negative externality costs, expressed in euros. According to their studies the informal recyclers generate 97.6 per cent of these externality costs in the case of Lima, Peru; 100 per cent in the case of Pune, Peru; 92.9 per cent in Quezon, China; and 83.4 per cent in Cairo, Egypt (Scheinberg *et al.*, 2010: 21).

8.5 Case study assessing the environmental contributions from cooperative recycling

The recyclers involved in the PSWM programme collectively identified the need to learn about their environmental contribution. The following collaborative research focused on the design of a tool to calculate greenhouse gas (GHG) emission reduction and energy savings from their recycling operations. A recycling cooperative (*Cooperpires*) in Ribeirão Pires, the metropolitan region of São Paulo, was involved in this case study, using a mixed methods and an action-oriented methodology (King and Gutberlet, 2013).

According to the Intergovernmental Panel on Climate Change (IPCC), solid waste and its management are considered to be key contributors to climate change. Greenhouse gas (GHG) emissions are emitted or avoided in the upstream and downstream stages in the life cycle of municipal solid waste management systems (US EPA, 2006). Upstream emissions can be avoided when recycled resources replace virgin resources in the fabrication of metal, glass, plastic and paper products. In addition, landfill gas (CH_4) and deforestation represent other upstream impacts that are reduced with recycling (Bogner *et al.*, 2008; Chester *et al.*, 2008; Pimenteira *et al.*, 2004; Thorneloe *et al.*, 2002).

Fossil-fuel greenhouse gas emissions are also associated with recycling operations, as energy and some virgin resources are consumed during the collection and transportation of materials, and processing and re-manufacturing (ICF Consulting, 2005). With recycling, however, both methane (CH_4) and carbon dioxide (CO_2) emissions are avoided through the diversion of resources from landfills, with resource recovery and recycling of paper, cardboards and other biodegradable material (Morris, 2005; US EPA, 2006), and with reducing the amount of waste to be deposited at landfills (see Figure 8.3).

The Clean Development Mechanism (CDM) is a carbon finance mechanism. It is a market-based vehicle through which municipal governments can catalyse sector investments to tackle GHG emission reduction, supported by the Kyoto Protocol. It was further designed to assist developing countries to also achieve GHG emissions mitigation through sustainable development measures (Barton *et al.*, 2008; Gurung and Polprasert, 2007).

Other methods for assessing GHG emissions from solid waste management activities are mostly based on the concept of Life Cycle Assessment (LCA). As to Morrissey and Browne (2004) neither the LCA nor the CDM greenhouse gas accounting methods can determine triple bottom line sustainability because they do not consider social aspects of waste management, or the socioeconomic

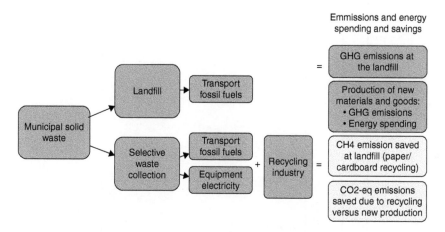

Figure 8.3 GHG emission and energy requirements in landfilling and recycling.

advantages of recycling, as highlighted by Baumann and Tillman (2004), Reddy and Assenza (2009) and Rogger *et al.* (2011) (see also Chapter 5). The case study involves an input–output analysis based on energy spending during collection, separation, transportation and recycling; compared to the spending during extraction of virgin resources and new material production. In our case study, we set up a standard calculation model allowing recycling cooperatives to roughly determine their contribution to GHG emission reduction and energy savings, based on their material inflow–outflow operations (see Table 8.1).

There are drawbacks of the CDM methodology in terms of accuracy. Perform-ing a full-scale LCA to assess the GHG impacts of recycling would provide a more precise result. However, the application of this method is complicated in the context of recycling cooperatives. The CDM method is focused on energy input and resultant GHG emissions only, and ignores other inputs and processes of the life cycle. Nevertheless, the case study shows that a considerable reduction in greenhouse gas emissions is achieved through recycling, besides generating a large array of social and other environmental benefits.

The findings underline the need to redefine clean development mechanisms (CDMs) to allow for the recognition of resource recovery for reuse and recycling as measures to reduce GHG emissions and save natural resources and energy (King and Gutberlet, 2013). Recycling has not yet been considered a CDM, while waste-to-energy and methane-to-energy projects, associated to landfills, are already financed under this mechanism (Forsyth, 2005). These shortcomings need to be addressed by including a social development agenda within CDM policy frameworks. Taking a social perspective on the thermal treatment of solid waste, the outcome is aggravated by the fact that this form of waste management destroys the resources and labour in waste and, thus, the source of income for waste pickers.

Table 8.1 Greenhouse gas (GHG) emissions reduction calculator for recycling groups[1]

Resource	Quantity (tonnes)	Baseline emissions		−	Project emissions		=	Emissions reduction
		Virgin resources Emissions/tonne (et)	Baseline emissions		Recycled resources Emissions/tonne	Project emissions		Emissions reduction*
HDPE/PP	0	0.767	0.000		0.183	0.000		−0.001
LDPE	0	0.906	0.000		0.183	0.000		−0.001
PET/PS	0	0.813	0.000		0.183	0.000		−0.001
Paper/card.	0	0.898	0.000		0.323	0.000		−0.001
Glass	0	0.935	0.000		0.922	0.000		−0.001
Aluminum	0	3.872	0.000		0.154	0.000		−0.001
Steel	0	1.264	0.000		0.392	0.000		−0.001
			0.000			0.000		−0.001
			Quantity (tonnes)					
Paper/cardboard (from composting organic matter at the landfill	0	5.877	0.000					

Total CO_2-eq. emissions avoided by the substitution of virgin resources by recycled resources   −0.001   t CO_2-eq./year

Total CH_4 emissions avoided by the landfill diversion of paper/cardboard   0.000   t CO_2-eq./year

TOTAL CO_2-eq. emissions reduction   −0.001   t CO_2-eq./year

[1] Source: King and Gutberlet (2013).

Note * includes subtraction of Leakage Emissions (LE) from electricity consumption = 0.001 t CO_2-eq./year.

8.6 Final considerations

Consumption-dependent economic growth is becoming increasingly criticized and scholars from different backgrounds study ways out of the growth dependent paradigm. The research discussed in this chapter points towards a radical economic and social shift away from growth-centred development, towards steady state development embracing de-acceleration, stability, sufficiency and sustainability. Selective waste collection and recycling performed by waste pickers is a form of resource recovery, redistribution of income and re-education of communities. Resource recovery aligns with the key principles of Ecological Economy, primarily by: (1) recognizing that economy happens within a complex human–environment system where non-renewable natural resources are limited, and (2) understanding that economic growth is also limited. Recovering materials for reuse or to transform into new products is a step towards sparing virgin resource extraction, thus diminishing the current accelerated pace of natural resource extraction. Prioritizing recycling means recognizing the fact that we cannot continue with business as usual, though there are limits to down-cycling and there are also environmental impacts generated by recycling. However, resource recovery is essential on the path towards de-accelerated growth. This chapter has discussed some of the environmental implications that accompany the most prominent forms of waste management. All of them, including recycling, point towards the necessity of a much more radical shift towards sufficiency and *de-growth*.

Greenhouse gas emission reductions from selective waste collection and recycling are important for climate change mitigation. Recycling reduces the need for new resource extraction, slowing down the pace of mineral extraction. Fundamental gains relate to the social aspects of recycling, with poverty alleviation and redistribution of income at the centre. Recycling creates work for many people and maintains their livelihoods.

To demonstrate the climate change mitigation factor of recycling, a method has been elaborated to determine the energy gains and losses as well as the greenhouse gas emission reductions achieved by the cooperative for specific materials that are collected, separated and recycled. The tool allows waste pickers, organized in cooperatives or associations to calculate the CO_2 emission reduction values and energy savings from their operations. With this information the recyclers can demonstrate the benefits to the environment and society at large. The application of this tool can provide users with a stronger voice in their negotiations for recognition and remuneration of the environmental and social services provided through their work. The calculator is an instrument, easily applicable by the workers themselves, which can be adjusted to specific local contexts and situations regarding the operations involved in collecting, separating and redirecting. The result demonstrates the fact that waste management systems reorganized for selective waste collection and recycling help save resources and reduce GHG emissions, and therefore qualify as a clean development mechanism.

Reduction and reorganization are key steps towards a post-growth economy. "Cutting down and slowing down" in terms of lengthening product life cycles and intensifying the use of products to the "extent that value could be created with no need for extra material production, resulting in a 'material zero-sum' game" could bring us closer to the vision of living in an Ecological Economy (Paech, 2009: 27). The work of waste pickers, as resource recoverers – for recycling and reuse – and the role they play as socio-environmental educators can be extended to gradually recover more of the materials that are still wasted in landfills, illegal dumps or incinerators, progressing towards more resilient and healthy communities.

9 Different ways of managing waste

From neoliberal to cooperative approaches

DOI: 10.4324/9781315686523-9

Summary

Inadequate social infrastructure and public services generate many inconveniences for residents but most importantly, the lack of service has significant long-term consequences for these communities and involves associated costs. Basic infrastructure and services are crucial public assets to a healthy life in every city. There are a number of related social problems associated with communities that lack good social infrastructure, including physical and mental health problems, fear of violence and crime and effects on community building and social cohesion. The local governance structure shapes the process of decision-making and the implementation of infrastructure. Neoliberal policies and politics have heavily impacted water and solid waste management in many cities in the world with privatization of these services on the rise since the 1980s. These political decisions impact residents and have serious consequences for those previously involved in providing services such as waste collection. This chapter discusses the problems that come with these transformations in the global South, specifically with regards to solid waste management. Key aspects are the absence of the state in providing services and infrastructure in poor and informal settlements and the trend towards privatization in waste management. Chapter 9 examines the challenges involved in service provision through partnerships in waste collection and recycling services, also called co-production. While studying everyday experiences from Southern cities, I will analyse assets of and barriers to community recycling organizations and their networks in working with local governments.

9.1 Introduction: the politics of infrastructure and services in solid waste management

In Chapter 8, I introduced the concept of cities understood as urban metabolisms with complex and dense flows of energy, food, water, sewerage and waste. Infrastructure networks and services are there to collect, transport and distribute these products between the human population and broader metabolic processes, with the aim of maintaining and guaranteeing public health (Gandy, 2005; Heynen *et al.*, 2006; Swyngedouw, 2004). Particularly in the absence of basic infrastructure, or the mismanagement of it, the everyday dimension becomes problematic to those who are affected by it. Infrastructure refers to the range of activities, organizations and facilities supporting the formation, development and maintenance of social relationships in a community and in society at large, including household waste collection and treatment as well as the maintainance of clean public spaces. Although rarely considered in public discourse and praxis, a healthy environment should also include the rights of other life forms (fauna, flora) with which we share the city space. For example, why don't birds have the same right to be in the city as humans? Focusing on the daily life experience of city inhabitants helps reveal the inequalities, resistance and struggles for change by and for city inhabitants (Graham and Thrift, 2007; Rigg, 2007). As Graham and McFarlane put it: "The everyday is both a key domain through which practices are regulated and normalised as well as an arena for negotiation, resistance and potential for difference" (2014: 2). Urban infrastructure and service provision are structured by the power relations and political economies that make up the city. These relationships become apparent when service provision is omitted, as is the reality in so many underprivileged, informal neighbourhoods in the global South.

The term *power* as used by Foucault (1977) expresses the ability to act and to exercise agency both collectively within a group and individually (Read and Shapiro, 2013). Power is often used synonymously with the word *control*, by which a dominant force monopolizes agency. Power, from the perspective of empowerment, means being able to resist and oppose and to struggle for the improvement of a given condition or circumstance (Tremblay and Gutberlet, 2011). Focusing on people's everyday city experiences helps identify and contest inequalities and socioecological inadequacies in urban production (Swyngedouw, 2004). Often the city's most vulnerable populations, those who inhabit informal settlements, suffer from inadequate living conditions, infrastructure and services, as well as from the absence or inadequacy of proper waste disposal methods. They are frequently the primary victims of environmental pollution and a whole spectrum of water-borne and other diseases linked to uncollected waste and sewage.

The provision of infrastructure and services and the lack thereof involves political and economic interests (Graham and McFarlane, 2014). Waste management implies a wide range of different actors and practices. The form in which waste is treated matters profoundly and decisions over which technology to apply can have detrimental and long-term consequences. Landfills and incineration are the most common methods for waste disposal, but they are problematic because they destroy resources and release pollutants in different quantities and of varying levels of toxicity. The range of these pollutants, their pathways of exposure, and the potential for synergism pose serious concerns for negative health effects (see Porta *et al.*, 2009; Rocher, 2008). Besides environmental concerns, waste pickers in the global South advocate against waste incineration because of the destruction of the employment opportunities created with selective waste collection, separation, reuse, transformation and recycling.

Several authors discuss the rising privatization trend in urban infrastructure, highlighting the emergence of a fragmented and uneven pattern of privatized services that exclude large populations within the city (Graham and Marvin, 2001; Moore, 2001; Page, 2005; Shove *et al.*, 2007; Guy *et al.*, 2011). Nevertheless, little attention has been given so far to the social impacts of the privatization of waste management infrastructure and services, particularly on vulnerable populations and those involved in providing 'informal' waste collection and recycling services. In some cases waste-to-energy incineration technology is replacing laborious selective waste collection and recycling arrangements, which have been in place for decades and which provide income for a large population.

Neoliberalism, the dominant economic, social and political approach under capitalism in 'both worlds', has created many structural imbalances, most visible in material poverty and in the development of informality (e.g. informal settlements). City authorities become administrators of poverty, usually within one department, instead of taking an integrated approach, pooling together different departments and jointly building opportunities for economic inclusion. Citizen participation is still very low in decision-making and implementation processes. Hirsch (1995) refers to the *national competitive state* where government takes priority in representing the interests of capital, while neglecting the popular sectors of society. There are plentiful examples of infrastructural decisions being taken in favour of a small elite, excluding the needs and vulnerabilities experienced by the urban majority living in informal settlements within these cities. Under neoliberalism, two major characteristics in solid waste management are visible: deficient and lacking basic services and infrastructure in many parts of the city and the trend towards privatization in the public sector.

A renewed idea of infrastructures as shared common goods is a pressing matter and 'informal' selective waste collectors and recyclers throughout the global South have important contributions to make in order to maintain these common goods. Particularly given the serious environmental and socioeconomic concerns cities are facing, especially in developing countries, infrastructure decisions have to become participatory, with the population being serviced equally but also with users taking greater responsibility for the maintenance and care of the system (Offenhuber, 2012). A growing number of municipalities have become interested in inclusive and more sustainable waste management alternatives. Grass-roots pressure from local communities expresses the demand for a radical reinterpretation of the role of policy-making and service delivery in the public domain. Community leaders and organized groups challenge conventional decision-making processes and insist on participating in policy design and in some cases also in service provision. As Bovaird puts it "[p]olicy making is no longer seen as a purely top-down process but rather as a negotiation among many interacting policy systems" (2007: 846).

As discussed in Chapter 4, 'informal' recyclers worldwide organize themselves into cooperatives, associations, and networks, focusing on the politics of selective waste collection, material transformation and collective commercialization operations. The recyclers themselves are city co-producers of selective waste collection services. These informal activities provide a livelihood for large numbers of workers, who would otherwise be unemployed and often become socially and economically excluded (Gutberlet 2013, 2012). The workers involved in organized forms of informal recycling, such as door-to-door household collections done by recycling cooperatives, act as environmental stewards and have the potential to educate the public, changing consumption and discard behaviours and promoting more responsible lifestyles. In recent years more groups and communities have partnered with local governments to perform the collection of recyclable materials, putting in place a system also called co-production. Innovative approaches to solid waste management require appropriate public policies to address the complex waste scenarios most large cities currently face. Co-production involving the local government and organized groups of recyclers (e.g. cooperatives or associations) in selective waste collection is an alternative waste management solution.

In the present chapter I introduce diverse situations of basic infrastructure and service provision regarding solid waste management as experienced in many cities in the global South. Herein the infrastructure controversy created by the absence or the implementation of appropriate technology becomes apparent. Then, neoliberal politics of waste characterized by a trend of privatization and the establishment of public private partnerships often to acquire costly infrastructure, is problematized. Finally, innovative ideas with collective and inclusive approaches, tackling environmental and socioeconomic aspects are presented with everyday experiences from the global South.

9.2 Lack of public services in waste collection and final destination

Most informal settlements don't have regular waste and sewage collection and then residents have to find their own solution for the disposal of their household and human waste. An estimated 70 million new residents are added to urban areas in the global South each year, most of whom will be living in informal settlements. Particularly in South Asia and Sub-Saharan Africa, the world's two poorest regions, urban growth is expected to double over the next two decades. The dimension of the challenge underlines the necessity to develop appropriate strategies and technologies to tackle waste-related issues, particularly in informal urban areas (UN-Habitat, 2015).

Informal settlements are residential areas that are commonly called *slums*. As noted by UN-Habitat (2015):

> Slums are the most deprived and excluded form of informal settlements characterized by poverty and large agglomerations of dilapidated housing often located in the most hazardous urban land. In addition to tenure insecurity, slum dwellers lack formal supply of basic infrastructure and services, public space and green areas, and are constantly exposed to eviction, disease and violence.

Despite significant improvements in the living conditions of urban populations during the past, around one-quarter of the world's urban population (approximately 875 million people) continues to live in slums (UN-Habitat, 2013). The most vulnerable sections of the population, particularly pregnant women, infants and children, are most affected by the precarious living conditions in slums – a reason why infant and child mortality rates are often many times higher than the average rate of the country (Hardoy *et al.*, 2001).

Municipalities have been held responsible for solid waste collection since the mid-nineteenth century, when public health issues were linked to a lack of sanitation and uncollected waste. There is strong evidence that the concentration of uncollected waste is linked to a higher incidence of infectious diseases (e.g. diarrhoea, cholera, the bubonic plague and respiratory diseases) and indirectly to flooding and the consequent spread of water-borne diseases (Wilson *et al.*, 2012). Uncollected waste accumulates in the streets and in dumpsites, where it is sometimes burned. A study conducted in a small city in Egypt, found that 89 per cent of the local population living downwind of the burning dumpsite was suffering from respiratory disease (UN-Habitat, 2010: 22) (see also Chapter 6). Lack of financial and material resources is a serious constraint to controlled solid waste management in many cities in the global South.

Research by Wilson *et al.* (2012), comparing collection coverage in different cities, shows that particularly in low-income cities, collection coverage ranges between 45 and 60 per cent, while even the poorest of the middle-income countries have waste collection service coverage of between 70 and 90 per cent. In low- and middle-income cities 'informal' workers or small to medium-scale businesses collect the garbage from the households. They take the waste either to communal collection points (skips) or to small transfer stations, from where it is taken in larger vehicles to the final destination. In this situation the household contracts the primary collection, while the municipal government is in charge of transporting the waste to the landfill or dumpsite. The government often does not empty the skips and transfer stations and these places turn into dumps. As a response to large waste accumulations, resident organizations – or other grass-roots initiatives, sometimes with local government support – conduct clean-ups in these communities (see Photograph 9.1).

The emergence of other private and 'informal' players in collecting and separating household waste often derives from the absence of official household waste collection in informal settlements (Thieme, 2015). Further on, I will take a closer look into these 'informal' and organized initiatives and the assets and barriers that affect their work.

9.3 Trends in waste management under neoliberal politics

9.3.1 Privatization of public services

The permeation of global neoliberal ideology in government decisions over running or upgrading the public sector through privatization is a prevailing development in the global South, mostly observed since the late 1980s. Privatization ranges from a complete sell out of the public assets, to a mix of public and private ownership and responsibility in providing the infrastructure and services. Public–private partnerships usually adopt private-sector principles. These arrangements are widely pursued for the purpose of cost recovery and to modernize the sector with new, often very expensive, technologies. Most partnerships ultimately are also a form of privatization, functioning by the principles of the private sector as the strongest member of the enterprise. Therefore in some contexts the establishment of these partnerships is also referred to as *corporatization* (Miraftab, 2004b). Tan (2012: 2552) discusses private participation in infrastructure as often "driven by political considerations related to rent-seeking and as part of broader

Photograph 9.1 Cleaning up the informal settlement Obunga, in Kisumu, Kenya.

accumulation processes that are invariably linked with corruption". The connection between privatization and corruption has to be contextualized as corruption can take different forms and scales. A common format of corruption, for example, is favouritism in the transfer of assets. Privatization may allow gains to both: the firms by way of large profits, and the governments, through increased tax revenues at the expense of the local population (Martimort and Straub, 2009).

Privatization has the potential to involve conflict as, in some cases, communities or specific stakeholder groups oppose these developments. Community mobilization and opposition to attempted privatization of common property assets is not uncommon in the Southern context. Bolivia's water wars, in 2000, became a celebrated landmark for the victory of the commons over privatization (Dwinell and Olivera, 2014). In this case indigenous community groups have resisted the sell out of the water rights in Cochabamba, setting an example for community-based organizations defending local control and autonomy over water rights.

9.3.2 Privatization in waste management

For 'informal' recyclers solid waste is a common good which maintains their livelihoods. Prohibiting the access to this resource jeopardizes the survival of the workers. This is the primary motivation of waste pickers throughout the world to oppose waste incineration. The municipal government of São Bernardo do Campo, southeast Brazil, has recently established a private–public partnership to buy a large-scale waste-to-energy facility. I became a close witness to the political developments on this contentious project and have observed the resistance of the local *catadores*, supported by their national movement (MNCR), during manifestations in opposition to the proposed facility.

As an immediate consequence the local government withdrew all support previously given to the two local recycling cooperatives, which destroyed one of the cooperatives and destabilized the other. Many cooperative members then moved on to different activities (Gutberlet, 2011, 2012). The local government was successful in creating a situation of abandonment, weakening the *catadores*. Until today, the national recyclers' movement (MNCR) and the local recyclers in São Bernardo do Campo, supported by grass-roots and non-governmental organizations, continue fighting the acquisition of the waste incinerator.

9.3.3 Introduction of high-tech approaches to waste management

There are cases were waste-to-energy has been defeated. From 1999, the Philippines became the first country worldwide to ban all forms of waste incineration. In Mozambique, a social movement has succeeded in stopping the incineration of pesticides in a cement kiln next to a residential neighbourhood. In 2001, incinerator proposals were defeated with public opposition in cities in France, Haiti, Ireland, Poland, Thailand, the United Kingdom and Venezuela (Tangri, 2003).

The speed with which the trend towards privatization has evolved is varied. Privatization has been around longer in the water sector than in waste management. The privatization of public services and assets is often accompanied by structural adjustment policies to facilitate and encourage foreign investment. Mostly silent and without social dialogue infrastructure and service privatization projects creep in and are to stay, unless citizens revolt. Miraftab (2004b) describes the differences in privatization processes for the public water and waste management sectors in South Africa. In the case of the highly urbanized and industrialized province Guateng (including Johannesburg and Pretoria), for example, the process occurred early and very quick, resulting in the multinational private water company *Suez Lyonnaise des Eaux* winning the state's water service contracts. In Cape Town, privatization of the municipal water services was conflicted and slow, with the opposition legally challenging the privatization of basic services. This required the city council to address internal service delivery mechanisms before considering the external mechanisms. In the end, however, the opposition was overruled and privatization proceeded despite noticeable opposition (Smith, 2002; Smith and Hanson, 2003).

9.3.4 Casualization of labour

Neoliberal politics has driven the privatization of solid waste management in Cape Town, South Africa. This decision has also generated the casualization of labour, heavily impacting the livelihood of those working with solid waste. Many waste workers lost their jobs and were then re-employed as, or replaced by, casual or

contract workers, under worse conditions. The Cape Town government had promoted short-term contracts for labour paying them minimum wages under precarious conditions, particularly for cost recovery purposes. Outsourcing and
privatizing municipal waste collection services reiterates the

> promotion of labor casualization and stratification of urban services is sub-
> stantiated by examining two aspects of the waste collection strategies: the
> disassociation of local government from the labor relations for municipal
> services, and the unequal distribution of basic municipal services.
>
> (Miraftab, 2004b: 885)

The privatization of public services does not necessarily guarantee equal services
in all parts of the city. In the case of Cape Town, outsourcing waste collection has
perpetuated uneven service provision and informal settlements, in particular,
remain without proper service.

Without protective labour regulations in place, as is frequently the case for
'informal' workers in the global South, private contracting allows for abusive labour
relations, taking advantage of poor and unemployed vulnerable individuals – often
women. In the context of South Africa, Miraftab discusses the concerns for such
entrenched casualization and flexibilization of workers employed by contractors
in the public sector, as a condition "that allows contractors' 'race to the bottom' to
pay only the minimum wage – which is not a living wage" (2004b: 886). Importantly, such precarious work situations challenge the collective bargaining power
of the service provision sector, thus maintaining the potential for, and reinstating,
exploitation by the contracting firms.

Despite the poor results described for privatization in infrastructure in many
countries in Asia, Africa and Latin America, many cities in the global South are
still privatizing their solid waste management, or part of it (Tan, 2012). Large
corporations in the waste sector are becoming the new brokers of waste management in developing countries. Sometimes local governments consider incineration
as a final household waste destination method. To them this technology is attractive because it quickly makes waste disappear, replacing landfilling and laborious
selective waste collection and recycling processes. Privatization in waste management matches with what David Harvey has termed *accumulation by dispossession*, translating into the aggressive appropriation of common resources, here
water and solid waste, as an ongoing required process that produces accumulation
(of capital) and keeps capitalism going. A similar analysis has been made by
Loftus (2009) in the context of recent water service privatizations.

Neoliberal political agendas argue for waste incineration in view of the possible
energy generation benefit and, thus, cost recovery component. Many cities, particularly large metropolitan areas in the global South, are urged by their updated
federal legislation to close waste dumps and move away from landfilling. Japan,
South Korea, Taiwan and Singapore are the countries with the largest number of
incinerators in Asia (Gohlke and Martin, 2007; Bai and Sutanto, 2002). In Latin
America the number of incinerators is still small and they are used mainly for
hospital and industrial waste.

9.3.5 Waste-to-energy

Private–public partnerships are considered to be an alternative to full privatization and a solution for municipalities to tackle basic infrastructure and service provision related to water, sewage and waste. With the acquisition of expensive waste-to-energy technology, governments lock themselves into long-term contracts in waste management (between ten and 15 years), without control over strategic decisions or over the quality and price of the service (Corvellec *et al.*, 2013). This type of infrastructure acquisition has *durable consequences*. Thus the notion of *path-dependence* applies to this situation. *Path-dependence* explains how future decisions may be limited by the decisions made in the past, even though past conditions may no longer be applicable (Martin and Sunley, 2006). Past decisions on infrastructure may slow down or even prevent the emergence of more sustainable urban infrastructures. This is true for the case of waste incineration facilities. Having a technology in place that is able to process large amounts of solid waste for energy recovery, with motives of cost recovery and profit generation, will most likely not be voluntarily underused. That translates into fewer incentives to diminish the generation of waste, but rather to maintain or even increase current generation and disposal rates.

A recent trend observed in Brazil and Nicaragua is the modernization of selective waste collection and recycling schemes following a logic that is primarily oriented towards market competition. In some of these cases, the local government has upgraded the cities' recycling programme with the introduction of new technologies for greater mechanization of the recycling process (trucks, moving belts, presses, etc.). These transformations have also been reflected in changed management structures within the groups working in these new mega-recycling centres. This allows for larger quantities of waste to be processed more effortlessly, but bears the risk of groups moving away from a social economy oriented cooperative approach towards a market-oriented industrial business mode. Observations recently made at Managua's *La Chureca* recycling plant and at the *megacentral* in Santo Amaro, São Paulo, confirm these concerns. Here, there are frequent complaints that the work has become de-humanized with participants now having to work at a very fast pace with little room for building social and human capital (e.g. by fostering solidarity, sharing stories and becoming politically engaged in the operation) affecting the wellbeing of the recyclers. Although upgrading for appropriate technology is essential, the positive aspects of collective separation and recycling for social and human development should not be lost.

9.4 Contracting recycling cooperatives and associations in waste management

The term co-production means that citizens and the state work together in producing public services. Ostrom describes the term co-production as: "the process through which inputs used to produce goods or services are contributed by individuals who are not 'in' the same organization" (1996: 1073). Co-production implies that citizens can actively participate in producing public goods and services, thus benefitting their communities. Ostrom's early work recognizes the importance of the bridging function in co-production. She further suggests that: "no market can survive without extensive public goods provided by governmental agencies. No government can be efficient and equitable without considerable input from citizens" (1996: 1083).

Co-management, which is the joint approach towards controlling and using natural resources, is primarily discussed in the context of natural sciences. Co-management literature often emphasises the praxis of bottom-up, participatory learning and community empowerment, usually in a natural resource setting; for example, in fisheries or forestry (see: Jentoft, 2005; Gutberlet *et al.*, 2007). The literature provides insights on how multi-stakeholder approaches can be incorporated in resource management and underlines the fact that, here, the collective approach to the process is as important as the expected service outcomes are (Carlsson and Berkes, 2005). Solid waste is also a resource with multiple actors and diverse stakeholder interests; therefore, the concept is useful for understanding ways in which we can integrate recycling cooperatives in selective waste collection and separation, with these groups having an active voice in the politics and praxis of waste management.

Both approaches, co-management and co-production, are strategic for improving the delivery of public services, particularly in those neighbourhoods that have long been neglected. Joshi and Moore observe that most of the co-production examples are rather undefined, informal and have to be renegotiated with the state and stakeholders almost continuously. They then describe formal or institutionalized co-production as the "provision of public services (broadly defined, to include regulation) through regular, long-term relationships between state agencies and organized groups of citizens, where both make substantial resource contributions" (Joshi and Moore, 2004: 40).

Some municipalities rely on the participation of the grass-roots sector in waste management to improve service delivery in informal settlements. Mitlin (2008) provides several examples of self-organized, co-production where community-based organizations and social movements have partnered with the state for service delivery. In some of these cases citizens have been successful only in the objective of helping the state in providing a service, thus lowering the cost for its delivery. In other cases the grass-roots movements were able to maintain a certain degree of autonomy and to also contribute towards wider issues of democratic practices. Mitlin concludes that "[c]o-production is attractive to movements both because it strengthens local organizations and because it equips these groups with an understanding of the changes in state delivery practices that are required if they are to address citizen needs" (2008: 357). It is more difficult to see bottom-up approaches in waste management co-production, with initiatives of the organized poor being contracted as autonomous operators to provide waste collection services.

Benefits of co-production are obvious in building public housing or in improving street security (Roy *et al.*, 2004). The *Slum/Shack Dwellers' Federation* in Africa provides many examples for co-production in housing and sanitation service provision (Sisulu, 2006; Satterthwaite and Mitlin, 2014). However, there are very few examples of the co-production in waste management. 'Informal' and organized recyclers are city constructors and co-producers of basic services, including house-hold collection and street sweeping in informal settlements, and selective waste collection with recycling throughout the city. This is very obvious in the urban global South. My colleagues and I describe an example of co-production for waste collection and recycling in Kisumu, Kenya (Gutberlet *et al.*, 2015).

While the significant social, environmental and economic contributions of infor-mal recycling are discussed in Chapter 4, the current chapter focuses primarily on institutionalized (or partially institutionalized) co-production. The case study illus-trated in Box 9.1 refers to the well-known, co-production experience from the city of Londrina, which is considered a groundbreaking, successful experience in Brazil. Other good examples for experiences in co-production in the Brazilian state of São Paulo are the cities Diadema, Assis, Arujá, Biritiba-Mirim, Araraquara, São Caetano do Sul, Sanatana de Parnaiba, Mauá and São José do Rio Preto.

BOX 9.1: Building resilience with formalized co-production in solid waste management: the case of Londrina, Brazil

Since 2001, Londrina's *Reciclando Vidas* (Recycling Lives) programme has become a benchmark for formalized co-production in solid waste manage-ment (Besen, 2006). Londrina is the second largest city in the state of Paraná, in the south of Brazil with approximately 510,000 inhabitants. The population is well serviced, with almost 100 per cent coverage for solid waste collection, 97 per cent for drinking water provision and 79 per cent for wastewater collection. The city is divided into 33 sectors, with one sort-ing centre in each sector. Federal law number 11.445/2007 authorizes the municipalities to hire recycling associations or cooperatives for the service provision in selective waste collection, processing and marketing. This legislation has enabled the co-production in Londrina as in several other cities in Brazil. The selective waste collection programme in Londrina involves approximately 500 recyclers organized in 33 recyclers' associa-tions, one for each sector. Household collection is done with electric carts (see Photograph 9.2).

The *catadores* separate the material into 25 different categories. Most of the material is cardboard, newspaper and other papers, followed by broken glass, PET bottles, Tetrapak, thin coloured plastics and other categories. The *catado-res* work on tables to separate the materials and not on moving belts, which reduces the loss of materials. The *catadores* commercialize close to 100 tons of separated materials every day, which is roughly 23 per cent of the total solid waste generated in the city. Only 4 per cent of the material collected for recycling has to be landfilled, which is low compared to other cities, where up to 50 per cent of the collected and separated material can not be recycled due to contamination. A study confirms that separating on tables generates less

Photograph 9.2 Electric cart for selective household waste collection in Londrina.

waste (around 5 per cent), while on moving belts a minimum of 25 to 30 per cent of rejected materials are produced (Pinto and González, 2008).

The associations created a Weighing and Sales Centre – CEPEVE (*Central de Pesagem e Vendas* – CEPEVE) to perform collective commercialization. This centre also allows those associations that don't have their own presses to compact the material using CEPEVE's presses. In 2007, CEPEVE charged between 3 and 5 per cent of the total value for the collective transactions, as maintenance cost. The door-to-door collection allows for a direct contact with the population, a key aspect in improving the quality of the selective waste collection. The *catadores* perform continuous community environmental education, which has reduced the percentage of rejected material from 15 per cent in 2001 to 4 per cent in 2005.

In 2011, the government paid R$ 64.00 (US$ 40.29) per ton of commercialized, recyclable material plus R$ 0.23 for each serviced household participant. In addition, the cooperative in charge receives a monthly amount of R$ 33,000 (US$ 20,772) for solid waste diversion from the landfill. This total value in addition to the income from the material commercialization is divided among the *catadores* according to their work effort. In 2010, the municipality invested an additional R$ 20,000 (US$ 12,589) every month to upgrade the infrastructure (trucks and electric carts) used in the collection of recyclables.

The government of Londrina is committed to selective waste collection with a consolidated public policy that is more than just a government programme based on a contractual relationship between government and recyclers. Another bonus in this experience is the strong communication system in the community (e.g. the recycling programme offers a *800 number to communicate with the population). Exemplary transparency and trustful relationships between *catadores* and the government have been vital in the success of this programme, contributing to the high self-esteem of the participant recyclers.

The precarious infrastructure in some separation centres is one of the remaining challenges to overcome. The *catadores* also point out logistical difficulties in working with the recycling industries. The experience of Londrina provides evidence for the feasibility of institutionalized co-production. Although some challenges remain, this case study suggests a win–win situation, with all major stakeholders involved benefitting from the arrangement. In order to build resilient and sustainable cities, local governments must go beyond short-term selective waste collection programmes and commit to long-term public policies for inclusive solid waste management.

Co-production is a political process and, when institutionalized, citizens engage with government and state agencies in addition to working on improvements in infrastructure or basic services. These processes are extremely important because they open up spaces for wider democratic and civic engagement and even political inclusion, altogether strengthening civil society and building social cohesion in the community (Abers, 1998). Nevertheless, everyday co-production often means challenging existing power relations and oppressive and discriminatory practices. The community-based organizations and social movements motivated for co-production frequently have to negotiate their participation beyond just fulfilling a service provision.

Zapata Campos and Zapata (2013) describe co-production arrangements for household waste collection services in informal settlements in Managua, Nicaragua. Here community groups as well as small-scale waste collection enterprises in partnership with the local government are able to improve the level of household waste collection in previously un-serviced informal neighbourhoods. These actors work under difficult circumstances, refining their entrepreneurial skills in the everyday praxis, which turns them into important co-producers.

However, without becoming anchored in public policy, co-production arrangements are rarely long term and sustainable. Local governments use and abandon the partnerships with community groups for political and/or economic reasons, as it pleases their convenience. Power distribution seems to be a frequent hurdle in co-production. Often local governments treat solid waste management as an engineering problem, to be tackled solely with technology solutions, and there is little perception of the social facets of waste and the willingness to involve community groups, cooperatives or associations in the management of municipal waste. Local governments' understanding of participatory approaches, required in co-production and co-management, is often tinted by prejudice, not valuing the input, experience and knowledge of 'informal' recyclers (Yates and Gutberlet, 2011a; 2011b).

Yet the community groups and social movements involved are not passive and they often engage in long struggles to improve their livelihoods and working conditions as city co-producers. The interdisciplinary research and community outreach experience of the *Participatory Sustainable Waste Management* programme (see Chapter 3) documents a wide range of initiatives in co-production and co-management involving recycling cooperatives and associations with local governments in Brazil (Gutberlet, 2014). The experience of these organized recyclers is one of constant struggle. Even in situations where their work has already been institutionalized, the recyclers have to persistently fight for better working conditions and decent remuneration for the service they provide (Gutberlet, 2013; 2012; 2008b; Yates and Gutberlet, 2011a; 2011b). The greater the organizational and networking skills, the more resilient the groups become and the more sustainable their work is. Box 9.2 provides detailed background information on co-production experiences of COOPCENT-ABC, a recycling cooperative network in the metropolitan region of São Paulo (also see the information on the recycling network in São Paulo see Chapter 3). For more details on public policies favouring the inclusion of organized recyclers in waste management see also Chapter 4.

BOX 9.2: Cooperative recycling networks stimulating co-production in waste management: the case of COOPCENT-ABC

Founded in 2008, COOPCENT-ABC is a second degree cooperative that networks several organized recycling groups from four cities in the metropolitan region of São Paulo, with around 200 affiliated recyclers. Key objectives are to improve the performance of the affiliates through democratic management, economic efficiency and excellence in the recycling process, and assuring safe and sustainable economic development conditions for recyclers in the region. The network emerges out of the specific historic and political context of the urban social movement of 'informal' and organized recyclers. COOPCENT-ABC was created with the support of the *Participatory Sustainable Waste Management* programme (see Chapter 3).

The network is committed to improving employment and income conditions, as well as to fight for the formal recognition of the *catadores*. The initial prime objective was to facilitate collective commercialization. Later the network also started to participate in the design of public waste management policies that practice social inclusion. COOPCENT-ABC defends

the principles of authentic cooperativism and Solidarity Economy. Participatory and democratic self-management (*autogestão*) is a key characteristic to ensure gender equity and the dignity of all recyclers. With the improvement and the promotion of the recycling chain the network tackles social and economic inequities, deriving from the effect of the current development model based primarily on economic growth and the concentration of income at the expense of social inequities and environmental degradation, which affects current and future generations.

(Coopcent-ABC website, 2014)

So far, COOPCENT-ABC collectively sells paper (white paper, mixed paper, cardboard, newspapers and magazines), plastics (PET, PEAD, separated by cleanliness and colour), and Tetra Pak beverage packaging (containing different layers of plastic and aluminium). In 2013, COOPCENT-ABC jointly commercialized approximately 1,586 tons of recyclable materials, in the value of R$ 600,000 (approximately US$ 200,000). As shown in the following figure, there is an overall trend to increasingly engage in collective commercialization (see Figure 9.1).

In addition, COOPCENT-ABC adds value to one of the materials by transforming PET plastic bottles into washing line and brooms. One 1 litre PET bottle produces 10 m of washing line, which is sold for the price of R$ 2.50 (US$ 0.83) (Photograph 9.3).

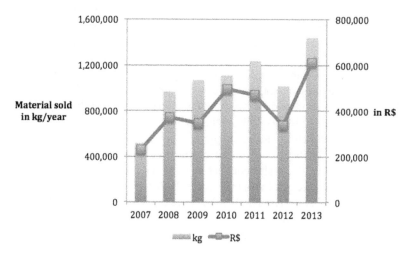

Figure 9.1 COOPCENT commercialization of paper and plastic since 2007.
Source: Data supplied by COOPCENT-ABC, 2014.

Photograph 9.3 The transformation of plastic bottles into washing line.

Three of the municipalities in which COOPCENT-ABC is active (Diadema, Mauá and Ribeirão Pires) have engaged in the process of formalizing co-production in selective household waste collection. The initiatives are still fragile and depend on supportive political constellations. In 2005, the municipality of Diadema created a law to remunerate the *catadores* for the material collected from the households (Decree No. 5.984/2005). Since then, frequent changes in the local political scene have hindered the consequent and continuous application of this law and often the *catadores* go without pay for months. The government of Ribeirão Pires grants the space for the recycling depot and provides a truck and driver to accompany the door-to-door household recyclable collection. Cooperative members underline the importance but also the vulnerability of this input. In April 2014, the city of Mauá signed a pre-contract for co-production with the cooperative *Coopercata,* promising remuneration for the service of the cooperative members (which was only fulfilled in April 2016). This contract includes the provision of the space for the recycling centre and transportation of the household collection in Mauá. However, as of now (April 2016) the recyclers have not been paid for the service they are providing.

As the recycler Monica puts it:

> at the beginning only collective commercialization involving all
> groups was the main objective of the network, but then we realized

that COOPCENT could do much more than this. At the time, the *catadores* already had problems with the local governments regarding the municipal separate waste collection programmes. Now we from COOPCENT's leadership normally help solve these cases. Dealing with these issues as a singular group is different than speaking as a network. Now with the presence of COOPCENT, it is possible to discuss at arms length and thus COOPCENT got another important function.

Importantly, Brazil has introduced a couple of important policies favouring the organization of recycling cooperatives and the formalization of co-production. In 2002, the federal government created the professional category *catador* for the person collecting recyclable materials (Code 5192-05). In 2007, the federal Law No. 11,445 authorized municipalities to contract out waste management to recycling associations and cooperatives. Law no. 12,305, regulated through Decree No. 7,404, 23 December 2010 is a key milestone establishing the national solid waste policy. The law creates a Steering Committee for the implementation of the reverse logistics systems. Finally, the federal Decree No. 7,405, 23 December 2010 instituted the programme called *Pro-Catador* and created the Joint Inter-ministerial Committee for social and economic inclusion of *catadores*. There are also municipal laws that promote the inclusion of recycling cooperatives in official programmes, like the cases mentioned for Diadema and Mauá. However, public policies alone are not sufficient to implement the necessary shift towards participatory, integrated waste management. Radical institutional change and the performance of democratic processes is equally important, allowing for the development of strong community-sector initiatives to participate in co-production.

Finally, there are several lessons to be learned from the experience of the trade union KKPKP (Kagad Kach Patra Kashtakari Panchayat) in Pune, India, which is one of many good experiences coming from India (see BOX 9.3).

BOX 9.3: Co-production experience of the waste pickers' trade union KKPKP in India

KKPKP (Kagad Kach Patra Kashtakari Panchayat) is a trade union of over 5,000 registered waste pickers and itinerant scrap buyers in Pune, India. With hard work, over many years since its creation in 1993, KKPKP has developed into a credible, responsible and mature organization, striving for the recognition of waste pickers as respected and valued workers. The union provides identity cards to secure access to waste and public services, including healthcare, for waste pickers. It undertakes educational and literacy programmes and has created credit cooperatives and group insurance for members. The union is a driver for collective mobilization around topics that concern the waste pickers, including uncovering exploitation and harassment, confronting extortion, fighting injustices and challenging stereotypes. It organizes around economic issues, establishing scrap collectors as workers and scrap collection as work that is recognized by the state and supported with resources (e.g. medical insurance). The union also mobilizes around social issues, including rape, child labour and child marriage, and political issues building political awareness and education amongst its members. KKPKP has established cooperative scrap stores to service the waste pickers and ensure better prices for the sale of the material; which is usually dominated and controlled by middlemen. About 400 members are involved in the collection of source separated waste from 40,000 households and commercial enterprises across the city (Chikarmane and Narayan, n.d.).

KKPKP has had remarkable successes in improving working and living conditions for the waste pickers and in raising awareness about their role in waste management. The union has been able to influence India's public policy on solid waste management. They are part of an expert committee on solid waste constituted by the Supreme Court of India. Their programme of door-to-door household collection is an inspiring example for co-production, where municipal authorities, residents and the waste picker members perform selective waste collection (Routh, 2014).

Another remarkable experience from India falls under an initiative of SEWA (Self Employed Women's Association), an internationally known organization for women informal workers. SEWA's main objective is to organize women workers for full employment and self-reliance; establishing work security, income security, food security and social security (at least healthcare, childcare and shelter). This association has also been successful in mobilizing waste pickers to secure access to healthcare and capacity building as well as to provide them with government-issued identity cards. SEWA operates three cooperatives of waste picker members. These cooperatives have established contracts with Vejalpur municipality, in the city of Ahmedabad – in the state of Gujarat – to provide selective waste collection services to 46,842 households (Routh, 2014).

CHINTAN Environmental Research and Action Group is a grass-roots organization based in Delhi that has partnered with the informal waste sector to support their struggle for inclusion in policies for better livelihoods. The organization is a strong vocal advocate for waste recycling instead of waste incineration. They argue that waste-to-energy plants can push waste pickers further into poverty by decreasing access to waste, a crucial livelihood source for many poor residents (CHINTAN, 2012). With the support of CHINTAN, waste pickers are now contracted to carry out selective waste collection service in parts of Delhi (Routh, 2014).

9.5 Concluding remarks

There are diverse collective and individual initiatives involved in the arena of public waste service delivery, particularly in circumstances where the government is unwilling or unable to provide the required infrastructure and service. Residents in informal settlements suffer most from the lack of waste collection and the consequent accumulation of waste, which creates severe health risks. Waste pickers searching for recyclables and waste collectors operate on different scales, from servicing specific streets and households or particular communities, primarily informal settlements, to providing waste collection in all parts of the city. The level of organization and entrepreneurship varies significantly, as does the support that these groups receive from governmental and non-governmental organizations. The literature describes cases where community groups participate in water, sanitation, electricity, housing and solid waste collection service provision. Sometimes these initiatives develop into successful co-production arrangements, between cooperatives or small-scale entrepreneurs and local governments, collaboratively responsible for the service provision in their neighbourhood or in other parts of the city.

It is common practice under neoliberalism for governments to privatize infrastructure and services and to involve large corporations. As a consequence, these communities and governments often become locked into costly technology for many years, even decades, despite the social and environmental impacts this technology generates. In this case the concept of *path-dependence* applies, inhibiting the government's ability to be flexible and adapt to new, more appropriate technology, in line with the cities' resilience and sustainability.

Despite the many difficulties and constraints attached to cooperative recycling, it generates an obvious, short- to long-term, win–win situation for city administrations, communities, the recyclers and the environment. Innovative experiences of co-production arrangements, primarily from the global South, demonstrate these opportunities and multiple social, economic and environmental benefits for the cities and their populations. The recyclers, who usually are the most socially and economically excluded, have the opportunity to work in a collective setting, which is self-managed and guided by principles of cooperation, solidarity, equity and reciprocity. Cooperative members engage in education and training activities that benefit their human development.

The recyclers, performing the tasks of resource recovery, act as environmental stewards and educators, particularly through door-to-door collection of household recyclables, but also by engaging in awareness building activities in schools, community centres, via radio and television, or other forms of media. With their work, they help to diminish the waste of resources, which reduces the need for further natural resource extraction. All these aspects ultimately benefit communities and build resilience.

The most successful cases of cooperative recycling are those with institutionalized co-production, where the local government signs a contract with an organized group of recyclers for them to formally execute the selective waste collection programme, and where the recyclers are paid for this service provision. For these recycling groups, participation does not only mean fulfilling the service, but it also means participating in planning, monitoring and the evaluation of solid waste management. Public policies formalizing these inclusive arrangements are crucial to guarantee a successful and lasting programme. Legislation has the potential to safeguard co-management arrangements, beyond party politics.

At the same time, praxis has highlighted multifarious challenges and difficulties related to this form of solid waste management, as has been described by the experiences of the COOPCENT-ABC network, which coordinates collective commercialization of recyclable materials for twelve cooperatives in four municipalities in the metropolitan region of São Paulo (see Box 9.2). This example, and many other cases, demonstrate the necessity to anchor co-production in comprehensive public policy and democratic processes. Securing the remuneration of organized recyclers for door-to-door collection services by law is essential; however it is not enough. The recyclers themselves need to be well organized and networked to use their agency and power to demand for their rights. Furthermore, the recyclers provide different environmental services related to waste diversion, which translates into greenhouse gas emission reduction and energy savings, obtained from recycling. These environmental gains are still widely ignored by governments, as is the aspect of cooperative recycling generating social goods and contributing to social cohesion within local communities.

10 Final outlook

A world without waste

DOI: 10.4324/9781315686523-10

Summary

This final chapter reminds us about the social, economic, cultural and environmental challenges caused by the current *waste regime* of industrial capitalism, shaping our contemporary times. The concept of *waste regime* is used here to help understand the politics, power structures, and social/cultural dimensions related to waste generation and waste management. In order to overcome the critical waste problems discussed in this book, a new *waste regime* needs to be cultivated, which is characterized by a radical transformation towards sustainable practices, equitable and just working conditions and appropriate technologies in production, consumption and waste management. This new paradigm has to embrace the idea of *zero waste* as environmental ethics by maximizing waste avoidance, reduction, repair, reuse and recycling. Some municipalities in the global South have contracted waste picker organizations, such as recycling cooperatives or associations to perform the city's household collection of recyclable materials. These forms of community-based, participatory arrangements in solid waste management, also termed co-production, represent important transitional ways of creating more resilient communities, as discussed in the previous chapter. The book concludes by highlighting some key benefits and remaining challenges of inclusive solid waste management, pointing towards ideas and concepts that need to be developed further.

10.1 Introduction: from waste as a problem to waste as a solution

In previous chapters I have discussed the current waste dilemma as a *fallout* of modern society that generates complex and often unanticipated social and environmental problems. Many collectives, writers and filmmakers have expressed their warnings about the problematic human impacts on Earth: Rachel Carson's *Silent Spring* (1962); *The Limits to Growth* (1972) prepared by the Club of Rome; Declarations from the *Earth Summits* in 1972, 1992 and 2012 and countless other reports and papers presented at conferences, congresses and seminars, to mention but a few. Ulrich Beck (1992) and Anthony Giddens (1990) have coined the term *risk society* for contemporary civilization, where environmental degradation has become an inadvertent side-effect of everyday conduct in industrialized societies. The dimension and severity of the contemporary environmental crisis is spelled out in the notion of the *Anthropocene*, a term that refers to an epoch of Earth's history during which human beings have become a major geological force (Crutzen and Stoermer, 2015). Human activities are generating wide-ranging environmental impacts; including biodiversity loss, global warming, ozone layer depletion, acidification of the oceans, and the production of extensive carpets of plastics and other non-biodegradable composite materials as new '*anthropocene* layers' on the ocean floors and on the lands, among others.

Waste, as a direct outcome of human production and consumption processes, has become infinitely more complex and convoluted, heightening the uncertainties that threaten the planet. Tackling waste problems is essential in addressing the consequences of negative human impacts. Throughout the book many case studies and examples from the literature, and from my own experience describe and analyse innovative ideas and strategies that address some of the everyday problems deriving from waste. In many cities in the global South, the organized informal recycling sector gives inspiring examples for changing current unsustainable waste management methods and policies. In India, for instance, the trade union (KKPKP) organizes over 5,000 registered waste pickers and itinerant scrap buyers in the city of Pune. The union has established cooperative scrap stores to service the waste pickers and some of the members are involved in the collection of source-separated waste from households and commercial enterprises across the city. Similar to Brazil's National Movement of Catadores (MNCR), KKPKP also influences solid waste management policies on behalf of waste picker organizations. Another remarkable experience from India concerns the three cooperatives run by SEWA, an organization for informal women workers. These cooperatives have established contracts with the Vejalpur municipality in Ahmedabad to provide selective waste collection services to its households. Activist groups such as CHINTAN have been active in educating, informing and researching contentious issues related to waste picking and the livelihoods behind it. They have also actively supported co-production schemes, for example in Delhi, where waste pickers are now contracted to carry out the selective waste collection service.

Many other examples from Brazil were described in previous chapters, such as practices in the municipalities of Londrina, Mauá and São Caetana do Sul which have contracted recycling cooperatives for the selective waste collection service. In Brazil, *catadores* are key protagonists in the defence of resource recovery for recycling. This social movement has significantly shaped the new national solid waste management policy, which legally pushes municipalities towards participatory waste management and co-production arrangements.

The concept of *waste regimes*, highlights the forms of waste generation, disposal and treatment that are characteristic for a specific historic time period, denoting a particular epoch (Gille, 2007). The concept emphasizes underlying social relations that shape the way we perceive waste and deal with it. Gille suggests that waste should thus also be analysed as something produced materially and theoretically by deeply social relations:

> Waste regimes consist of social institutions and conventions that not only determine what wastes are considered valuable but also regulate their production and

distribution. Waste regimes, therefore, differ from each other according to the production, representation and politics of waste.

(Gille, 2013: 29)

We currently live in a *waste regime* that is characterized by an exponential increase in volume and material diversification of discarded objects and substances, as a consequence of increases in packaging, shorter product durability, programmed obsolescence, economic growth logic, consumerism and mass consumption. Our present *waste regime* is based on unsustainable production, lack of producer responsibility, lack of consumer consciousness, economic growth-oriented development and socially and environmentally unjust power relations with regard to how we deal with waste. For many decades a widely devalued perception of trash and the externalization of environmental costs related to waste disposal and management have maintained the prevailing status quo.

"Waste regimes consist of social institutions and conventions that not only determine what wastes are considered valuable but also regulate their production and distribution" (Gille, 2013: 29) and, further, shape decisions over how to treat waste. Most current governments still primarily invest in end-of-pipe solutions and technological fixes, promoting large-scale, expensive technology. Instead of solving the waste problem they only make waste disappear quickly. Regulations that promote more sustainable forms of production, consumption and discard would tackle the transformation of our current *waste regime* at its roots.

A closer look at the politics of solid waste reveals the protagonists involved in decision-making and the extent to which waste issues are a subject of public discourse. Waste management politics under the current *waste regime* are driven by economic rather than ecological or social principles. In the context of the global North, this means following a trend towards high-tech methods and privatization in waste management. Whilst in the global South the *waste regime* is characterized by neglect and informality; for example, with the absence of waste collection in informal settlements, with garbage being deposited in waste dumps, and with numerous individuals salvaging resources for recycling out of dumps and garbage bags.

The *waste regime* concept is also helpful to identify the actors that mobilize and participate in waste issues. While in the global North, mostly government agents and private businesses are the main protagonists in solid waste management; in the global South it is communities and particularly individuals and groups from the informal sector who are mobilized by waste issues. Here also, other actors become involved in waste management, such as middlemen and scrap dealers, small- to large-scale waste and recycling entrepreneurs, public and grassroots organizations, non-governmental organizations and medium to large enterprises in waste management, besides the many and diversified sizes of different recycling industries. These actors have their own histories, perspectives, aims, ambitions and politics regarding waste; sometimes these are highly controversial regarding the aspirations of 'informal' waste workers. Under these circumstances a participatory, democratic and transparent approach to waste becomes even more pressing in order to hear all voices and find the most just, appropriate and fair solutions. Economic recession, political turmoil and uneven development is also creating visible 'informal' actors in waste recycling activities in the global North. While historically these activities used to be related primarily to ethnic minorities, e.g. the Sinti and Roma, more recently a diverse spectrum of actors engages with resource recovery also in Southern and Eastern European countries.

The following section discusses *zero waste* as a new *waste regime*. Potentials and challenges related to such a paradigm shift are briefly outlined. Then the contributions from informal waste pickers, recycling cooperatives and alternative forms of resource recovery as important transitional steps towards *zero waste* are outlined. The chapter concludes with considerations about a future without waste.

10.2 A new *waste regime*: change in culture for *zero waste*

Recycling is not the final solution but rather a transitional phase towards a radical change in production and consumption. Obviously there are material limits to endless recyclability, there are negative impacts from recycling and there remain technological obstacles to implementing *zero waste*. The biggest challenge, however, comes with the required political and cultural change, as will be discussed later on. In addition, the everyday problem of mixing different materialities and increasing complexity of waste materials makes reuse and recycling extremely difficult and expensive. *Zero waste* is more than waste diversion into recycling. *Zero waste* encompasses a paradigm shift – away from unsustainable consumerism and discard-oriented linear production and consumption patterns, concentrated primarily on downstream responses towards a re-definition of production and consumption based on a post-humanist ethics and centering on social and environmental justice. The concept comprehends a radical political change away from acting largely on citizens' waste management needs with industrial and technological innovations towards a fresh perspective of framing waste as a matter of deliberation and critique on issues such as over-consumption, economic growth-based logic or technological fix. Not generating waste, by avoiding the use of substances and materials that are not recyclable or require expensive and inefficient recycling technologies, should be mandatory. Most often pro-active prevention is not sufficiently rewarded.

Those who work with waste know that the term 'waste' is relative: one person's waste is another person's livelihood or profit. Incineration, landfilling and dumping puts waste quickly out of sight. In the end, however, each one of these forms creates different environmental impacts. Landfilled and dumped materials, for example, resist differently and are transformed into other substances, including toxic leachate and air pollutants which are usually not captured at most landfill sites in the global South. Waste incineration, including waste-to-energy plants, generate different degrees and complexities of air pollutants and toxic ashes, and destroy resources that could be recycled or reused. Erroneously, governments, businesses, and the general public often interpret *zero waste* as no waste being deposited at landfills, but rather diverted into waste-to-energy. This interpretation creates resistance and opposition in many places in the global South, where waste pickers mobilize against waste incineration (see Photograph 10.1).

Photograph 10.1 Catadores resist against the introduction of a waste-to-energy facility in São Paulo.

The current linear economic development model, dominant in most of the global South and global North, is mainly based on resource abundance, modernization and expensive technology. These deceptions, suit those with political and economic interests and widely dominate the decision making and public perception. The proposed technological waste management solutions generally do not put in question people's lifestyles, but rather tend to cocoon the consumption bubble.

Challenging the status quo of current economic development means disrupting business as usual, breaking off the growth-oriented myths about unlimited resources and ever-growing economies. *Zero waste* comes in tandem with *de-growth* approaches to de-accelerate economic development, which means less resources are used more efficiently, to result in an overall better quality of life (Sjöströma and Östblom, 2010). The term *de-growth* has recently been coined to signify planned reduction in economic output (Jackson, 2009b). *De-growth* challenges the conventional understanding of economic growth as ultimate status and as maximum achievement (Fournier, 2008; Jackson, 2009b).

Slowing down, in the context of affluent societies, translates into less consumption and less generation of unwanted outcomes. This encompasses a philosophical perspective where less materiality means more quality of life. New ethical and moral values in social and environmental justice and solidarity can derive from a re-orientation towards *de-growth*.

The *zero-waste* paradigm implies expanding human awareness in the sense of Paulo Freire's *conscientization,* which generates consequent responsible actions

(Freire, 1972). The process of developing a critical awareness of one's social and environmental reality evolves with spiraling reflection, followed by action. It is widely recognized that communications that activate social norms can be effective in producing beneficial societal behaviours. When adequately formulated, the reinforcement of values and new social norms that cherish sufficiency, solidarity, equity or justice can optimize human behaviour (Cialdini, 2003). For Paulo Freire, aside from dialogue and reflection, action (in particular) is considered a fundamental stage in changing reality. Objection and action are the required ingredients for addressing current power hegemonies, which have created our waste dilemma in the first place. McBride (2012) uses the term *busy-ness* to avoid over-emphasizing the idea that small individual actions can sum up and make a difference, giving people the sense that a lot is already being done to address a serious problem.

Critical reflection about long-acquired and widely disseminated environmental and economic myths alone may not provoke change. Besides a better understanding of the facts and processes that shape current developments and social relations, actions are required to generate greater responsibility and actions that revert the negative impacts on this planet. These actions comprehend not only conscious lifestyle changes, but also need to happen on the government level (e.g. rewarding low-carbon actions and penalizing wasteful behaviours, installing safe bike lanes and low-cost access to bicycles, stimulating circular economy initiatives, exercising deliberation in decision-making and critically questioning why we generate so much waste).

The learning process, aiming at reduction for *less is more*, sufficiency and solidarity can also be nurtured by re-setting values and social norms. Important change is stirred by "cognitions, affect, and motivation that underlie interpersonal behavior and social interaction" (Van Lange *et al.*, 2007: 541). Social norms can be changed in order to stimulate a cultural transformation towards valuing environmental integrity and promoting sustainability. In praxis, new social norms can demand innovations beyond waste diversion, tackling the root causes for our current waste predicament before the problem arises and needs to be managed. New standards of what is environmentally, culturally and socially appropriate can influence strategies and behaviours in resource use and re-distribution within society. Redistribution between the rich and the poor is key to achieving *zero waste* in the global South.

These new values can then be supported by and communicated via creative and inclusive strategies (education, public events, cultural activities, social media, etc.). This is already happening worldwide and in multiple forms. Through active participation the desired information becomes meaningful knowledge and has the potential to travel quickly. Actively disseminated and reinforced new social values become norms that address required behavioral and lifestyle changes, turning away from unhealthy production and consumption patterns. Dialogue and engagement with the community, as well as updated information on waste separation, are important measures for receiving the support of households for source separation and recycling. We find examples from different contexts where members of the public perceive the praxis of recycling to be characterizing them as good citizens; sometimes even recycling adherence is seen as contributing to community wellbeing. Creative educational campaigns and citizens' participation can multiply these commitments and perceptions. A scrutinized political reflection on the powers involved in setting our waste management agenda is essential to uncover why most recycling programmes are still so far from being efficient, or why not enough is invested in avoidance and reuse.

It is impossible to down-cycle infinitely. Recycling may produce hazardous byproducts, it involves substantial transportation and certain processes require a lot of energy. Furthermore, recycling can also reinforce unsustainable consumption behaviours; we see examples everywhere, of increased recycling rates coming hand in hand with increased packaging and growing consumption, justified by the attitude of *being good in recycling*. Existing diversion processes also need to be critically looked at. Public policies are essential to prescribe the transition towards upstream solutions with a focus on avoidance, reduction and reuse. Economic instruments, in particular, can provide incentives to enforce legislation on carbon emission reduction and natural resources conservation. How informal sector recycling can become a stepping-stone in changing culture towards *zero waste* is discussed in the following section.

10.3 Recycling cooperatives and resource recovery

In many countries in the global South, waste pickers organize into cooperatives, associations or unions, and engage in selective waste collection, sometimes with the support of non-governmental or governmental organizations. Widespread institutional inertia subverting collective initiatives of 'informal' recyclers and preventing them from participating in the city's solid waste management is still a frequent challenge to these workers. Darbas (2008) labels this tendency *deliberative truncation*, to capture the process by which discussions become sabotaged by rigid norms, standards and understandings (see also Chapter 7). Those groups that have collectively organized into networks refer to heightened negotiating power and are potentially more successful in engaging with local government agencies in co-managing solid waste.

Despite the many undeniable benefits of collective processes, they are often conflict-laden, time consuming and difficult to implement. Working in a cooperative system implies facing multiple complexities on a daily basis. However, these everyday experiences also generate personal growth, agency, individual empowerment and transformation, steering professional and political achievement, as well as heightened human benefits (human capital). These social benefits (social capital) are unquestionable and it is time to recognize and value their contribution to solid waste management, to the economy and to the community.

The collective approach to work is challenging and requires continuous conflict resolution. As Freire (1972) notes during the initial stage of the struggle for emancipation, the oppressed tend to become oppressors themselves (*sub-oppressors*), as a consequence of being conditioned by the contradictions of the concrete situation by which they were shaped (*oppressed*). Discussions over participatory forms of co-management in waste recycling are still timid and tend to happen in unorthodox circles. Nevertheless, there is a growing momentum for these circles – particularly through social media and community-based organizations – to expand. The dialogue is a broad one and includes the different sectors of society; providing equal voices and recognizing power structures. These dialogues create opportunities for local governments to address multiple themes and problems that can be related to waste.

A shift towards integrated, collaborative forms of governance is vital to make participatory selective waste collection and recycling work. The notion of participatory ecological governance, addressing the *Anthropocene* complexities as well as the social justice realities, is imperative. The praxis of recycling groups working in tandem with local governments to recover recyclable waste fits this idea and is also in line with the aims set by *zero waste* movements (Zero Waste Europe, 2015). Furthermore, inclusive waste management provides many extra jobs and thus also addresses social justice demands. For example, under a current maximum resource recovery scenario in the metropolitan region of São Paulo, Brazil, and with current technology available to the cooperatives, one job could be created in collecting recyclables from 600 households and one job in the separation of 200 kg of recyclable materials per day. This would result in approximately one job in resource recovery (collection and separation) for every 550 inhabitants in this metropolitan region (Oliveira, 2014). This would mean more than 20,000 jobs in resource recovery just in the city of São Paulo.

The activity helps close the material loop, reduces dependency on imports, reduces environmental impacts associated with waste disposal, drives innovation in product design, involves citizens in creating a better world and helps educate and generate greater awareness (and possibly *conscientization*). Organic waste can be composted and used in urban agriculture, bringing nutrients back to the soils in urban and peri-urban spaces (see Chapter 7), or it can generate heat, used as energy. In a transition away from wastefulness towards resource recovery, the proposed concept of inclusive solid waste management with worker aggregations such as cooperatives, associations, or unions tackles the objectives of a "low-carbon, resource efficient, resilient and socially inclusive economy" (Zero Waste Europe, 2015) and a society with greater social cohesion (Zaman and Lehmann, 2011).

10.4 A future without waste?

Knowing that we already have significantly less resources at hand to be used by a growing population should provide enough motivation to induce a shifting of gears towards a culture of *zero waste*. The reconceptualization of waste as a resource has already happened. Urban mining, or recovering what is deeply buried in old and active landfills, is a reality. The prospects involved in this activity are discussed at conferences and are researched from different disciplinary backgrounds. The scale of the involvement of the private sector in mining those resources discarded decades ago also demonstrates the economic interest in retrieving resources embedded in waste. Solid waste has become a commodity, disputed by different interest groups, following the same capitalist logic of profit orientation in terms of its materiality (e.g. maximizing profits by increasing waste flows). The market economy tends to squeeze the 'informal' recyclers out of this niche. Nevertheless, in the global South in particular, organized waste pickers are contesting these moves and they are successful at times.

In the global North, community-based initiatives in resource recovery are mostly still stand-alone experiences. Examples are: the recycling and reuse centres in the Gulf islands in western Canada, the recyclers cooperative *Les Valoristes* in Montreal and *United-We-Can* bottle depot run as social enterprise in Vancouver

(Tremblay *et al.*, 2010). These experiences also generate social benefits and build social cohesion in the city. The trend for those who recover resources from waste, be it waste pickers in the South or *binners* in the North, is to become more visible and, consequently, to organize and gain in voice and political power.

The cooperative recycling examples demonstrate that there is not just one model for redesigning waste management. It is time to upscale and expand the scope of these initiatives to have a more significant impact by avoiding and reducing waste generation, maximizing recovery rates and increasing the awareness level (*conscientization*) of government, industry and the public at large. The current waste dilemma can be addressed through innovative ways, transforming society in positive forms at a global level.

Trans-disciplinary research, inter-sectorial policy approaches and participatory praxis come into play when addressing citizens on the practicalities of waste reduction and waste disposal; and when creating municipal, provincial/state and national/international regulations for avoidance, reduction, reuse and recycling. Such an integrated approach can also inform industry and business in creating viable products, thus mitigating environmental problems.

If humans are willing to collectively shift away from a regime of waste accumulation, moulded by practices that exploit labour and the environment, towards new sets of social, economic and institutional arrangements guided by a *zero waste* culture, then there will be a future without waste. Circular economy aims at keeping products, components and materials at their highest utility and value at all times, following the principle of *what goes around comes around*. Finally, it has been argued throughout this book that using resources more efficiently brings new jobs, which is important given the problematic involved in unemployment – a pressing social and economic issue worldwide. Reusing, repairing, refurbishing and recycling are also good for the local economy.

This circular logic implies changing infrastructures, technologies, policies and, primarily, cultures towards waste prevention, reduction, reuse, recycling and extended producer responsibility. City spaces need to be adjusted to fit decentralized transfer stations of recyclable materials (e.g. *ecopontos*) and recycling centres or depots, as well as decentralized composting and gardens to practice urban agriculture and biodigestion. Building resilient cities translates into urban design for reuse, repair and recycling, with adequate infrastructure, logistics and appropriate technology. If the topography allows curbside collection of recyclable materials can be done with bicycles and tricycles and other low carbon solutions.

Continuous education and training are required – as well as research – to always diminish what is generated as waste from production and consumption (Bartl, 2011, 2014b; King *et al.*, 2006; Lehmann, 2011; Levin *et al.*, 2012). Initiatives pointing towards *zero waste* should be observed, supported and disseminated to inspire other places and people to do better. It seems to be the most logical and necessary transformation in order to avoid the severe consequences from our waste dilemma and to mitigate the broader environmental and climate concerns that characterize everyday realities. Resource recovery and recycling are only stepping stones towards shaping resilient communities in resilient cities. Multiple lessons can be learned from waste pickers in the global South.

References

Abers, R. (1998) From Clientelism to Cooperation: Local Government, Participatory Policy and Civil Organizing in Porto Alegre, Brazil. *Politics and Society* 26 (4): 511–537.

ABRELPE (Associação Brasileira de Empresas de Limpeza Pública e Resíduos Especiais) (2011) *Panorama dos Resíduos Sólidos no Brasil 2011*. São Paulo (report).

Achankeng, E. (2003) Globalization, Urbanization and Municipal Solid Waste Management in Africa. *African Studies Association of Australasia and the Pacific 2003 Conference Proceedings – African on a Global Stage*. Last accessed 15 April 2015 at: http://wiego. org/sites/wiego.org/files/publications/files/Achankeng_Globalization_Urbanization_ MSWMgmt_Africa.pdf.

Ackerman, F. and Mirza, S. (2001) Waste in the Inner city: Asset or Assault? *Local Environment: The International Journal of Justice and Sustainability* 6 (2): 113–120.

Ahmed, S. (2004) Affective Economies. *Social Text* 22 2 (79): 117–139.

Ahmed, S. A. and Ali, M. (2004) Partnerships for Solid Waste Management in Developing Countries: Linking Theories to Realities. *Habitat International* 28 (3): 467–479.

Akenji, L., Hotta, Y., Bengtsson, M. and Hayashi, S. (2011) EPR Policies for Electronics in Developing Asia: An Adapted Phase-in Approach. *Waste Management & Research* 29 (9): 919–930.

Alberti, M. (2008) *Advances in Urban Ecology: Integrating Humans and Ecological Processes in Urban Ecosystems*, New York: Springer.

Ali, M. (2003) Community-based Enterprises: Constraints to Scaling Up and Sustainability. In: *Report of the Workshop on Solid Waste Collection that Benefits the Urban Poor*, Collaborative Working Group on Solid Waste Management in Low- and Middle-income Countries.

Ali, M. (2006) Urban Waste Management as if People Matter. *Habitat International* 30 (4): 729–730.

Alison, M. and Cunningham, G. (2003) From Clients to Citizens: Asset-based Community Development as a Strategy for Community-driven Development. *Development in Practice* 13 (5): 474–486.

Alter, K. (2006) *Social Enterprise Typology*. Last accessed 2 November 2015 at: www. virtueventures.com/setypology/semg.aspx.

Altieri, M. A. and Funes-Monzote, F. (2012) The Paradox of Cuban Agriculture. *Monthly Review An Independent Socialist Magazine* 63 (8). Last accessed 1 May 2015 at: http:// monthlyreview.org/2012/01/01/the-paradox-of-cuban-agriculture/.

Alvarado-Esquivel, C., Liesenfeld, O., Márquez-Conde, J. Á., Cisneros-Camacho, A., Estrada-Martínez, S., Martínez-García, S. A., González-Herrera, A. and García-Corral, N. (2008) Seroepidemiology of Infection with *Toxoplasma gondii* in Waste Pickers and Waste Workers in Durango, Mexico. *Zoonoses and Public Health* 55 (6): 306–312.

Amengual, L. (2014) 25 Years of Waste Management in Mallorca, Balearic Islands, Spain: Time to Brush up on History. *Zero Waste International Alliance Conference and Dialogue 2014*, Nanaimo, Canada, 2–4 October 2014.

Aparcana, S. and Salhofer, S. (2013) Application of a Methodology for the Social Life Cycle Assessment of Recycling Systems in Low Income Countries: Three Peruvian Case Studies. *International Journal of Life Cycle Assessment* 18 (5): 1116–1128.

Arieli, D., Friedman, V. J. and Agbaria, K. (2009) The Paradox of Participation in Action Research. *Action Research* 7 (3): 263–290.

Arini, J. (2012) Reciclagem ainda engatinha em São Paulo e Rio. In Veja – Ambiente, 21 June 2012. Last accessed 2 November 2015 at: http://veja.abril.com.br/noticia/ciencia/reciclagem-ainda-engatinha-em-sao-paulo-e-rio.

Armitage, D. (2005) Adaptive Capacity and Community-based Natural Resource Management, *Environmental Management* 35 (6): 703–715.

Arnstein, S. (1969) A Ladder of Citizen Participation. *Journal of American Institute of Planners* 35 (4): 216–224.

Arruda, M. (2008) Exchanging Visions on a Responsible, Plural and Solidarity-based Economy. *Third World Planning Review* 19 (2): 139–161.

Asomani-Boateng, R. (2007) Closing the Loop: Community-based Organic Solid Waste Recycling, Urban Gardening, and Land Use Planning in Ghana, West Africa. *Journal of Planning Education and Research* 27 (2): 132–145.

Bai, R. and Sutanto, M. (2002) The Practice and Challenges of Solid Waste Management in Singapore. *Waste Management* 22 (5): 557–567.

Baldasano, J. M. and Soriano, C. (2000) Emission of Greenhouse Gases from Anaerobic Digestion Processes: Comparison with Other Municipal Solid Waste Treatments. *Water Science and Technology* 41 (3): 275–282.

Barkin, D. and Lemus, B. (2014) Rethinking the Social and Solidarity Society in Light of Community Practice. *Sustainability* 6: 6432–6445. DOI: 10.3390/su6096432.

Bartl, A. (2011) Barriers towards Achieving a Zero Waste. *Waste Management* 31 (12) (Editorial): 2369–2370.

Bartl, A. (2014a) Ways and Entanglements of the Waste Hierarchy. *Waste Management* 34 (1): 1–2.

Bartl, A. (2014b) Moving from Recycling to Waste Prevention: A Review of Barriers and Enablers. *Waste Management & Research* 32 (9): 3–18.

Barton, J. R., Issaias, I. and Stentiford, E. I. (2008) Carbon – Making the Right Choice for Waste Management in Developing Countries. *Waste Management* 28 (4): 690–698.

Bauder, H. and Engel-Di Mauro, S. (eds) (2008) Critical Geographies: A Collection of Readings. *Critical topographies series*. E-edition. Last accessed 2 November 2015 at: www.praxis-epress.org/availablebooks/introcriticalgeog.html.

Baumann, H. and Tillman, A. M. (2004) *The Hitch Hiker's Guide to LCA. An Orientation in Life Cycle Assessment Methodology and Application*, Lund: Studentlitteratur.

Beck, U. (1992) *Risk Society: Towards a New Modernity*, London: Sage.

Bennett, L. (2002) *Using Empowerment and Social Inclusion For Pro-poor Growth: A Theory of Social Change*. Background Paper for the Social Development Sector Strategy. World Bank. Last accessed 2 November 2015 at: http://file.upi.edu/Direktori/FIP/JUR._PEND._LUAR_SEKOLAH/195207251978031-ACE_SURYADI/bennet.pdf.

Besen, R. (2006) Programa de coleta seletiva de Londrina e caminhos inovadores rumo à sustentabilidade. In P. Jacobi (Ed.), *Gestão Compartilhada dos Resíduos Sólidos no Brasil*. São Paulo: Anna Blume.

Blackburn, J. Chambers, R. and Gaventa, J. (2001) Mainstreaming Participation in Development. *OED Working Paper Series No. 10*. Washington, DC: Operations Evaluation Department, The World Bank.

Blomley, N. (2006) Uncritical Critical Geography? *Progress in Human Geography* 30 (1): 87–94.

BNDS (Banco Nacional de Desenvolvimento Social) (2012) *Relatório final do perfil institucional, quadro legal e políticas públicas relacionados a resíduos sólidos urbanos no exterior e no Brasil.* Fundação de Apoio ao Desenvolvimento da Universidade Federal de Pernambuco – FADE. Pesquisa Científica BNDS FEP No 02/2010 (report).

Boggs, C. (1976) *Gramsci's Marxism*, London: Pluto Press.

Bogner, J., Abdelrafie, A. M., Diaz, C., Faaij, A., Gao, Q., Hashimoto, S., Mareckova, K., Pipatti, R. and Zhang, T. (2007) Waste Management. In *Climate Change 2007: Mitigation. Contribution of Working Group III to the Fourth Assessment Report of the Intergovernmental Panel on Climate Change*, Metz, B., Davidson, O. R., Bosch, P. R., Dave, R. and Meyer, L. A. (eds), Cambridge: Cambridge University Press.

Bogner, J., Pipatti, R., Hashimoto, S., Diaz, C., Mareckova, K., Diaz L., Kjeldsen, P., Monni, S., Faaij, A., Gao, Q., Zhang, T., Ahmed, M. A., Sutamihardja, R. T. and Gregory, R. (2008) Mitigation of Global Greenhouse Gas Emissions from Waste: Conclusions and Strategies from the Intergovernmental Panel on Climate Change (IPCC) Fourth Assessment Report. Working Group III (Mitigation). *Waste Management Resources* 26 (1): 11–32.

Botheju, D. and Bakke, R. (2011) Oxygen Effects in Anaerobic Digestion – A Review. *The Open Waste Management Journal* 4 (1): 1–19.

Bourdieu, P. (1986) The Forms of Capital. In Richardson, J. (ed.) *Handbook of Theory and Research for the Sociology of Education*, Westport CT: Greenwood Press.

Bovaird, T. (2007) Beyond Engagement and Participation: User and Community Coproduction of Public Service. *Public Administration Review* 67 (5): 846–860.

Brandão, C. R. (ed.) (1982) *Pesquisa Participante*. 2nd edn. Brasiliense, São Paulo, Brazil: 1982, p. 211.

Brandão, C. R. (ed.) (1987) *Repensando a pesquisa participante*; Brasiliense: São Paulo, Brazil.

Braun, B. and Castree, N. (eds) (1998) *Remaking Reality: Nature at the Millennium*, London and New York: Routledge.

Briceño-León, R., Villaveces, A. and Concha-Eastman, A. (2008) Understanding the Uneven Distribution of the Incidence of Homicide in Latin America. *Int. J. Epidemiology* 37 (4): 751–757. Last accessed 2 November 2015 at: http://ije.oxfordjournals.org/content/37/4/751.full.

Bryant, R. L. (1998) Power, Knowledge and Political Ecology in the Third World: A Review. *Progress in Physical Geography* 22 (1): 79–94.

Cahill, C. (2007) Including Excluded Perspectives in Participatory Action Research. *Design Studies* 28 (3): 325–340.

Callari, A. and Ruccio D. F. (2008) Socialism, Community, and Democracy: A Postmodern Marxian Perspective. In Harvey, J. T. and Garnett, R. F. (eds) *Future Directions for Heterodox Economics*, The University of Michigan Press, chapter 13.

Cargo, M. and Mercer, S. L. (2008) The Value and Challenges of Participatory Research: Strengthening Its Practice. *Annual Rev. Public Health* 29: 325–250.

Carlsson, L. and Berkes, F. (2005) Co-management: Concepts and Methodological Implications. *Journal of Environmental Management* 75 (1): 65–76.

Carson, R. (1962) *Silent Spring*, Boston: Houghton Mifflin.

Caruana, M. and Srnec, C. (2013) Public Policies Addressed to the Social And Solidarity Economy in South America. Toward a New Model? *Voluntas* 24 (3): 713–732. DOI: 10.1007/s11266-012-9276-y.

Castree, N., Kitchin, R. and Rogers, A. (2013) *A Dictionary of Human Geography*, Oxford University Press Print. Online Version: eISBN: 9780191758065. Last accessed: 2 November 2015 at: www.oxfordreference.com.

Cavalcante, S. and Franco, M. F. A. (2007) Profissão Perigo; Percepção de Risco à Saúde entre os Catadores do Lixão do Jangurussu. *Revista Mal-Estar e Subjetividade* 7 (1): 211–231.

Cavé, J. (2014) Who Owns Urban Waste? Appropriation Conflicts in Emerging Countries. *Waste Management & Research* 32 (9): 813–821.

Chambers R. (1994) The Origins and Practice of Participatory Rural Appraisal. *World Development* 22: 953–969.

Chaskin, R. J., Goerge, R. M., Skyles, A. and Guiltinan, S. (2006) Measuring Social Capital: An Exploration in Community–Research Partnership. *Journal of Community Psychology* 34 (4): 489–514.

Chester, M., Martin, E. and Sathaye, N. (2008) Energy, Greenhouse Gas, and Cost Reductions for Municipal Recycling Systems. *Environmental Science & Technology* 42 (6): 2142–2149.

Chikarmane, P. and Narayan, L. (n.d.) Organising the Unorganised: A Case Study of the Kagad Kach Patra Kashtakari Panchayat (Trade Union of Waste-pickers). Last accessed 30 October 2015 at: http://wiego.org/sites/wiego.org/files/resources/files/Chikarmane_Narayan_case-kkpkp.pdf.

CHINTAN (2009) *Cooling Agents: An Analysis of Climate Change Mitigation by the Informal Recycling Sector in India.* Report prepared in association with The Advocacy Project, Washington, DC.

CHINTAN (2012) Give back our waste. What the Okhla Waste-to-Energy plant has done to local waste pickers. CHINTAN Environmental Research and Action Group. New Delhi, India. Last accessed 8 April 2016 at: www.chintan-india.org/documents/research_and_reports/chintan-report-give-back-our-waste.pdf

Cialdini, R. (2003) Crafting Normative Messages to Protect the Environment. *Current Directions in Psychological Science* 12 (4): 105–109.

Club of Rome (n.d.) Last accessed 2 November 2015 at: www.clubofrome.org.

Cointreau, S. (2006) Occupational and Environmental Health Issues of Solid Waste Management: Special Emphasis on Middle and Lower-income Countries. *World Bank Urban Paper* No. 2, July. Last accessed 2 November 2015 at: www.worldbank.org/urban/uswm/healtheffects.pdf.

Coleman, J. (1988) Social Capital and the Creation of Human Capital. *American Journal of Sociology* 94, Supplement: S95–S120 (Suppl.)

Conceição, M. M. (2005) *Os empresários do lixo: um paradoxo da modernidade*, 2nd edn. Átomo: Campinas.

Cooperativa Central do ABC (COOPCENT-ABC) (2014) COOPCENT-ABC Website. Last accessed 26 October 2015 at: www.coopcentabc.org.br.

Cooperativa Central do ABC (COOPCENT-ABC) (2015) *Experiências da Coleta Seletiva e Subsídios para a Implementação da Política Nacional de Resíduos Sólidos.* Public Seminar 28.08.2015, Universidade Federal do ABC (UFABC). Last accessed 2 November 2015 at: http://coopcentabc.org.br/?pg=evento_hangout_implentacao_politica_residuos_solidos.

Cooperrider, D. L. and Whitney, D. (2005) *Appreciative Inquiry: A Positive Revolution in Change*, San Francisco: Berrett-Koehler.

Corvellec, H., Zapata Campos, M. J. and Zapata, P. (2013) Infrastructures, Lock-in, and Sustainable Urban Development and the Case of Waste Incineration in the Göteborg Metropolitan Area. *Journal of Cleaner Production* 50 (1): 32–39.

Costanza, R. (1991) *Ecological Economics: The Science and Management of Sustainability*, New York: Columbia University Press.

Crowther, J., Galloway, V. and Martin, I. (eds) (2005) *Popular Education: Engaging the Academy: International Perspectives*, Leicester: Niace.

Crutzen, P. and Stoermer, E. (2015) Have We Entered the "Anthropocene"? *Global International Geosphere-Biosphere Programme.* Last accessed 2 November 2015 at: www.igbp.net/5.d8b4c3c12bf3be638a8000578.html.

Czech, B. and Daly, H. E. (2004) The Steady State Economy – What it is, Entails, and Connotes. *Wildlife Society Bulletin* 32 (2): 598–605.

Da Silva, M. C., Fassa, A. G., Siqueira, C. E. and Kriebel, D. (2005) World at Work: Brazilian Ragpickers. *Occupational and Environmental Medicine* 62 (10): 736–740.

Dall'Agnol, C. M. and Fernandes, F. dos S. (2007) Saúde e autocuidado entre catadores de lixo: vivências no trabalho em uma cooperativa de lixo reciclável. *Rev. Latino-Americana de Enfermagem* 15 (Special Issue, September/October 2007): 729–735.

Daly, H. E. (1996) *Beyond Growth: The Economics of Sustainable Development.* Boston: Beacon Press.

Daly, H. E. and Farley, J. (2011) *Ecological Economics: Principles and Applications*, 2nd edn, Washington, DC: Island Press.

Darbas, T. (2004) Reflexive Governance of Urban Catchments: A Case of Deliberative Truncation. *Urban Policy Program Research Paper* 1, Griffith University Brisbane.

Darbas, T. (2008) Reflexive Governance of Urban Catchments: A Case of Deliberative Truncation. *Environment and Planning A* 40 (6): 1454–1469.

Das, R. (2004) Social Capital and Poverty of the Wage-labour Class: Problems with the Social Capital Theory. *Transactions of the Institute of British Geographers* New Series, 29 (1): 27–45.

Deutsche Gesellschaft für Internationale Zusammenarbeit (GIZ) (2011) *Recovering Resources, Creating Opportunities. Integrating the Informal Sector into Solid Waste Management.* Eschborn: GIZ: Eschborn.

Dwinell, A. and Olivera, M. (2014) The Water is Ours Damn it! Water Commoning in Bolivia. *Community Development Journal* 49 (S1): i44–i52.

Eade, D. (1997) Capacity-Building: An Approach to People-centred Development, Oxford Development Guidelines. Oxford: Oxfam.

Economic Commission for Latin America and the Caribbean (ECLAC) and International Labour Organization (ILO) (2012) *The Employment Situation in Latin America and the Caribbean.* October 2012, (7): 27. Last accessed: 2 November 2015 at: www.skillsforemployment.org/wcmstest4/idcplg?IdcService=GET_FILE&dID=45427&dDocName=WCMSTEST4_029827&allowInterrupt=1.

Emmett, T. (2000) Beyond Community Participation. Alternative Routes to Civil Engagement and Development in South Africa. *Development Southern Africa* 17 (4): 501–518.

Erdmann, G. and Engel, U. (2006) Neopatrimonialism Revisited – Beyond a Catch-All Concept. *German Institute of Global and Area Studies (GIGA) Working Papers*, No. 16. Hamburg: GIGA.

Ericson, J. A. (2006) A Participatory Approach to Conservation in the Calakmul Biosphere Reserve, Campeche Mexico. *Landscape and Urban Planning* 74 (3–4): 242–266. DOI: 10.1016/j.landurbplan.2004.09.006.

European Environment Agency (EEA) (2013) Managing Municipal Solid Waste – A Review of Achievements in 32 European Countries EEA Report No. 2. Copenhagen: EEA.

E-wasteguide.info (n.d.) Global Knowledge Partnerships in e-Waste Recycling programme. *Swiss State Secretariat for Economic Affairs (SECO) and Swiss Federal Laboratories for Materials Science and Technology (Empa).* Last accessed: 2 November 2015 at: http://ewasteguide.info.

Ezeah, C., Fazakerley, J. A. and Roberts, C. L. (2013) Emerging Trends in Informal Sector Recycling in Developing and Transition Countries. *Waste Management* 33 (11): 2509–2519.

Fahmi, W. S. (2005) The Impact of Privatization of Solid Waste Management on the Zabaleen Garbage Contractors in Cairo. *Environment and Urbanization* 17 (2): 155–170.

Fahmi, W. S. and Sutton, K. (2006) Cairo's Zabaleen Garbage Recyclers: Multi-nationals' Takeover and State Relocation Plans. *Habitat International* 30 (4): 809–837.

Fals Borda, O. (2001) Participatory Action Research in Social Theory. In Reason, P. and Bradbury, H. (eds) *Handbook of Action Research*, London: Sage, pp. 27–37.

Fals-Borda, O. and Rahman, M. A. (1991) *Action and Knowledge: Breaking the Monopoly with Participatory Action Research*, New York: Intermediate Technology Pubs/Apex.

Fetterman, D. M. and Wandersman, A. (2005) *Empowerment Evaluation Principles in Practice*, New York: Guilford, p. 231.

Fischer, F. and Hajer, M. A. (eds) (1999) *Living with Nature. Environmental Politics as Cultural Discourse*, New York: Oxford University Press.

Flicker, S., Savan, B., Kolenda, B. and Mildenberger, M. (2007) A Snapshot of Community-based Research in Canada: Who? What? Why? How? *Health Education Research* 9. Last accessed 2 November 2015 at: http://depts.washington.edu/ccph/commbas.html#Conf.

Forsyth, T. (2005) Building Deliberative Public–Private Partnerships for Waste Management in Asia. *Science* 36 (4): 429–439.

Foucault, M. (1977) *Discipline and Punishment*, London: Tavistock

Foucault, M. (1982) The Subject and Power. *Critical Inquiry* 8 (4): 777–795.

Fournier, V. (2008) Escaping from the Economy: The Politics of Degrowth. *International Journal of Sociology and Social Policy* 28 (11/12): 528–545.

Freire, P. (1972) *Pedagogy of the Oppressed*. London: Penguin.

Freire, P. (1973) *Education for Critical Consciousness*. New York: Seabury.

Fuks, M. (2012) Reflections on the Paradigm of Ecological Economics for Environmental Management. *Estudos Avançados* 26 (74): 105–119.

Furedy, C. and Whitney, J. (1997) Food from Waste: Urban Pressures and Opportunities for Food Production in Asian Cities. *International Conference on Sustainable Urban Food Systems*. Ryerson Polytechnic University, Toronto, Canada.

Gambina, J. and Roffinelli, G. (2013) Building Alternatives Beyond Capitalism. In Piñeiro Harnecker, C. (ed.) *Cooperatives and Socialism, A View from Cuba*. Palgrave Macmillan, pp. 46–59. DOI: 10.1057/9781137277756.

Gandy, M. (2004) Rethinking Urban Metabolism: Water, Space and the Modern City. *City* 8 (3): 363–379.

Gandy, M. (2005) Cyborg Urbanization: Complexity and Monstrosity in the Contemporary City. *International Journal of Urban and Regional Research* 29 (1): 26–49.

Gandy, M. (2006) Urban Nature and the Ecological Imaginary. In Heynen, N. C., Kaika, M. and Swyngedouw, E. (eds) *The Nature of Cities: Urban Political Ecology and the Politics of Urban Metabolism*, Questioning cities series. Abingdon: Routledge, pp. 62–72.

Gebreeziabher, Z., Naik, L., Melamu, R. and Balana, B. B. (2014) Prospects and Challenges for Urban Application of Biogas Installations in Sub-Saharan Africa. *Biomass and Bioenergy* 70: 130–140.

Georgescu-Roegen, N. (1971) *The Entropy Law and the Economic Process*. Cambridge MA: Harvard University Press.

Gibbs, D. and Jonas, A. E. G. (2000) Governance and Regulation in Local Environmental Policy: The Utility of a Regime Approach. *Geoforum* 31 (3): 299–313.

Gibson-Graham, J. K. (2008) Diverse Economies: Performative Practices for "Other Worlds." *Progress in Human Geography* 32 (5): 613–632.

Giddens, A. (1990) *The Consequences of Modernity*, Stanford CA: Stanford University Press.

Giddens, A. (1997) *Sociology*, 3rd edn, Cambridge: Polity Press.

Gijzen, H. J. (2002) Anaerobic Digestion for Sustainable Development: A Natural Approach. *Water Research and Technology* 45 (10): 321–328.

Gille, Z. (2007) *From the Cult of Waste to the Trash Heap of History: The Politics of Waste in Socialist and Postsocialist Hungary*, Bloomington: Indiana University Press.

Gille, Z. (2013) From Risk to Waste: Global Food Waste Regimes. *The Sociological Review* 60 (S2): 27–46. DOI: 10.1111/1467-954X.12036.

Gohlke, O. and Martin, J. (2007) Drivers for Innovation in Waste-to-Energy Technology. *Waste Management Research* 25 (3): 214–219.

Gomez-Correa, J., Agudelo-Suarez, A. and Ronda-Perez, E. (2008) Social Conditions and Health Profile of Recyclers from Medellín. *Rev. Salud Pública* 10 (5): 706–715.

Graham, S. and Marvin, S. (2001) *Splintering Urbanism: Networked Infrastructures, Technological Mobilities and the Urban Condition*, London: Routledge.

Graham, S. and McFarlane, C. (eds) (2014) *Infrastructural Lives. Urban Infrastructure in Context*, London and New York: Routledge.

Graham, S. and Thrift, N. (2007) Out of Order: Understanding Repair and Maintenance. *Theory Culture & Society* 24 (3): 1–25.

Greben, H. A. and Oelofse, S. H. H. (2009) Unlocking the Resource Potential of Organic Waste: a South African Perspective. *Waste Management & Research* 27 (7): 676–684.

Guijt, I. and Braden, S. (1999) Ensuring Reflection in Participatory Processes. In *PLA Notes*, No. 34. International Institute for Environment and Development (IIED), Sustainable Agriculture Program, London, 18–24 February 1999.

Gunsilius, E., Chaturvedi, B. and Scheinberg, A. (2011) *The Economics of the Informal Sector in Solid Waste Management*. Collaborative Working Group on Solid Waste Management in Low- and Middle-income Countries (CWG), Publication Series No 5. Last accessed 4 February 2016 at www.giz.de/en/downloads/giz2011-cwg-booklet-economic aspects.pdf.

Gurung, I. and Polprasert, C. (2007) Application of Clean Development Mechanism (CDM) for Solid Waste Management in Developing Countries: A Case Study for Bangkok, Thailand. *Proceedings of the International Conference on Sustainable Solid Waste Management* 5–7 September 2007, Chennai, India, pp. 511–518.

Gutberlet, J. (2008a) *Recycling Citizenship, Recovering Resources: Urban Poverty Reduction in Latin America*, Aldershot: Ashgate.

Gutberlet, J. (2008b) Empowering Collective Recycling Initiatives: Video Documentation and Action Research with a Recycling Co-op in Brazil. *Resources Conservation and Recycling* 52: 659–670.

Gutberlet, J. (2011) Waste to Energy, Wasting Resources and Livelihoods. In Kumar, S. (ed.) *InTech: Integrated Waste Management*, Vol. 1, Croatia: INTECH, pp. 219–236.

Gutberlet, J. (2012) Informal and Cooperative Recycling as a Poverty Eradication Strategy. *Geography Compass* 6 (1): 19–34.

Gutberlet, J. (2013) Briefing: Social Facets of Solid Waste: Insights from the global South. *Waste and Resource Management* 166 (3): 110–113.

Gutberlet, J. (2014) More Inclusive and Cleaner Cities with Waste Management Co-production: Insights from Participatory Epistemologies and Methods. *Habitat International*

46: 234–243. Last accessed 2 November 2015 at: http://dx.doi.org/10.1016/j.habitatint. 2014.10.004.

Gutberlet, J. and Baeder, A. (2008) Informal Recycling and Occupational Health in Santo Andrê, Brazil. *International Journal of Environmental Health Research*, 18 (1): 1–15.

Gutberlet, J. and Jayme, B. O. (2010) The Story of my Face. How Environmental Stewards Perceive Stigmatization (Re)produced by the Media. *Sustainability* 2 (11): 3339–3353.

Gutberlet, J., Seixas, S. C., Glinfkoi Thé, A. M. and Carolsfeld, K. (2007) Resource Conflicts and Co-management: Challenges in the São Francisco Watershed, Brazil. *Human Ecology* 35 (5): 623–638.

Gutberlet, J., Baeder, A. M., Pontuschka, N. N., Felipone, S. M. N. and dos Santos, T. L. F. (2013) Participatory Research Revealing the Work and Occupational Health Hazards of Cooperative Recyclers in Brazil. *International Journal of Environmental Research Public Health* 10 (10): 4607–4627. Last accessed 2 November 2015 at: http://dx.doi.org/ 10.3390/ijerph10104607.

Gutberlet, J., Kain, J.-H., Nyakinda, B., Oshieng, D. H., Odhiambo, N., Oloko, M., Omolo, J., Omondi, E., Otieno, S., Zapata, P. and Zapata Campos, M. J. (2016) Socio-environmental Entrepreneurship and the Provision of Critical Services in Informal Settlements. *Environment and Urbanization*.

Guy, S., Marvin, S., Medd, W. and Moss, T. (2011) *Shaping Urban Infrastructures: Intermediaries and the Governance of Socio-technical Networks*. London: Earthscan.

Hall, B. (1981) Participatory Research, Popular Knowledge and Power: A Personal Reflection. *Convergence* 14 (3): 6–17.

Hall, B. (2005) In from the Cold? Reflections on Participatory Research from 1970–2005. *Convergence* 38 (1): 5–24.

Hamilton, C., Gemenne, F. and Bonneuil, C. (eds) (2015) *The Anthropocene and the Global Environmental Crisis: Rethinking Modernity in a New Epoch*, London: Routledge.

Hara, Y., Furutani, T., Murakami A., Palijon A. M. and Yokohari, M. (2011) Current Organic Waste Recycling and the Potential for Local Recycling through Urban Agriculture in Metro Manila. *Waste Management & Research* 29 (11): 1213–1221.

Hardoy J. E., Mitlin, D. and Satterthwaite D. (2001) *Environmental Problems in an Urbanizing World: Finding Solutions for Cities in Africa, Asia and Latin America*, London: Earthscan Publications.

Harnecker, C. P. (2005) The New Co-Operative Movement in Venezuela's Bolivarian Process, 17 December 2005. Last accessed 2 November 2015 at: www.venezuelanalysis. com/analysis/1531.

Harrison, P. (2000) Making Sense: Embodiment and the Sensibilities of the Everyday. *Environment and Planning D* 18 (4): 497–517.

Hartmann, H. and Ahring, B. K. (2006) Strategies for the Anaerobic Digestion of the Organic Fraction of Municipal Solid Waste: An Overview. *Water Science and Technology* 53 (8): 7–22. DOI: 10.2166/wst.2006.231.

Harvey, D. (2001) *Spaces of Capital. Towards a Critical Geography*. Edinburgh: Edinburgh University Press.

Harvey, D. (2012) Rebel Cities: From the Right to the City to the Urban Revolution. London and New York: Verso.

Heart, S. and Agamuthu, P. (2012) E-waste: A Problem or an Opportunity? Review of Issues, Challenges and Solutions in Asian Countries. *Waste Management & Research* 30 (11): 1113–1129.

Heintz, J. and Razavi, S. (2012) Social Policy and Employment: Rebuilding the Connections. *UNRISD Research and Policy Brief* 17 (December 2012) Last accessed 2 November 2015 at: www.unrisd.org/80256B3C005BCCF9/search/AEB4A2E095603CCCC1257B09004A 005E?OpenDocument.

Henriksen, A. Z., Sandvik, A., Bergh, K., Reiersen, R. and Natås, O. (1993) Severe Gastro-enteritis after Domestic Infection with Vibrio Cholerae Non-O1. *Tidsskrift for den Norske Laegeforening: Tidsskrift for Praktisk Medicin, ny Raekke* 113 (24): 3017–3018.

Heynen, N., Kaika, M. and Swyngedouw, E. (eds) (2006) *In the Nature of Cities: Urban Political Ecology and the Politics of Urban Metabolism*, London: Routledge.

Hirsch, J. (1995) Nation-state, International Regulation and the Question of Democracy. *Review of International Political Economy* 2 (2): 267–284.

Hjorth, P. (2003) Knowledge Development and Management for Urban Poverty Alleviation. *Habitat International* 27 (3): 381–392.

Hoekstra, A. Y., Chapagain, A. K., Aldaya, M. A. and Mekonnen, M. M. (2009) *Water Footprint Manual. State of the Art 2009*, Enschede: Water Footprint Network.

Hoornweg, D. and Bhada-Tata, P. (2012) What a Waste: A Global Review of Solid Waste Management. *Urban Development Series Knowledge Papers*. Nr. 15. Urban Development and Local Government Unit, Washington, DC: World Bank DC. Last accessed 15 April 2015 at: www.scribd.com/doc/97467178/What-a-Waste-A-Global-Review-of-Solid-Waste-Management.

IBGE (Instituto Brasileiro de Geografia e Estatística) (2010) Pesquisa Nacional por Amostra de Domicílio Síntese de indicadores 2009. Rio de Janeiro: IBGE.

IBGE (Instituto Brasileiro de Geografia e Estatística) (2012) *Censo Demográfico 2010*. Rio de Janeiro: IBGE.

IBGE (Instituto Brasileiro de Geografia e Estatística) (2012a) *Pesquisa Nacional por Amostra de Domicílio 2012*. Rio de Janeiro: IBGE.

ICF Consulting (2005) Determination of the Impact of Waste Management Activities on Greenhouse Gas Emission: 2005 Update. Final Report. Submitted to: Environment Canada and Natural Resources Canada. Last accessed 9 February 2016 at: www.rcbc.ca/files/u3/ICF-final-report.pdf.

Instituto de Pesquisa Econômica Aplicada (IPEA) (2010) Pesquisa sobre pagamento por serviços ambientais urbanos para gestão de resíduos sólidos, Relatório de pesquisa. Brasil: IPEA.

Instituto de Pesquisa Economica Aplicada (IPEA) (2013) Situação Social das Catadoras e dos Catadores de Material Reciclável e Reutilizável, Brasil: IPEA.

International Labour Office (ILO) (2002) *Decent Work and the Informal Economy*–Report VI presented for the General Discussion at the International Labour Conference 2002, Geneva: International Labour Office. ISBN 92-2-112429-0. Last accessed 2 November 2015 at: www.ilo.org/public/english/standards/relm/ilc/ilc90/pdf/rep-vi.pdf.

International Labour Office (ILO) (2007) *Toolkit for Mainstreaming Employment and Decent Work/United Nations System Chief Executives Board for Coordination*, 1st edn, Geneva: International Labour Office. Last accessed 2 November 2015 at: http://ilo.org/integration/themes/dw_mainstreaming/lang--en/index.htm.

International Labour Office (ILO) (2013) *The Informal Economy and Decent Work: A Policy Resource Guide Supporting Transitions to Formality*. International Labour Office, Employment Policy Department, Geneva: ILO.

International Labour Office (ILO) (2014) *World of Work Report 2014: Developing with Jobs*, Geneva: ILO. Last accessed 2 November 2015 at: www.ilo.org/publns.

International Solid Waste Association (ISWA) (2012) *Globalization and Waste Management*. Phase 1: Concepts and facts. ISWA. PDF Last accessed 3 November 2015 at: www.iswa.org/index.php?eID=tx_iswatfg_download&fileUid=36.

Israel, B. A., Eng, E., Schulz, A. and Parker, E. A. (eds) (2005) *Methods in Community-based Participatory Research for Health*. San Francisco: Jossey–Bass.

Israel, B. A., Schulz, A. J., Parker, E. A. and Becker, A. B. (1998) Review of Community-based Research: Assessing Partnership Approaches to Improve Public Health. *Annu. Rev. Public Health* 19: 173–202.

Israel, B. A., Schulz, A. J., Parker, E. A. and Becker, A. B. (2001) Community-based Participatory Research: Policy Recommendations for Promoting a Partnership Approach in Health Research. *Education for Health* 14 (2): 182–197.

Itzhaky, H. and York, A. S. (2000) Empowerment and Community Participation: Does Gender Make a Difference? *Social Work Research* 24 (4): 225–234.

Jackson, T. (2009a) Confronting Structure. In Jackson, T. (ed.) *Prosperity without growth? The Transition to a Sustainable Economy*. Sustainable Development Commission, Surrey, England: SDC, pp. 59–66. Last accessed 8 April 2016 at: http://ontario-sea.org/Storage/32/2351_Prosperity_Without_Growth_-_The_transition_to_a_sustainable_economy.pdf

Jackson, T. (2009b) *Prosperity without Growth: Economics for a Finite Planet*, London: Earthscan.

Jentoft, S. (2005) Fisheries Co-management as Empowerment. *Marine Policy* 29 (1): 1–7.

Joshi, A. and Moore, N. (2004) Institutionalised Co-production: Unorthodox Public Service Delivery in Challenging Environments, *The Journal of Development Studies* 40 (4): 31–49.

Kaika, M. and Swyngedouw, E. (2000) Fetishizing the Modern City: The Phantasmagoria of Urban Technological Networks. *International Journal of Urban and Regional Research* 24 (1): 120–138.

Keil, R. (2013) Progress Report—Urban Political Ecology. *Urban Geography* 26 (7): 640–651. DOI: 10.2747/0272-3638.26.7.640.

Kellner, D. (n.d.) Critical Theory Today: Revisiting the Classics. Last accessed 2 November 2015 at: www.gseis.ucla.edu/faculty/kellner/kellner.html.

Kemmis, S. and McTaggart, R. (2000) Participatory Action Research. In Denzin, N. K. and Lincoln, Y. S. (eds) *Handbook of Qualitative Research*, Thousand Oaks, CA: Sage, pp. 567–605.

Kennedy, S., Copes R., Bartlett, K. and Brauer, M. (2004) Point-of-sale Glass Bottle Recycling: Indoor Airborne Exposures and Symptoms among Employees. *Occupational and Environmental Medicine* 61 (7): 628–635.

Kerstenetzky, C. L. (2003) Sobre associativismo, desigualdades e democracia (About associativism, inequality, and democracy). *Revista Brasileira de Ciências Sociais* 18 (53): 131–142.

Kerstenetzky, C. L. (2007) About Associativism, Inequality, and Democracy. *Revista Brasileira de Ciências Sociais* 18 (53): 131–142.

King, A., Burgess, S., Ijomah, W. and McMahon, C. (2006) Reducing Waste: Repair, Recondition, Remanufacture or Recycle? *Sustainable Development* 14 (4): 257–267.

King, M. and Gutberlet, J. (2013) Contribution of Cooperative Sector Recycling to Greenhouse Gas Emissions Reduction: A Case Study of Ribeirão Pires, Brazil, *Waste Management* 33 (12): 2771–2780.

Kooiman, J. (2003) *Governing as Governance*. London: Sage.

Kühn, S., Bravo Rebolledo, E. L. and Van Franeker, J. A. (2015) Deleterious effects of litter on marine life. In: Bergmann, M., Gutow, L. and Klages, M. (eds) *Marine Anthropogenic Litter*, Springer Verlag: Berlin.

Kuppinger, P. (2013) Crushed? Cairo's Garbage Collectors and Neoliberal Urban Politics. *Journal of Urban Affairs* 36 (S2): 621–633.

Kurzban, R. and Leary, M. R. (2001) Evolutionary Origins of Stigmatization: The Functions of Social Exclusion. *Psychological Bulletin* 127 (2): 187–208.

Lane, R. (2011) The Waste Commons in an Emerging Resource Recovery Waste Regime: Contesting Property and Value in Melbourne's Hard Rubbish Collections. *Geographical Research* 49 (4): 395–407.

Lavalle, A. G., Acharya, A. and Houtzager, P. P. (2005) Beyond Comparative Anecdotalism: Lessons on Civil Society and Participation from São Paulo, Brazil. *World Development* 33 (6): 951–964.

Laverack, G. (2001) An Identification and Interpretation of the Organizational Aspects of Community Empowerment. *Community Development Journal* 36 (2): 134–145.

Laville, J. -L. (1992) *Les services de proximité en Europe*, Paris: Vuibert.

Law, J. (1992) Notes on the Theory of the Actor Network: Ordering, Strategy and Heterogeneity. *Systems Practice* 5: 379–393. Last accessed 2 November 2015 at: www.heterogeneities.net/publications/Law1992NotesOnTheTheoryOfTheActorNetwork.pdf.

Lefebvre, H. (1976) *The Survival of Capitalism: Reproduction of the Relations of Production*, London: Allison and Busby Limited.

Lehmann, S. (2010) Green Urbanism: Formulating a Series of Holistic Principles. *Sapiens* 3 (2). Last accessed 1 May 2015 at: http://sapiens.revues.org/1057.

Lehmann, S. (2011) Optimizing Urban Material Flows and Waste Streams in Urban Development through Principles of Zero Waste and Sustainable Consumption. *Sustainability* 3 (1): 155–183. DOI:10.3390/su3010155.

Lennie, J. (2005) An Evaluation Capacity-building Process for Sustainable Community IT Initiatives: Empowering and Disempowering Impacts. *Evaluation* 11 (4): 390–414.

Levin, K., Cashore, B., Bernstein, S. and Auld, G. (2012) Overcoming the Tragedy of Super Wicked Problems: Constraining our Future Selves to Ameliorate Global Climate Change. *Policy Science* 45 (2): 123–152.

Levine, D. M., Becker, D. M. and Bone, L. R. (1994) Community–Academic Health Center Partnerships for Underserved Minority Populations. *Journal of the American Medical Association* 272 (4): 309–311.

Loftus, A. (2009) Rethinking Political Ecologies of Water. *Third World Quarterly* 30 (5): 953–968.

Loftus, A. (2012) *Everyday Environmentalism: Creating an Urban Political Ecology*, Minneapolis: University of Minnesota Press.

Ma, J., Cheng, J., Wang, W., Kunisue, T., Wu, M. and Kannan, K. (2011) Elevated Concentrations of Polychlorinated Dibenzo-p-dioxins and Polychlorinated Dibenzofurans and Polybrominated Diphenyl Ethers in Hair from Workers at an Electronic Waste Recycling Facility in Eastern China. *Journal of Hazardous Materials* 186 (2–3): 1966–1971.

MacBride, S. (2012) *Recycling Reconsidered: The Present Failure and Future Promise of Environmental Action in the United States*, Cambridge, MA, USA: The MIT Press.

McGurty, E. M. (1998) Trashy Women: Gender and the Politics of Garbage in Chicago, 1890–1917. *Historical Geography* 26, 27–43.

Mckenna, A. (2007) Computer Waste: A Forgotten and Hidden Side to the Global Information Society. *Environmental Law Review* 9: 116–131.

Malmros, P., Sigsgaard, T. and Bach, B. (1992) Occupational Health Problems due to Garbage Sorting. *Waste Management & Research* 10 (3): 227–234.

Marcotullio, P. J. and Boyle, G. (2003) *Defining an Ecosystem Approach to Urban Management and Policy Development*, Tokyo: United Nations University Institute of Advanced Studies.

Martimort, D. and Straub, S. (2009) Infrastructure Privatization and Changes in Corruption Patterns: The Roots of Public Discontent, *Journal of Development Economics* 90 (1): 69–84.

Martin, I., Ruggerio, C., Mino, M., Flores P. and Walter M. (2007) Vulnerabilidad y riesgos de los recuperadores de residuos de la Ciudad Autonoma de Buenos Aires. In Schamber and Suárez. Editors. *Recicloscopio: Miradas sobre recuperadores urbanos de residuos de America Latina.* Buenos Aires: Universidade Nacional de General Sarmiento, pp. 285–302.

Martin, R. and Sunley, P. (2006) Path Dependence and Regional Economic Evolution. *Journal of Economic Geography* 6 (4): 395–437.

Maslow, A. H. (1970) *Motivation and Personality*, 2nd edn, New York: Harper & Row.

Mason, P. (2015) *PostCapitalism. A Guide to Our Future*, London: Allen Lane.

Matthews, E. and Themelis, N. J. (2007) Potential for Reducing Global Methane Emissions From Landfills, 2000–2030. *Proceedings Sardinia 2007*, 11. International Waste Management and Landfill Symposium S. Margherita di Pula, Cagliari, Italy, 1–5 October 2007. Last accessed 15 April 2015 at: www.necec.org/files/Matthews_Themelis_ Sardinia2007.pdf.

Mayer, J. D. (1996) The Political Ecology of Disease as One New Focus for Medical Geography. *Progress in Human Geography* 20 (4): 441–456.

Medina, M. (2000) Scavenger Cooperatives in Asia and Latin America. *Resources, Conservation and Recycling* 31 (1): 51–69.

Miller, R. L. and Campbell R. (2006) Taking Stock of Empowerment Evaluation: An Empirical Review. *American Journal of Evaluation* 27 (3): 296–319.

Minkler, M. and Wallerstein, N. (2003) *Community-Based Participatory Research for Health*, San Francisco: Jossey-Bass.

Miraftab, F. (2004a) Neoliberalism and Casualization of Public Sector Services: The Case of Waste Collection Services in Cape Town, South Africa. *International Journal of Urban and Regional Research*, 28 (4): 874–892.

Miraftab, F. (2004b) Public–Private Partnerships: The Trojan Horse of Neoliberal Development? *Journal of Planning Education and Research* 24 (1): 89–101.

Mitlin, D. (2008) With and beyond the State – Co-production as a Route to Political Influence, Power and Transformation for Grassroots Organizations. *Environment and Urbanization* 20 (2): 339–360.

MNCR (2012) Declaração de princípios e objetivos do MNCR. Last accessed: 2 November 2015 at: www.mncr.org.br/.

Moore, D. (2001) Neoliberal Globalization and the Triple Crisis of "Modernisation" in Africa: Zimbabwe, the Democratic Republic of the Congo and South Africa, *Third World Quarterly* 22 (6): 909–929.

Morris, J. (1996) Recycling versus Incineration: An Energy Conservation Analysis. *Journal of Hazardous Materials* 47: 277–293.

Morris, J. (2005) In LCA: Case Studies – Using LCA to Compare Alternatives Comparative LCAs for Curbside Recycling Versus Either Landfilling or Incineration with Energy Recovery. *International Journal* 10 (4): 273–284.

Morrissey, A. J. and Browne, J. (2004) Waste Management Models and their Application to Sustainable Waste Management. *Waste Management* 24 (3): 297–308.

Moser, C. O. N. (1998) The Asset Vulnerability Framework: Reassessing Urban Poverty Reduction Strategies. *World Development* 26 (1): 1–19.

Moulaert, F. and Ailenei, O. (2005) Social Economy, Third Sector and Solidarity Relations: A Conceptual Synthesis from History to Present, *Urban Studies* 42 (11): 2037–2053.

Moulaert, F. and Nussbaumer, J. (2005) Defining the Social Economy and its Governance at the Neighbourhood Level: A Methodological Reflection. *Urban Studies* 42 (11): 2071–2088.

Movimento Nacional de Catadores(as) de Material Reciclável (MNCR) (2006) Relatório do Encontro dos 700, 2006. Last accessed 2 November 2015 at: www.mncr.org.br.

Myers, N. and Kent, J. (2003) New Consumers: The Influence of Affluence on the Environment. *Proceedings of the National Academy of Sciences, USA*, 100: 4963–4968. DOI:10.1073/pnas.0438061100.

Nayono, S. E. (2010) *Anaerobic Digestion of Organic Solid Waste for Energy Production, Karlsruher Berichte zur Ingenieurbiologie No 46*, Institut für Ingenieurbiologie und Biotechnologie des Abwassers. Karlsruher Institut für Technologie (KIT), Karlsruhe: Scientific Publishing.

Newman, P. and Jennings, I. (2008) *Cities as Sustainable Ecosystems: Principles and Practices*, Washington, DC: Island Press.

News Nunavut (2014) *Nunavut to Iqaluit: Extinguish Dumpcano With Your Own Money.* 1 August 2014 – 12:04 p.m. Last accessed 1 May 2015 at: www.nunatsiaqonline.ca/stories/article/65674nunavut_to_iqaluit_extinguish_dumpcano_with_your_own_money/.

Nguyen, H., Chalin, C., Lam, T. and Maclaren, V. (2003) Health and Social Needs of Waste Pickers in Vietnam. Research paper WASTE-ECON program in South East Asia. Last accessed 3 November 2015 at: http://idm.org.in/attachments/article/17/waste%20Picker%20Study.pdf.

Niemann, J., Tichkiewitch, S. and Westkämper, E. (eds) (2009) *Design of Sustainable Product Life Cycles*, Stuttgart: Springer.

Nunan, F. (2000) Urban Organic Waste Markets: Responding to Change in Hubli Dharward, India. *Habitat International* 24 (3): 347–360.

Nunn, N. and Gutberlet, J. (2013) Cooperative Recycling in São Paulo, Brazil: Towards an Emotional Consideration of Empowerment. *Area*, 45 (4): 452–458. DOI: 10.1111/area.12052.

Oberlin, A. S. (2012) Involvement of Community-based Organization in Household Waste Management in Dar es Salaam. *Journal of Science and Technology* 2 (Special Issue) 195–206.

Oberlin, A. S. and Szántó, G. L. (2011) Community Level Composting in a Developing Country: Case Study of KIWODET, Tanzania. *Waste Management & Research* 29 (10): 993–1113.

OECD Development Centre (2009) *Is Informal Normal?* ILO LABORSTA database; ILO Global Employment Trends, January 2009. Last accessed 2. November 2015 at: www.oecd.org/dev/poverty/42528124.pdf.

Offenhuber, D. (2012) On Infrastructure Legibility. In Offenhuber, D. and Schechtner, K. (eds) *Inscribing a Square: Urban Data as Public Space*, Vienna and New York: Springer, pp. 37–48.

Oliveira, C. H. (2014) Diagnóstico da Coleta Seletiva no Grande ABC e as perspectivas quanto às ações do PPA Regional Participativo Implantação e Fortalecimento da Coleta Seletiva no ABCDMRR. Conferência temática regional: saúde mental – coleta seletiva/catadores e economia solidária, III CONAES. Mauá – SP 14 March 2014. *(unpublished conference paper).*

Ostrom, E. (1996) Crossing the Great Divide: Coproduction, Synergy, and Development. *World Development* 24 (6): 1073–1087.

Paech, N. (2009) The 'Economy in the Aftermath of Growth. *Einblicke Carl von Ossietzky Universität Oldenburg* 49 (Frühjahr): 24–27.

Page, B. (2005) Paying for Water and the Geography of Commodities. *Transactions of the Institute of British Geographers* 30 (3): 293–306.

Parizeau, K. (2013) Formalization Beckons: A Baseline of Informal Recycling Work in Buenos Aires, 2007–2011. *Environment and Urbanization* 25 (2): 501–521.

Parizeau, K. (2015) When Assets are Vulnerabilities: An Assessment of Informal Recyclers' Livelihood Strategies in Buenos Aires, Argentina. *World Development* 67: 161–173.

Patwary, M. A., O'Hare, W. T. and Sarker, M. H. (2011) Assessment of Occupational and Environmental Safety Associated with Medical Waste Disposal in Developing Countries: A Qualitative Approach. *Safety Science* 49 (8–9): 1200–1207.

Peet, R. (ed.) (1977) *Radical Geography: Alternative Viewpoints on Contemporary Social Issues*, Chicago: Maaroufa Press.

Peet, R. (1998) *Modern Geographical Thought*, Oxford: Blackwell.

Pelling, M. (2011) *Adaptation to Climate Change: From Resilience to Transformation*, London: Routledge.

Pelling, M., Navarrete, M. D. and Redclift, M. (2011) *Climate Change and the Crisis of Capitalism: A Chance to Reclaim Self, Society and Nature*, London: Routledge.

Pérez-Belis, V., Bovea, M. D. and Ibáñez-Forés, V. (2014) An In-depth Literature Review of the Waste Electrical and Electronic Equipment Context: Trends and Evolution. *Waste Management & Research* 33 (1): 3–29.

Pezzey, J. (1992) Sustainability: An Interdisciplinary Guide. *Environmental Values* 1: 321–362.

Piacentini, R. D., Bracalenti, L., Salum, G., Zimmerman E., Lattuca, A., Terrile, R., Bartolomé, S., Vega, M., Tosello, L., Di Leo, N., Feldman, S. and Coronel, A. (2014) Monitoring the Climate Change Impacts of Urban Agriculture in Rosario, Argentina. *Urban Agriculture magazine* 27 (March). Last accessed 2 November 2015 at: www.ruaf.org.

Pimenteira, C. A. P., Pereira, A. S., Oliveira, L. B., Rosa, L. P., Reis, M. M. and Henriques, R. M. (2004) Energy Conservation and CO_2 Emission Reductions Due to Recycling in Brazil. *Waste Management* 24: 889–897.

Pinto, T. de P. and González, J. L. R. (2008) Elementos para a organização da coleta seletiva e projeto dos galpões de triagem. Ministerio das Cidades & Ministerio do Meio Ambiente. Brasilia. Last accessed 9 February 2016 at: www.mma.gov.br/estruturas/srhu_urbano/_publicacao/125_publicacao20012011032243.pdf.

Polanyi, K. (1944) *The Great Transformation: The Political and Economic Origins of our Time*, New York: Farrar & Rinehart.

Porta, D., Milani, S., Lazzarino, A., Perucci, C. A. and Forastiere, F. (2009) Systematic Review of Epidemiological Studies on Health Effects Associated with Management of Solid Waste, *Environmental Health* 8 (60): 1–14.

Porto, M., Junca, D., Goncalves, R. and Filhote, M. (2004) Lixo, trabalho e saude: um estudo de caso com catadores em um aterro metropolitano no Rio de Janeiro, Brasil. *Cad. Saúde Pública* 20 (6): 1503–1514.

Premakumara, D. G. J. (2012) Best Practices and Innovations in Community-based Solid Waste Management in Cebu. *Kitakyushu International Techno-cooperative Association*. Report, pp. 1–29. Last accessed 1 May 2015 at: http://pub.iges.or.jp/modules/envirolib/upload/4336/attach/Dickella_Premakumara_final_Best_Practices.pdf.

Pretty, J. and Ward, H. (2001) Social Capital and the Environment. *World Development* 29 (2): 209–227.

Pritchard, C. and Sanders, P. (2002) Weaving Our Stories as They Weave Us. *New Directions for Adult and Continuing Education*, 94 (Summer): 63–72.

Puntasen, T., Kleiman, F., Taylor, P. and Boothroyd, P. (2008) Higher Education and Participatory Development: Opportunities for Strengthening the Linkage. Presented to Asia Pacific Sub-Regional Preparatory Conference for the 2009 World Conference on Higher Education "Facing Global and Local Challenges: The New Dynamics for Higher Education." 24–26 September 2008, Macao SAR, PR China.

Putnam, R. D. (1993) *Making Democracy Work: Civic Traditions in Modern Italy*, Princeton: Princeton University Press.

Putnam, R. D. (2000) *Bowling Alone: The Collapse and the Revival of American Society*, New York: Simon and Schuster.

Putnam, R. D. (1995) Bowling Alone: America's Declining Social Capital. *Journal of Democracy* 6 (1): 65–78.

Ramos, N. F., Castilhos, Jr A. B. de, Forcellini, F. A. and Graciolli, O. D. (2013) Profile Survey of Waste Pickers in Brazil: Requirements for the Development of a Collection Vehicle and Optimized Routing. *Journal of Urban and Environmental Engineering* 7 (2): 231–246.

Ray, M. R., Mukherjee, G., Roychowdhury, S. and Lahiri, T. (2004) Respiratory and General Health Impairments of Ragpickers in India: A Study in Delhi. *International Archives of Occupational and Environmental Health* 77 (8): 595–598.

Read, J. and Shapiro, I. (2013) Transforming Power Relationships: Leadership, Risk, and Hope. *Political Science Series* No. 135, Wien: Institut für Höhere Studien.

Reason, P. and Bradbury, H. (eds) (2008) *The Handbook of Action Research: Participative Inquiry and Practice*, 2nd edn, Thousand Oaks, CA: Sage.

Reddy, B. S. and Assenza, G. B. (2009) Climate Change – A Developing Country Perspective. *Current Science* 97 (1): 50–62.

Rigg, J. (2007) *An Everyday Geography of the Global South*, London: Routledge.

Rocher, L. (2008) Les contradictions de la gestion intégrée des déchets urbains: l'incinération entre valorization énergétique et refus social. *Flux* 4 (74): 22–29.

Rogger, C., Beaurain, F. and Schmidt, T. S. (2011) Composting Projects under the Clean Development Mechanism: Sustainable Contribution to Mitigate Climate Change. *Waste Management* 31 (1): 138–146.

Røpke, I. (2005) Trends in the Development of Ecological Economics from the late 1980s to the early 2000s. *Ecological Economics* 55 (2): 262–290.

Rosa, M. C. (2014) Theories of the South: Limits and Perspectives of an Emergent Movement in Social Sciences. *Current Sociology*, 62 (6): 851–867.

Routh, S. (2014) *Enhancing Capabilities through Labour Law: Informal Workers in India*, New York: Routledge.

Roy, A. N., Jockin, A. and Javed, A. (2004) Community Police Stations in Mumbai's Slums, *Environment and Urbanization* 16 (2): 135–138.

Saegert, S. (2006) Building Civic Capacity in Urban Neighborhoods: An Empirically Grounded Anatomy. *Journal of Urban Affairs* 28 (3): 275–294.

Samson, M. (2003) *Dumping on Women: Gender and Privatization of Waste Management*, Cape Town: Municipal Services Project (MSPO) and the South African Municipal Workers' Union (SAMWU).

Samson, M. (2009) *Refusing to be Cast Aside: Waste Pickers Organising around the World*. Women in Informal Employment: Globalizing and Organizing (WIEGO), Cambridge, MA, USA.

Sarkar, P. (2003) Solid Waste Management In Delhi – A Social Vulnerability Study. *Third International Conference on Environment and Health*. Chennai, India, pp. 451–464.

Satterthwaite, D. (2009) The implications of population growth and urbanization for climate change. *Environment and Urban* 21 (2): 545–567.

Satterthwaite, D. and Mitlin, D. (2014) *Reducing Urban Poverty in the Global South*. London & New York: Routledge,

Schamber, P. and Suárez, F. (2007) *Recicloscopio. Miradas sobre recuperadores urbanos de residuos de América Latina*, eds. UNLa/UNGS/Prometeo: Buenos Aires, Argentina.

Scheinberg, A., Wilson, D. C. and Rodic-Wiersma, L. (2010) *Solid Waste Management in the World's Cities*. London and Washington, DC: Earthscan for UN-Habitat.

Schmink, M. and Wood, C. H. (1987) The "Political Ecology" of Amazonia. In Little, P. D. and Horowitz, M. M. (eds) *Lands at Risk in The Third World: Local-Level Perspectives*, Boulder, CO: Westview Press, pp. 38–57.

Schor, J. B. (2010) *Plenitude: The New Economics of True Wealth*, New York, NY: Penguin Press.

Schulz, A., Israel, B. A., Zimmerman, M. A. and Checkoway, B. (1995) Empowerment as a Multi-level Construct: Perceived Control at the Individual, Organizational and Community Levels. *Health Education Research* 10 (3): 309–327.

Schwarzer, S., Bono, A. D., Peduzzi, P., Giuliani G. and Kluser S. (2005) E-waste, the Hidden Side of IT Equipment's Manufacturing and Use. *UNEP Environment Alert Bulletin*: United Nations Environment Programme. Last accessed 9 February 2016 at: www.grid. unep.ch/products/3_Reports/ew_ewaste.en.pdf.

Self Employed Women's Association (SEWA) (n.d.) Last accessed 30 October 2015 at: www.sewa.org.

Shove, E., Watson, M., Hand, M. and Ingram, J. (2007) *The Design of Everyday Life*, Oxford: Berg.

Sidorenko, A. (2006) Empowerment and Participation in Policy Action on Ageing. *UN Program on Ageing*. Paper presented at the International Design for All Conference 2006, Rovaniemi, Finland.

Silva, P. C. S. (2012) O direito humano à moradia digna e o programa 'Minha Casa Minha Vida' no município de Ilhéus. In *Anais III Encontro Nacional de Pesquisa e Extensão em Direitos Humanos e Fundamentos da UESC*. 26–29 November 2012, Universidade Estadual do Sudoeste da Bahia UESC.

Simon, D. R. (2000) Corporate Environmental Crimes and Social Inequality: New Directions for Environmental Justice Research. In White, R. (ed.) (2009) *Environmental Crime: A Reader*, Cullompton: Willan Publishing, pp. 103–116.

Singh, K. J. and Sooch, S. S. (2004) Comparative Study of Economics of Different Models of Family Size Biogas Plants for State of Punjab, India. *Energy Conversion and Management* 45 (9–10): 1329–1341.

Sisulu, L. (2006) Partnerships between Government and Slum/Shack Dwellers' Federation. *Environment & Urbanization* 18 (2): 401–405.

Sjöströma, M. and Östblom, G. (2010) Decoupling Waste Generation from Economic Growth – A CGE Analysis of the Swedish Case. *Ecological Economics* 69 (7): 1545–1552.

Smit, J. and Nasr, J. (1992) Urban Agriculture for Sustainable Cities: Using Wastes and Idle Land and Water Bodies as Resources. *Environment and Urbanization* 4 (2): 141–152.

Smit, J., Ratta, A. and Nasr, J. (1996) *Urban Agriculture: Food, Jobs and Sustainable Cities*. Publication Series for Habitat II, Volume One. New York: United Nations Development Programme.

Smith, A., Brown, K., Ogilvie, S., Rushton, K. and Bates, J. (2001) *Waste Management Options and Climate Change*. Final report to the European Commission, DG. Environment Luxembourg: Office for Official Publications of the European Communities.

Smith, L. (1999) *Decolonizing Methodologies: Research and Indigenous Peoples*, London: Zed Books.

Smith, L. (2002) The Corporatization of Water. In McDonald, D. and Smith, L. *Privatizing Cape Town: Service Delivery and Policy Reforms Since 1996*, Occasional Paper Series, No. 7, Municipal Services Project, Cape Town.

Smith, L. and Hanson, S. (2003) Access to Water for the Urban Poor in Cape Town: where Equity Meets Cost-recovery. *Urban Studies* 40 (8): 1517–1532.

SNDT Women's University, Chintan Group (n.d.) Recycling Livelihoods. Integration of the Informal Sector in Solid waste Management in India. Last accessed 2 November 2015 at: www.gtz.de/informal-recycling-india.pdf.

Snyman, H., Van Niekerk, A. M. and Rajasakran, N. (2006) Sustainable Wastewater Treatment – What Has Gone Wrong and How Do We Get Back on Track? In *Proc. WISA 2006 Conference*. Water Institute South Africa, Midrand, SA.

Speer, P., Jackson, C. and Peterson, A. (2001) The Relationship between Social Cohesion and Empowerment: Support and New Implication for Theory. *Health Education & Behaviour* 28 (6): 716–732.

Sreberny, A. (2006) Gender, Empowerment, and Communication: Looking Backwards and Forwards. *International Social Science Journal* 57 (184): 197–201.

Stern, D. I. (1997) The Capital Theory Approach to Sustainability: A Critical Appraisal. *Journal of Economic Issues* 31 (1): 145–173.

Stringer, E. and Dwyer, R. (2005) *Action Research in Human Services*, Upper Saddle River, NJ: Prentice Hall.

Swyngedouw, E. (2004) *Social Power and the Urbanization of Water: Flows of Power*, Oxford: Oxford University Press.

Swyngedouw, E. (2009) The Antinomies of the Postpolitical City: In Search of a Democratic Politics of Environmental Production. *International Journal of Urban and Regional Research* 33 (3): 601–620.

Swyngedouw, E. and Heynen, N. C. (2003) Urban Political Ecology, Justice and the Politics of Scale. *Antipode* 35 (5): 898–918.

Szreter, S. and Woolcock, M. (2004) Health by Association? Social Capital, Social Theory, and the Political Economy of Public Health. *International Journal of Epidemiology* 33 (4): 650–667.

Tan, J. (2012) The Pitfalls of Water Privatization: Failure and Reform in Malaysia. *World Development* 40 (12): 2552–2563.

Tangri, N. (2003) *Waste Incineration: A Dying Technology*. Philippines & Berkley, US: Global Anti-Incinerator Alliance & Global Alliance for Incinerator Alternatives. Last accessed 3 November 2015 at: www.no-burn.org/downloads/Waste%20Incineration%20 -%20A%20Dying%20Technology.pdf.

Tembo, F. (2003) *Participation, Negotiation and Poverty: Encountering the Power of Images*. Hampshire: Ashgate.

Terraza, H. and Sturzenegger, G. (2010) *Dinámicas de organización de los Recicladores informales: tres casos de estudio en América Latina*, Banco Interamericano de Desarrollo, Sector de Infraestructura y Medio Ambiente. Nota Técnica No. 117. Last accessed 3 November 2015 at: http://idbdocs.iadb.org/wsdocs/getdocument.aspx?docnum=35325785.

Thieme, T. A. (2015) Turning Hustlers into Entrepreneurs, and Social Needs into Market. *Geoforum* 59: 228–239. DOI: 10.1016/j.geoforum.2014.11.010.

Thiollent, M. (2008) *Metodologia da pesquisa-ação*, 16th edn, São Paulo, Brazil: Cortez.

Thorneloe, S. A., Weitz, K. A., Nishtala, S. R., Yarkosky, S. and Zannes, M. (2002) The Impact of Municipal Solid Waste Management on Greenhouse Gas Emissions in the United States. *Air & Waste Management Association* 52, 1000–1011.

Toakley, A. R. (2004) Globalization, Sustainable Development and Universities. *Higher Education Policy*, 17: 311–324. DOI: 10.1057/palgrave.hep.8300058.

Tokman, V. (2007) The Informal Economy, Insecurity and Social Cohesion in Latin America. *International Labour Review* 146 (1–2), 81–107.

Tremblay, C. and Gutberlet, J. (2011) Empowerment through Participation: Assessing the Voices of Leaders from Recycling Cooperatives in São Paulo, Brazil. *Community Development Journal* 46 (3): 282–302. DOI: 10.1093/cdj/bsq040.

Tremblay, C., Gutberlet, J. and Peredo, A. M. (2010) United We Can: Resource Recovery, Place and Social Enterprise, *Resources, Conservation & Recycling*, 54 (7): 422–428.

Tremblay, C., Hall, B. and Tandon, R. (2014) *Global Trends in Support Structures for Community University Research Partnerships. Survey Results* – September 2014. UNESCO, UVic & PRIA.

Turner, B. L., Kasperson, R. E., Matson, P. A., McCarthy, J. J., Corell, R. W., Christensen, L., Eckley, N., Kasperson, J. X., Luers, A., Martello, M. L., Polsky, C., Pulsipher, A. and Schiller, A. (2003) A Framework for Vulnerability Analysis in Sustainability Science. *PNAS*, 100 (14): 8074–8079.

United Nations Children's Fund (UNICEF) (n.d.) *Fast facts on Adolescents and Youth in Latin America and the Caribbean.* Last accessed 2 November 2015 at: www.unicef.org/media/files/Fast_facts__EN.doc.

United Nations Development Programme (UNDP) (2006) *El costo económico de la violencia en Guatemala.* PNUD-Guatemala. Cuánto le cuesta la violencia a El Salvador? *Cuadernos sobre Desarrollo Humano* No. 4.

United Nations Development Programme (UNDP) (2011) *Engaging with the Urban Poor and their Organizations for Poverty Reduction and Urban Governance.* An issues paper for the United Nations Development Programme. By Satterthwaite, D., Mitlin, D. and Patel, S.

United Nations Environment Programme (UNEP) (2010) Waste and Climate Change: Global trends and strategy framework. United Nations Environmental Programme Division of Technology, Industry and Economics International Environmental Technology Centre Osaka/Shiga. Last accessed 15 April 2015 at: www.unep.or.jp/ietc/Publications/spc/Waste&ClimateChange/Waste&ClimateChange.pdf.

United Nations Environment Programme (UNEP) (2011) *Waste Investing in Energy and Resource Efficiency.* Green Economy. Last accessed 2 November 2015 at: www.unep.org/greeneconomy/Portals/88/documents/ger/GER_8_Waste.pdf.

United Nations Human Settlement Programme (UN-HABITAT) (2010) *Solid Waste Management in the World's Cities.* London: Gutenberg Press.

United Nations Human Settlement Programme (UN-Habitat) (2013) *Streets as Public Spaces and Drivers of Urban Prosperity.* Nairobi, Kenya: UN-Habitat. Last accessed 26 October 2015 at: http://unhabitat.org/?wpdmact=process&did=MTYzLmhvdGxpbms.

United Nations Human Settlements Programme (UN-Habitat) (2015) Informal settlements. *Habitat III Issue Papers* 22. Last accessed 26 October 2015 at: http://unhabitat.org/wp-content/uploads/2015/04/Habitat-III-Issue-Paper-22_Informal-Settlements.pdf.

United States Enivronmental Protection Agency (US EPA) (2006) *Solid Waste Management and Greenhouse Gases. A Life-cycle Assessment of Emissions and Sinks.* Last accessed 15 April 2015 at: www.epa.gov/climatechange/wycd/waste/SWMGHGreport.html.

University of Washington. (n.d.) Developing and Sustaining A Community-based Participatory Research Partnership: A Skill-building Curriculum. Last accessed 2 November 2015 at: http://depts.washington.edu/ccph/cbpr/index.php.

Utting, P., van Dijk, N. and Matheï, M. (2014) Participation and Collective Action. In *Social and Solidarity Economy: Is There a New Economy in the Making? Occasional Paper 10 Potential and Limits of Social and Solidarity Economy*, Geneva, Switzerland: UNRISD, pp. 41–50.

Van Eerd, M. (1997) The Occupational Health Aspects of Waste Collection and Recycling. A Survey of the Literature. WASTE Working Document. Urban Waste Expertise Program (UWEP).

Van Lange, P., De Cremer, D., Van Dijk, E. and Van Vugt, M. (2007) Self-interest and Beyond: Basic Principles of Social Interaction. In *Social Psychology: Handbook of*

Basic Principles, edited by Kruglanski, A. and Higgins, T., New York, NY: Guilford Press, pp. 540–561.

Vergara, S. E. and Tchobanoglous, G. (2012) Municipal Solid Waste and the Environment: A Global Perspective. *Annual Review of Environment and Resources* 37 (1): 277–309.

Wackernagel, M. and Rees, W. E. (1996) *Our Ecological Footprint: Reducing Human Impact on Earth*, Philadelphia, PA: New Society.

Waiselfisz, J. (2012) *Mapa da Violência: A cor dos homicídios no Brasil*. Last accessed 2 November 2015 at: www.mapadaviolencia.org.br/mapa2012_cor.php.

Walker, B., Holling, C. S., Carpenter, R. and Kinzig, A. (2004) Resilience, Adaptability and Transformability in Social–ecological Systems. *Ecology and Society* 9 (2): 5. Last accessed 20 April 2015 at: www.ecologyandsociety.org/vol9/iss2/art5.

Wallerstein, N. (2006) What is the Evidence on Effectiveness of Empowerment to Improve Health? Copenhagen, World Health Organization (WHO), Regional Office for Europe. Health Evidence Network report. Last accessed 2 November 2015 at: www.euro.who.int/__data/assets/pdf_file/0010/74656/E88086.pdf.

Walsh, D. C. (2002) Urban Residential Refuse Composition and Generation Rates for the 20th Century. *Environ. Sci. Technol.* 36 (22): 4936–4942.

Walton, M. and Smulovitz, C. (2003) Evaluating Empowerment. *Working paper*, presented at the Workshop on "Measuring Empowerment: Cross-Disciplinary Perspectives", Washington, DC: The World Bank, 4–5 February.

Wang, T., Fu, J., Wang, Y., Liao, C., Tao, Y. and Jiang, G. (2009) Use of Scalp Hair as Indicator of Human Exposure to Heavy Metals in an Electronic Waste Recycling Area. *Environmental Pollution* 157 (8–9): 2445–2451.

Wéry, N. (2014) Bioaerosols from Composting Facilities – A Review. *Frontiers in Cellular and Infection Microbiology* 4 (42). Last accessed 20 April 2015 at: www.ncbi.nlm.nih.gov/pmc/articles/PMC3983499/.

Widmer, R., Oswald-Krapf, H., Sinha-Khetriwal, A., Scnellmann, M. and Boni, H. (2005) Global Perspectives on the E-waste. *Environmental Impact Assessment Review* 25 (5): 436–458.

Wiggershaus, R. (1986) *Die Frankfurter Schule*, Munich: Hanser.

Wilson, D., Velis, C. and Cheeseman, C. (2006) Role of Informal Sector Recycling in Waste Management in Developing Countries, *Habitat International* 30 (4): 797–808.

Wilson, D., Rodic, L., Scheinberg, A., Velis, C. and Alabaster, G. (2012) Comparative Analysis of Solid Waste Management in 20 Cities. *Waste Management and Research* 30 (3): 237–254.

Women in Informal Employment Globalizing and Organizing (WIEGO) (2014) Statistics on the Informal Economy. *WIEGO Working Paper (Statistics)* N. 2, April 2014. WIEGO Cambridge. Last accessed 2 November 2015 at: http://wiego.org/organizing/waste-pickers-networks.

Women in Informal Employment Globalizing and Organizing (WIEGO) (n.d.) Waste Pickers' Network. WIEGO homepage. Last accessed 2 February 2016 at: http://wiego.org/organizing/waste-pickers-networks.

Woolcock, M. and Narayan, D. (2000) Social Capital Theory: Implications for Development Theory, Research and Policy. *The World Bank Research Observer* 15 (2): 225–249.

Yates, J. S. and Gutberlet, J. (2011a) Re-claiming and Re-circulating Urban Natures: Integrated Organic Waste Management in Diadema, Brazil. *Environment and Planning A*, 43 (9): 2109–2124.

Yates, J. S. and Gutberlet, J. (2011b) Enhancing Livelihoods and the Urban Environment: The Local Political Framework for Integrated Organic Waste Management in Diadema, Brazil. *Journal of Development Studies* 47 (4): 1–18.

Yoshida, H., Gable, J. J. and Park, J. K. (2012) Evaluation of Organic Waste Diversion Alternatives for Greenhouse Gas Reduction. *Resources, Conservation and Recycling* 60: 1–9.

Zaman A. U. and Lehmann, S. (2011) Urban Growth and Waste Management Optimization towards "Zero Waste City". *City, Culture and Society* 2 (4): 177–187.

Zaman, A. U. and Lehmann, S. (2013) The Zero Waste Index: A Performance Measurement Tool for Waste Management Systems in a "Zero Waste City". *Journal of Cleaner Production* 50 (1): 123–132.

Zapata Campos, M. J. and Hall, M. (2013) *Organising Waste in the City: International Perspectives on Narratives and Practices*, Bristol: The Policy Press.

Zapata Campos, M. J. and Zapata, P. (2013) Switching Managua on! Connecting Informal Settlements to the Formal City through Household Waste Collection. *Environment and Urbanization* 25 (1): 1–18.

Zero Waste Europe (2015) "Zero Waste?". Last accessed 2 November 2015 at: www.zerowasteeurope.eu/about/principles-zw-europe/.

Zimmerman, M. (2000) Empowerment Theory: Psychological, Organizational and Community Level of Analysis. In Rappaport, J. and Seidman, E. (eds) *Handbook of Community Psychology*, New York: Kluwer, pp. 43–63.

Index

 Taylor & Francis eBooks

Helping you to choose the right eBooks for your Library

Add Routledge titles to your library's digital collection today. Taylor and Francis ebooks contains over 50,000 titles in the Humanities, Social Sciences, Behavioural Sciences, Built Environment and Law.

Choose from a range of subject packages or create your own!

Benefits for you

» Free MARC records
» COUNTER-compliant usage statistics
» Flexible purchase and pricing options
» All titles DRM-free.

Benefits for your user

» Off-site, anytime access via Athens or referring URL
» Print or copy pages or chapters
» Full content search
» Bookmark, highlight and annotate text
» Access to thousands of pages of quality research at the click of a button.

 REQUEST YOUR **FREE** INSTITUTIONAL TRIAL TODAY

Free Trials Available
We offer free trials to qualifying academic, corporate and government customers.

eCollections – Choose from over 30 subject eCollections, including:

Archaeology	Language Learning
Architecture	Law
Asian Studies	Literature
Business & Management	Media & Communication
Classical Studies	Middle East Studies
Construction	Music
Creative & Media Arts	Philosophy
Criminology & Criminal Justice	Planning
Economics	Politics
Education	Psychology & Mental Health
Energy	Religion
Engineering	Security
English Language & Linguistics	Social Work
Environment & Sustainability	Sociology
Geography	Sport
Health Studies	Theatre & Performance
History	Tourism, Hospitality & Events

For more information, pricing enquiries or to order a free trial, please contact your local sales team: www.tandfebooks.com/page/sales

 Routledge
Taylor & Francis Group

The home of
Routledge books

www.tandfebooks.com

For Product Safety Concerns and Information please contact our EU
representative GPSR@taylorandfrancis.com
Taylor & Francis Verlag GmbH, Kaufingerstraße 24, 80331 München, Germany

www.ingramcontent.com/pod-product-compliance
Ingram Content Group UK Ltd.
Pitfield, Milton Keynes, MK11 3LW, UK
UKHW020951180425
457613UK00019B/621